ACCORDING TO ME

ACCORDING TO ME

by
Orla J. Pedersen

According To Me

Copyright ©2011 Orla Pedersen
ISBN 978-0-578-08678-1

Author: Orla J. Pedersen
Edited by LaVonne Quinth and Darla Pedersen
Design by LaVonne Quinth

Printed in the United States of America

Dedicated to the memory of me!

For my grandchildren
Jonathan
Erik
Nicolas
Stephanie
Oliver
Lydia
Mallory

CONTENTS

DENMARK

I was born in Denmark, at very early age, to Jens and Ellen Pedersen. All people are born at an early age, but I like to point that out. The sun was not shining on the day of my birth, December 19, 1934. Not unusual, since the sun rarely shines in Denmark in December. The location for my arrival was a small town called Roust. I use the term "town" liberally; it was actually just a store, a creamery, a school, a hair salon and a blacksmith. My father used to say that we lived at the end of the world where even the crows turned around to return to wherever they came from.

These days when women have babies they go to the hospital, but I was born at home right there in bed with my mother. Can you imagine that? I feel sorry for my father. Where was he going to sleep that night and many nights thereafter? The bed must have been a mess. There was never a doctor involved. When the time came, the midwife, usually an older woman from the village was called to the house to help deliver the baby. The father was sent off to boil water, keeping him well out of the way.

ACCORDING TO ME

I'm told that I was a very beautiful baby, really something to behold. So proud of what they had produced, my parents displayed me at every opportunity. Terrified at this parade of strange faces constantly passing before me, I screamed until I developed a hernia and, when I was nine months old, ended up in the hospital for surgery. Actually, I was probably pre-disposed to problems having been born with un-descended testicles, a condition that placed them in my lower abdomen instead of where they were supposed to be. It's a condition that has bothered me one way or another all my life. But I was a sturdy little tyke and survived the torment.

We could have all suffocated my first New Year's morning. New Year's Eve in Denmark was a time of reveling. Young people gathered having a lot of fun setting off firecrackers and playing pranks on their neighbors. A common prank was to sneak into the kitchen while the homeowners were sitting in the living room, steal the coffee pot and hide it somewhere. Another favorite was to enter the barn, take the wheelbarrow and hide it in the field so that the farmer couldn't muck out for the animals in the morning. But the prank they played on us was not so innocent. My father's first chore every morning was to light a fire in the kitchen stove. That morning when he lit the fire smoke billowed out and we were soon completely engulfed. He couldn't imagine what the problem could be, but climbed up on the roof to look in the chimney and found that someone had stuffed a burlap sack in the flue as a New Years greeting. He pulled the sack out and the chimney worked fine, but it took a while to get the smoke out of the house.

When I was a year and a half, I wandered away from my parents, out to the pasture where the horses were grazing. Not a good place to be for a small tyke. One of the horses kicked me in the head and I was lying there, out for the count, when my Father found me. I guess for a few days they worried about whether I was going to survive, and, if I did, would I suffer any permanent damage? Of course I pulled through, but I now have

2

amnesia. I can't remember anything that happened before that time. I've often wondered if I'd have been any different if I hadn't gotten that big bump on my head at such a formative age.

I've also often questioned my parent's abilities regarding childcare, especially concerning me. When they were working, they would leave me sitting on the edge of the field. Hungry, I would grab the first thing available, dirt. Good stuff, it was fortified from the manure pile. My mother told me later that my diapers would be full of dirt instead of….well, you know. Later, apparently worried that I was depleting the good soil, they locked me

My parent's wedding
November 21, 1933

in the house instead. Bad decision. I found a can of paint that I managed to open, spilling it all over the floor. Then I walked through it, traipsing it all over the house. I can just imagine the mess.

I have few memories from my earliest years. I think that I remember standing in a big wooden box that I couldn't get out of. It was a kind of playpen, but not much fun. I can also remember a visit to the photographer when I was three years old. Trying to get me to smile, he gave me a big foxtail reed and told me to tickle grandma. Those pictures are now hanging on our wall to remind me of yesteryear.

Once I surprised my parents by walking into their bedroom and caught them really getting it on in bed. I told them that they were not supposed to play around in the bed, because that's what they had told me. I had no idea what they were doing, but somehow it made enough of an impression on me to remember it and figure it out later when I was older.

ACCORDING TO ME

Being the firstborn really wasn't so great. My mother had determined that I was to be the perfect little child and when I wasn't she felt it was an awful reflection on her. The kitchen ceiling in our old farmhouse had rough wooden beams with many nails, on which hung all manner of things. One of those things was the switch, a thin branch that was used for disciplining me. Often, my pants were pulled down and I was given several whacks with that switch. To this day I can still feel the sting of it and remember the nausea I felt at the mere sight of it. I was always happy when my favorite aunt, Ragna, who was my mother's youngest sister, came to visit because she always took down that wicked instrument of torture and burned it in the wood stove.

My mother's severe discipline continued for years. I remember one time we had been to a party at a neighbor's and I must have been exceptionally wild. When we came home again, I was too sleepy to get a spanking. Not to worry, the next morning I received a real working over which left welts lasting for days. Today she would have been reported for child abuse. Eventually she graduated to using a belt. I'm thankful that she didn't hit me with the buckle end.

Years later while, traveling in the car, the four of us siblings would sit in the backseat while my parents sat up in front. As is inevitable when children are kept in cramped quarters we would begin squabbling. Without warning my mother would reach over to my father, undo his belt and yank it off his pants, and begin flailing us with it. When we later arrived at our destination the first thing my father had to do was to put his belt back on so he wouldn't drop his pants.

I was about 16 the last time she tried to hit me with a belt. When I grabbed it and took it away from her I think she realized that I had become too big to spank any more. I do not look back on my childhood with great fondness. There were times that I didn't want to come home from school for fear that I had done something wrong and I would have a turn with the switch again, but there was no place else to go. I was sometimes so upset with my mother that I wished her dead, and was later plagued with remorse over having had such ghastly thoughts.

Despite the ill feelings that I had towards my mother, I felt closer to her than I did to my father, even though he almost never did any harm to me physically. I have often wondered about the dichotomy in that, but I think it stems from a need to protect her from my father's abuse. Maybe it was a kind of a Stockholm syndrome where the captives ally themselves with their captors. He was never physically abusive, but would become enraged with my mother, yelling at her, sometimes for days, calling her such terrible names that I cannot repeat them here.

I was probably no more than three years old when I was awakened in the middle of the night by the sound of shouting. My father was yelling at my mother saying he wanted to take her out in the barn and "spare her." The word "spare" in our Danish dialect could mean to "save someone," but it could also mean to "cut with a knife." To this day I have no idea what he really meant. I'm now 75 years old and this event is as vivid to me now as it was then. I really thought that he was going to take my mother out to the barn and stab her. I remember screaming in panic, and I believe that was the onset of my deep concern for my mother's welfare, because no matter how badly she treated me, I would always be on her side against him.

Now and then my mother would come to the end of her rope and she would grab the switch that she used on me and work him over with it. She even broke a broom handle on him and once locked him out of the house for a whole day!

Because of the situation at home, much of my childhood was a living a nightmare and I've never wanted it back. My friend's families seemed to be so much nicer than ours and I wished for things to be healthier at home. I longed for a relationship with my father and every now and then when we would be working together in the field, we got along quite well, and I wished it could continue. But as soon he got around my mother, the hostility would begin again and my distain for him would come

5

over me anew. My siblings never seemed to be bothered by any of this. Maybe it's because they were never awakened in the middle of the night, hearing Father threaten to stab Mother, or perhaps, as the oldest, I felt more responsibility.

These conflicting feelings towards my parents followed me into adulthood unresolved until long after I was married. Drifting off to sleep I was sometimes jolted awake by the memory of my father's voice berating my mother. Although we lived more than 100 miles away I could her him as clearly as if he were in the next room.

It has been painful to write about this part of my life but, as with many childhood experiences, it is a part of who I have become. Now I will leave the negative behind and focus on the positive. There were many good times. I often saw my parents hug and kiss each other. My mother hugged me often and told me I was a good boy. At those times I felt that life was wonderful and wished it would just continue that way.

As I grew into adulthood my relationship with my mother improved. She was proud of me and of my accomplishments and the anger and criticism was replaced with joy and praise.

CHRISTMAS

Some of my earliest memories are of Christmases in Denmark. On Christmas Eve, after the barn chores were completed and all the animals had been fed, my parents would put me in the little seat that hung on the handlebars of my father's bike and we would bicycle to my maternal grandparents. Christmas was the highlight of the year for me, something I looked forward to for months. Coming into my grandparent's home was delightful. Memories of the aroma of delectable food still makes my teeth water. In the dining room a long table was set with the finest china and silverware for the large and growing family. A Christmas tree dressed with live candles stood in the corner. That might seem hazardous, but the tree had been cut that morning and was fresh and green so it was not going to catch on fire.

When everyone was seated, before we could begin eating, we sang the doxology, mindful of the Lord who is the provider of all good things. The meal began with rice porridge, served from a large bowl that had been placed in the middle of the table. Someone would dish it up and serve each of us. Sprinkled with sugar and cinnamon and covered with milk, it tasted very good. To this very day I still adore a good portion of rice porridge with sugar and cinnamon. When we had finished our porridge a large roasted goose was served along with boiled potatoes, red cabbage and some other vegetable. Goose is wonderful, all dark meat, and my grandmother was an expert at preparing it!

The meal finished, our bellies full, the men went to the barn to admire the animals and to relieve themselves while the women cleared the table and helped each other to clean up the kitchen. There were no dishwashers, but the laughter and camaraderie made the work easy. When the kitchen was clean it was the women's turn to retire to the barn to admire the animals. Later we gathered in the living and dining rooms and sang Christmas hymns and carols, while I waited impatiently for the highlight of the evening and the arrival of a most important guest, Santa Claus.

Looking back on it, he really didn't look like the Santas I'd seen in pictures but, since my real interest was the gifts, it didn't seem to matter. I was usually sent out of the room on some pretense and when I returned Santa Claus would be sitting near the tree. Dressed in a bathrobe and a paper hat, he seemed like an awfully old creature and had a really strange voice that I supposed was due to age and exposure to the elements. He distributed the presents that were already lying under the tree when he arrived. One year, I remember, I got a car that could be wound up. Another year I got a four-engine airplane, also a wind up. For some reason they never lasted very long.

Funny thing though, my uncle Eske, who is less than 12 years older than me, was always missing. I do remember that I asked about him once and was told that he was out in the barn tying up a cow that had gotten loose. That sounded reasonable. One year however, I found out what was going on. I happened to go into the guest room and there, lying on the bed, was that old bathrobe and the paper hat. I was probably just 4 years old, but I was able to put two and two together and come up with the conclusion that Santa was a charlatan; he was only Uncle Eske in disguise. My mother told me that I shouldn't have gone snooping around the house, but Eske opined that it was high time that I learned the truth. I think he was tired of being Santa Claus. I was the only grandchild and would remain so for several years, yet I don't recall that he played Santa for anyone else later.

Our presents opened and admired, Santa would take his leave and we returned to the table for desert. We had Danish apple cake that was kind of like a pie except, instead of a crust, it was layered with breadcrumbs and was served in a bowl. There was also layer cake, coffee cake and lots of different kinds of cookies. We didn't have ice cream since we had didn't have a freezer or even a refrigerator. Late at night the crowd thanked my grandparents for a wonderful evening, wished each other Merry Christmas and found their way home along the dark, muddy and rutted tracks masquerading as roads.

Christmas day, when the barn chores had been done, we gathered once again at my Grandparents home to eat the leftovers, which were still as good as the night before. I imagine that is why I have always liked leftovers.

My grandparent's home was always a wonderful place to visit. There wasn't anybody my age to play with, but I didn't have anybody at home to play with either. I liked everybody there,

My favorite aunt, Ragna

especially my Aunt Ragna, she was always so much fun. She was a little on the plump side, enjoyed the tasty farm food a little too much perhaps, so she would go and do exercises with a group in the village. Not that it did much good.

My grandparents had a little motherless lamb that they were bottle-feeding. I guess it was a little bit of a rascal because they called it "Skittemett"– Naughty Lamb. When I was there I had the great honor of feeding Skittemett. I was given a big bottle filled with milk with a rubber nipple on top. One day when I was feeding him he pulled the nipple off and ate it. I was beside myself with fright. I thought that the lamb was going to die and ran crying to my Aunt Ragna and told her what had happened. She hugged me and comforted me and told me not to worry about it. Skittemet wasn't going to die and the nipple would be coming out the other end in a couple of days.

ACCORDING TO ME

OUR FARM

Our farm was about 10 miles east of Esbjerg, a city with the largest harbor on the west coast where ships of all sizes came and went from all over the world. My parents had to work very hard. They purchased the farm just a year prior to my arrival. It had been terribly neglected, run down and overgrown. There was very little machinery to work with and they didn't have much money, besides, it was in the middle of the Great Depression. They did what they could with what they had and in a short time their efforts began to pay off. Tractors were almost unheard of in those days, but they had a couple horses to do the work. They also raised pigs and chickens and had a few cows for milk. Slowly they built up the farm and by the time I was a young boy we had about a dozen cows, 20-30 pigs, a bunch of chickens and two huge Belgian workhorses.

The house I was born in was over 100 years old with a thatched roof. I remember a little about the old house. I remember I slept in my parent's room in a large crib until I was about six or seven years old when my brother came along and I was given a bigger bed. I remember also that my mother painted the mudroom floor in multi-colors and that she grew cacti in the dining room. I have a vivid memory of running smack into an especially spiny specimen that my aunt was carrying through to another room.

My parents had been planning to tear down the old house and build a new one. They had even purchased the materials, bricks, sand, cement, etc., but then the war started in 1940 and the project was put on hold. An inspector showed up in 1942, wondering why they hadn't built the house and advised them to go ahead with the project, otherwise the Germans would take the materials. So, in the summer of '42, they tore down the old farmhouse and built a new one in its place. In the meantime we lived in the chicken house, a cold and drafty building. Once they got started, they built the house very quickly and we were able to move in by Christmas of '42.

Our farm. The small building on the far left was the equipment house where we kept the machinery. The large white building was the barn. The new farm house is seen from the back. The first two windows were my parents bedroom windows, followed by two dining room windows and two living room windows. The low white building to the right of the farmhouse was the chicken house where we lived while they were building the new house.

Built with bricks, the house had doubled exterior walls with about two inches of air between them for insulation. Even the interior walls were brick covered with plaster. The floor plan was similar to the old house, except larger. We entered through the mudroom where we removed our shoes or boots. There was also a basin to wash in, but no running water. From there we entered the kitchen, which was the heart of the home. There was wood stove for cooking and heating and a big, six-foot table with an "L" shaped bench in the corner. From the kitchen a small hallway led to the "formal entrance" where guests entered. Most

11

people entering the house came through the mudroom, though. But if you came in through the "formal entrance," you would have the kitchen to your right, a small guest room to your left and straight ahead was the living room with an adjoining dining room, neither of which was ever used except on very special occasions, like Christmas. My parent's bedroom was next to the dining room but was usually entered through the mudroom. A small stairway led up from the mudroom to the loft where we had two small bedrooms. I had one of the bedrooms, which I later shared with my brother. The only heat source was in the kitchen, a wood stove. There were also tile ovens in the living and dining rooms, but they were seldom used.

We had no running water or indoor toilet. Instead we would go out in the barn. Behind the cows was a trough for their elimination. It also served as a toilet for the family, since we didn't have a bathroom or even an outhouse. Squatting, we would have to keep a sharp eye on the cow behind us, in case she had the notion to go at the same time as we did. Many times I had to scoot sideways, like a sand crab running for its hole, with my pants down around my ankles to get out of the line of fire. It was especially perilous in the springtime, when the cows had been out on new clover; their range could be as great as four feet plus collateral splash effect. If you got hit, you would look like a walking pile of guacamole, but the aroma would be considerably different. Toilet paper had not been invented, at least not as far as we were concerned. Instead, a handful of straw was pressed into service. In 1948 running water was installed in the kitchen, but only a cold tap, we still didn't have a bathroom or hot running water.

The house was connected to the barn by a small room, which did have a type of shower, a pipe hanging from the ceiling with a cold-water tap. There was also a large kettle that was heated by a fire underneath to boil water for washing clothes. My mother boiled the laundry first, scrubbed it clean on a washboard, and then rinsed it several times before hanging it on the line to dry.

Entering the barn you first encountered the horses, two huge Belgium horses in their stalls. After that the cows were lined up on one wall of the barn, and on the other side were the small calf stalls and the pigsties.

Our day began at 5:00 or 5:30 in the morning with the barn chores. The pigsty had to be mucked and fresh straw laid out every morning. Pigs are really neat animals, despite ideas to the contrary. They did their dirty business in the corner of the sty where there was a drain and left the rest of the area nice and clean and comfortable. We also mucked out behind a long row of cows. Then the animals had to be fed. Depending on how many animals there were, it could take my father and mother a couple of hours to finish the chores. They usually had about a dozen cows to milk by hand as we didn't have milk machines until the late '40's. The cows were milked twice daily, morning and evening, and some of them could produce as much as 5-6 gallons of milk per day. Milking was done by hand till 1948 when my father finally bought a milking machine, which helped a lot. The machine milked two cows at a time, freeing him to do other chores. There were no days off or holidays, as far as the barn was concerned, every day was the same and they seldom had any hired help.

Cows "come into season" sometime in early summer and the farmer had to make sure she met a friendly bull. I often saw someone walking down the road, leading a cow to be serviced by a bull. I have also seen a person leading a bull along the road to a farm somewhere, where he was needed for several cows.

Early in the spring, mid-March or early April, as soon as the frost was out of the ground, we began preparing the fields. The climate in Denmark is usually quite wet, which made farming challenging. Many times it was impossible to get on the fields, because one would get mired down, but in due course the fields dried up.

Farmers in Denmark, when I was growing up, grew many crops and were almost self-sufficient. There was very little that they needed to buy from the store. They grew four kinds of grain, rye, oats, wheat and barley. Kohlrabi, a large beet used for cow fodder, was also sown in long rows over several acres. There would also be a couple of acres of potatoes to fortify the family for a year. It was all a lot of hard work, mostly done by hand.

The big dung heap was the first thing to be loaded on wagons and hauled out on the field where it was spread around with a fork before being plowed down as fertilizer for the crops.

Horses could only draw a one-furrow plow, so it took a long time to cultivate the many fields. The farmers had to be in good physical shape, walking behind the horses all day long. In fact, while I was growing up, I never saw a farmer with a potbelly.

When the plowing was finished, the ground had to be leveled with a harrow that, even though it was about 10 feet wide, still required a lot of walking behind the horses. With that done the fields were ready for seeding. The grain fields pretty much took care of themselves until harvest time, but we had to spend a lot of time hoeing the weeds out of the rows of beets.

Fall was the time to harvest the crops. Again, most was done by hand. We had a machine that cut the grain and bound it into sheaves so we could pick them up with a fork and load them onto a wagon for transport to the storage building.

The beets were a lot more work. First we had to walk along each row, cutting the tops off, before we could come with a plow, digging them up out of the ground. Bringing out the horse drawn wagon, we picked them up one at a time and threw them in the wagon until it was full. We unloaded them by the barn in a large pile about five or six feet high and about 100 feet long. A whole lot of beets! To keep them from freezing during the winter my father covered the pile with a layer of straw which he carried in armloads from the barn, and then piled two or three feet of dirt over the whole thing. From time to time we loaded up the wagon with beets and brought them to a room in the barn where there was a big rasp, which chopped up the beets so that they could be fed to the cows. During the winter the cows were kept inside all the time. They were fed chopped beets, hay and some feed supplements to maximize milk production.

There were other animals on the farm. We raised chickens, of course, and also a few turkeys. The birds ran free in our yard. We had a Tom turkey that was especially aggressive, attacking anyone who dared to step outside the house. My mother took to carrying a broomstick, swatting him away with the skill of Babe Ruth. One day he attacked her just as she was stepping out the door, all dressed up for a party. Grabbing the broomstick, she hit him over the head and he dropped dead on the spot. She yelled for my father to bring the butcher knife to bleed the turkey and we feasted on turkey for several days. That was the end of that Tom turkey.

We also had a relatively large herd of geese, considering the size of the little farm. When I was between eight and ten years old, I was given the job of goose herder, keeping them on the pasture and out of the grain field. Not my idea of fun. I remember the frustration of trying to corral those unruly birds. For some reason the geese liked what was in the grain field much more than what the pasture had to offer. Geese are very smart and they realized splitting up gave them a fantastic advantage over me. While I was busy chasing one group out of the grain field, the other group wandered in to take their place. I remember at one time they simply took to wing and flew over my head, far into the forbidden area.

One of the ganders was especially mean and would nip me every chance he got. Somebody told me to grab him by the neck and drag him over to a bucket of water and hold his head under for a little while. That seemed to work. I don't know if he minded the water as much as being grabbed by the neck, but eventually he left me alone.

When my father decided to raise pigs on a larger scale, he converted the calf stalls into pigsties, but they were so tiny that there was barely room for the sow to move around. We had about a half dozen sows with little piglets. By the time I was twelve I had become a fairly skilled swine midwife, delivering dozens of pig babies, which probably didn't weigh much more than a pound. As soon as they came out I grabbed them, cut the umbilical cord and rubbed them with straw. If they didn't start breathing right away, I'd blow in their throats to get them going. Cleaned up and breathing I laid them by their mother's teat, so they could begin nursing right away. I had a favorite sow that was fairly small and sweet. Although she raised many litters in one of those small sties, she never crushed a single piglet.

We didn't usually have a boar, but a farmer about a mile down the road had one. When a sow came into season, I had to walk her over to visit her boyfriend. For a while we did have our own boar and, when he was needed on another farm, it was my job to take him there. Pigs are harder to herd than geese. I'm glad I only had one pig to drive at a time. They always want to do exactly the opposite of what you asked them. If I wanted them to go north, they wanted to go south. I even tried to drive one in the opposite direction to see if that would work better. It probably didn't. One time a boar got really mad at me and turned around slammed his head in to my leg. If he had had tusks I would have been in real trouble. These examples are of the old adage: Misery plus time equals comedy.

I decided at a very early age that farming was not for me. There had to be something else that I could do for a living. In school I liked woodshop and I toyed with the idea of becoming a finish carpenter, which was a nice clean job where you worked indoors and were always warm.

Like most farm families, we had a dog, a cross between a golden retriever and a German Shepherd. Her name was Fons and she was my friend. We were the same age and were pretty much inseparable. Sometimes I'd try to ride her, but that didn't work very well. She just sat down and looked at me like I was out of my mind. Sometimes she would go astray and before long we would have pups. My parents always managed to get rid of them, except for once, when they

decided to keep one. I had a lot of fun with the two dogs. Harnessing Fons to my little red wagon, the puppy would ride in style as the three of us traveled up and down the road. Until Fons saw a rabbit and chased it over the fields with the poor puppy bouncing around behind her. Other times I put Fons in the wagon and pulled her around the yard. Having little confidence in my driving skills, she usually bailed before we'd come very far.

Fons was getting older, so my parents decided to get a Fox Terrier. It was a much smaller dog and was great at catching mice, which we had in abundance. We called him Quick, because he was so fast and sharp. He took immediate control of the cats when he arrived and was generally the boss of his realm. I have always thought that Fons taught him to bark and to chase the occasional cars that came along.

As I mentioned before we had about half a dozen sows that would each have a litter or two of piglets every year. When the piglets were about two months old we sold them to a man who came to the farm and picked them up in his pickup truck. When he left, Quick would chase after him barking like mad and biting at the tires. One time when he was leaving, Quick gave him his normal farewell. Somehow losing his footing by the front tire, he was run over by both wheels. He had a bit of a stomachache for a few days but, other than that, nothing was hurt but his pride. From then on, though, whenever the man would come to pick up piglets, Quick would jump up in one of the barn windowsills as far away as possible, growling and shaking until the man was ready to leave. As the truck began to pull away Quick would

17

emerge from his fortress barking as usual, but still keeping his distance. No more biting at the tires.

When I became a teenager I was expected to do more of the work on the farm. We got up early and worked long hours, 15 hours was normal, especially in the summertime. There was little time for play during the week. One winter, though, I borrowed some ice skates. They were the kind that you strap on boots with hard soles, but I only had rubber boots and they kept falling off. The weather wasn't very cooperative either. It seems that all during the week the pond would freeze, but come Sunday the weather would warm up and there would be a couple of inches of water on top of the ice. I decided that I was going to skate anyway and got really soaked from falling in the icy water.

NO LONGER AN ONLY CHILD

My brother, Omar, arrived on the scene on October 9, 1940. I was almost six years old, but I remember it quite well. At the time I had no idea what was happening, except that something was out of the ordinary. My dad's brother, Thorvald, who was working for us at the time, was told to take me over to my maternal grandparents early in the morning. This was unusual but not traumatic since I enjoyed going to my grandparent's house. I heard Thorvald talking with my Uncle Peter, saying something like "She is having a little one."

"A little what?" I wondered, but didn't concern myself with adult matters.

I am six years old. My Aunt Tinne is holding Omar.

18

A couple of days later they took me home and I was informed that I now had a little brother. Entering the master bedroom I found my mother in bed with a little baby nursing at her breast. I didn't really know what to think. He didn't look like much of a playmate and I was not impressed.

As the years passed we tried to play together, but there was really too much of an age difference between us. I was always being told to be careful not to hurt him. One time I took him for a ride on my bicycle, probably riding too fast, and we crashed. I thought I'd never hear the end of that! Later, I attached a small seat to the crossbar in front of my seat for him to sit on, which worked much better.

Birgit was born February 21, 1945. This time my mother went to the hospital for the delivery, leaving my father at home as the sole caretaker. It can't have been easy for him, having to do all the chores in the barn and all the cooking for us. As I remember, he was not the best cook in the world by any stretch of the imagination. He cooked a chicken one evening, but it was only half done when he served it. The only thing worse than a half cooked chicken, is a half cooked turkey, which I was once subjected to while serving in the American army.

Birgit was a twin, but her sister was stillborn. My father went to the hospital, picked up her tiny body and placed her in a miniature white casket and brought it home and put it on the dining room table. The next day he put the casket on his bicycle

and rode to the church where she was buried in the churchyard.

We hadn't seen our mother for several days and Omar must have missed her terribly. We had been told that we now had a little sister. I, the experienced older brother, knew what to expect but Omar thought that he would now have a real playmate and was looking forward to meeting his new sister. When we came into my mother's room Omar was so excited to see her. Climbing up in her bed he hugged and kissed her repeatedly. After a while he slid down and we went to see the new addition to the family. She was not exactly what Omar had in mind, small and a little jaundiced, with a wrinkled head and a yellow face. He was so disappointed he was almost in tears. Angry and disillusioned, he refused to go back to my mother's room and say goodbye, wanting nothing to do with her. Things improved when they came home and later, when Birgit got a little bigger, Omar did get a little playmate.

In 1951 she was six years old and had learned how to ride a bike. For some reason, she preferred to ride mine. Although she wasn't tall enough to put her leg over the crossbar or sit on the saddle, she would merely put her leg underneath the bar and ride the bike on an angle. I told her umpteen times that I didn't want her to ride my bike, I even twisted the handlebars so that I could barely ride it myself, but she was not deterred, she got on and rode it crooked! I think she could have been a circus star! She has many other talents, too. She is artistic and outgoing and has always had a sweet disposition.

Jytte came along a couple of years later on January 17, 1947. She was always a spunky child, always happy and full of fun. She and Birgit became inseparable and remained good friends all their lives. Although they sometimes fought like cats, they always stood united against the world, sticking up for each other, particularly when it concerned a conflict with our mother. Jytte grew into a vivacious and gregarious woman who could brighten a room simply by entering it. Sadly, she died in 2003, at the age of 56.

When I was twelve my parents decided that I was old enough to take care of my siblings when they were away for a few hours or even a whole day. Omar could be quite unruly at times, as little boys often are. One afternoon he heaved a piece of carrot across the room shattering the big kitchen window. I was mortified. Thinking that I would be blamed for it, I feared I was in for a beating but, for once, my parents realized that it wasn't my fault.

After we immigrated to America in 1951 my younger siblings were enrolled in school. Being so much older I was not required or even expected to go to school. Instead I helped my father on the farm where he first was hired and later acquired employment of my own, working several odd jobs at a time. I was seldom home and had very little contact with the younger kids. Surprisingly, my mother, who had

21

so often been critical of me, now used me as an example, often admonishing them with, "Why can't you be more like Orla?"

We all grew up, of course, Omar still lives in the Sacramento area and has three children, Kelly, Jamie Beth and Clinton. Birgit is now living in Carlsbad, California and has a daughter, Kristen, and Jytte resides in heaven but is survived by her daughter, Susan. All of those children have, of course, grown up and are dispersed around the country.

First row from left: Omar with Clinton Dewey, Omar's wife Carol with Jamie Beth, Kelly, Birgit, Kristen. Second Row from left: LaVonne, Orla Jens, May-Britt, Jytte, Susan. I am standing behind my family and Jytte's husband Bill is standing behind Susan.

WW2

The 9th of April 1940, when I was five years old, remains vivid in my memory. We were awakened about 4 am by a noise we had never heard before. Outside, the sky was filled with airplanes. I had never seen anything like it before. We seldom saw airplanes, except once in a great while and they always generated excitement. Even automobiles were rare, if we saw one it was a real occasion. We soon learned that the Germans were in the process of invading our little country. It only took them four hours with very little bloodshed. We lost a few border guards, who decided to become heroes before the order came to stand down. There was nothing anybody could do to stem the assault of the Nazi juggernaut. My father and his farmhand got on their bicycles and rode the 10 miles to Esbjerg harbor to see what was happening. When they came back, they said that the harbor was full of warships and the highway was crowded with German military equipment. This was the beginning of a different way of life that would last for five years, until the Nazis finally got their just reward and walked back to their ruined homeland.

Towards the end of the war the Germans occupied the two classrooms in the school and the village community hall, and many soldiers were also housed at neighboring homes and farms, where they lived as part of the families. We were lucky not to get any in our home, although some representatives did come to inspect our place. They told us to expect to get a couple of soldiers, but they never showed up. We were not at all unhappy about that. They would have ruined our hardwood floors with their hobnailed boots and nobody would have dared to ask them to take them off.

As a small boy I was impressed with the soldiers we saw every time we came to town. I liked the uniforms they were wearing, especially the officers with their high caps and their shiny black riding boots. They really looked sharp. I made a gun using a broomstick for the barrel and a piece of wood that I shaped just right for the stock. Putting a small nail on the end of the barrel for a sight and a string on it for a shoulder strap, I slung my weapon over my shoulder and marched after the soldiers. I was an army of one.

Every morning, as we arrived at the school, the soldiers would line up for formation with something resembling stovepipes. They were qualifying to use this new weapon, the six foot long Bazooka. After receiving a lecture from the commanding officer, they marched out a couple of kilometers to a gravel pit at the bottom of our little farm. A couple hundred soldiers marched in the column singing their marching songs so loud that the noise carried for miles on the wind. I never saw them shoot the Bazooka, but I could hear the report from them and poor Fons nearly went out of her mind from fear. Always frightened of gunshots, she retreated to the farthest corner of the barn and lay there shivering.

While the Germans didn't do as much damage in Denmark as they did in other countries, they were still a fear-provoking horde. An unpleasant incident occurred when the Germans had just occupied our school. A younger teacher was walking across the schoolyard when a German officer asked a question. Ignoring him, the teacher kept walking away. The officer called a loud and menacing halt. Turning around, the teacher saw the officer, pistol aimed and ready to shoot. Immediately remorseful the young teacher apologized and lived to see the end of the war.

One of the farmers in our area had been involved in the resistance movement and somebody reported him to the Gestapo. Barely escaping out the back door as the Gestapo drove up to his farm, he went into hiding somewhere in Denmark and they never found him. Our family doctor was arrested for treating a freedom fighter. He was taken to a concentration camp in Germany and we never saw him again. Many books have been written about that time in Denmark's history. There were so many brave freedom fighters, which I'm sure made a difference in the war effort.

Denmark's deliverance came on May 4, 1945. I was at the general store the day before and overheard our neighbor lady saying that she had heard on the radio that the allies were at our southern border ready to go into Denmark and fight the Germans. It didn't make a whole lot of sense to me. The war was over, I knew that Germany was ruined, why would they come to Denmark to fight? The next day General Eisenhower, with his beautiful smile, was pictured on the front page of the newspaper. I had never seen pictures of him before, but from that day forward he became my hero. My dad had always bragged about how wonderful the Americans were. Maybe that is why they seemed more interesting to me than the Brits

A real tragedy occurred on the 5th of May that surely could have been averted. A couple of teenage boys, who I knew slightly, had gone to a location where there was a young German guard. They began to taunt him about losing the war. "Germany is kaput, completely ruined. Why are you still here? Go back where you came from." As they were walking away the guard called halt, but they just ignored him, something one should never do. Frustrated and trigger-happy the guard shot and killed one of them.

SCHOOL

I began school on May 1, 1941, the year I turned seven. My mother took me by the hand and we walked the one-kilometer to the village school. I was seated at a desk on the front row with a boy, who was slightly older than me. His name was Arne. We became very good friends all through our school years and we were often together at each other's homes. I visited him on his farm fifty years later, when I was in Denmark for a short visit.

According To Me

The teacher was an old man named Mr. Bastholm, who had been at the school since 1909. I had met him before because he was a friend of my parents. I had even been in his living quarters at the school, where he lived his wife, Karen. Mr. Bastholm ran the school with an iron hand. If anybody misbehaved, they risked getting a slap along side of the head by one of Mr. Bastholm's ham sized hands. Consequently there wasn't much disruption in class, definitely no talking to anybody except the teacher. One could even get in trouble during recess. One time I had been running out on the road too many times and when I came back to class, he was all over me like a dark ominous cloud. He told me that he was going to teach me about running out in the road and slapped me around so hard that I wet my pants, more from the surprise of the attack than him hurting me. Sometimes, when he had worked some kid over a little too much, he would later invite him in to his private quarters and atone for his deed by offering apples or a very delicious pear. Mr. Bastholm was really a good man. He wanted to train us the best way he knew how and I think he did a wonderful job. We could definitely use some of that discipline in schools today. I visited him in his home every time I returned to Denmark until he was up in his nineties. He always enjoyed seeing his former students and hearing how they were doing.

From November till May we were in school Monday through Friday and a half-day on Saturday. But from May till November we only attended school two half days per week with six weeks off for summer vacation. It was a rural farming area and all hands were needed at home to work. We had two classrooms. The small kids up to 10 years old were in one classroom, while the rest up till age 14 were in the other. We arrived at school at 8 am and were there until 4 pm. The first thing we did was line up against the wall, boys on one side and girls on the other. Mr. Bastholm would say a short prayer to begin the day. We followed a simple curriculum. We studied math, Bible, Danish history, handwriting, spelling and grammar. There was also a short period of singing with the teacher accompanying us on the old pump organ. A couple of times per week we had art. I always hated that class. I also had little interest in grammar. It was no different when I went to school in America and had to do it in English. It was a simple education, but it had always been quite adequate for agrarian people. After seven years our education was complete. If you were gifted and so inclined you could continue onto higher education, but most of us started working.

School picture from around 1947. I am standing in the middle row, farthest to the left with the light from the window blinds shining on my face. Ruth, my future fiancee, is standing on the top row, farthest to the right.

ACCORDING TO ME

Sometime during my first years in school they decided to build a new two-story structure with a woodshop above and bathrooms below. Up until then we only had outhouses, which was better than what we had at home, where we didn't have anything that even resembled a toilet.

I was looking forward to being in the woodshop, but you had to be ten years old before you could start. I didn't think I would ever turn ten, and when I eventually arrived at that magnificent age the Germans had taken over the school. The woodshop was converted into regular classrooms and shop class was canceled. A year later the war was over, the Germans gone home, and we were given back our school.

One day, when I was 13 years old, I walked into Mr. Bastholm's home and asked him if he could teach us English, he said that he would be happy to do that. Only half a dozen students were interested, but he said that he would still meet with us for an hour after school a couple of times per week. Mr. Bastholm taught us the correct pronunciation of the English words. I did, however, come in conflict with my dad on the subject of the "Th" sounds. My dad said that Mr. Bastholm didn't know what he was talking about. Dad had been in America and he knew how it was said. I didn't really believe him, but I wasn't sure who was really right. When my Uncle Søren and Aunt Esther came to visit from California I figured I would get it straight from the horse's mouth. One day I was sitting together with Søren on the sofa and I asked him how he pronounced "three."

"Tree," he said.

Then I asked him how he said "thirty."

"Turdy," he answered.

Confident that I now knew the correct pronunciation, I discounted some of what Mr. Bastholm was teaching us. Years later, when we immigrated to America, I found out that Mr. Bastholm had been correct after all.

THE CHURCH

The church in our village was, like most churches in Denmark, a very old stone building. Constructed in the 13th century, it was built like a fortress with walls at least 3 feet thick and small stained glass windows up high. Constructed not only for worship, the church also served as a fortification to protect the people in case of war. The windows were narrow on the inside and wider on the outside, giving people inside a wider view and better coverage with arrows, and the enemy outside a smaller target. There was a large, heavy door, about 6 inches thick, made of oak. Entering through the heavy door you came into what was called the weapon room. Today people don't carry weapons, but in bygone days they did. They were not allowed to bring their weapons into the church so they would hang their swords and lean their spears against the wall of the weapon room before entering the small sanctuary, which could probably seat a little over 100 people.

At the back of the church was a loft that held a large pump organ. I don't know what they used before they had the organ, perhaps minstrels. It took two people to play that organ. One person had to work the bellows by standing on a big pedal pumping it up and down, while the organist played the instrument. We often came to the church with our school class and our teacher would play the organ while my mother's former teacher led the singing of the ancient hymns. I got a kick out of watching these old men who were both about the same age and I found that intriguing.

When the church was built, Denmark, like most of Europe, was Catholic. Churches were very ornate with paintings and statues and golden altars carved with images of the Godhead and Saint Mary. The Catholic Church, often oppressive, became

29

especially abusive during the 16th century. The Pope, needing money for his favorite project in Rome, the construction of Saint Peter's Cathedral, sent his monks around Europe with wagons drawn by a team of oxen. On the wagon was a casket. Entering the town square, the monk would open the lid of the hideous casket, ring a bell and call to the people that the sooner they filled the casket with money, the sooner their dead loved ones would be rescued out of Purgatory, a place Catholics believe people go after they die to atone for their sins. Money paid to the church, the monk promised, would shorten the agony for yourself or your loved ones.

When the reformation came to Denmark in 1534 people converted to Lutheranism. Wanting to erase all memories of Catholicism, the churches were completely stripped of their ornate decorations and anything that would remind the public of the old ways. However, the little church in Grimstrup survived the holocaust of that time. For some mysterious reason it was never touched. To this very day the original altar is still standing where it has stood since the time the church was built. If you visit, you will see Father God, the Crucified Christ and Mary, the Mother of Jesus.

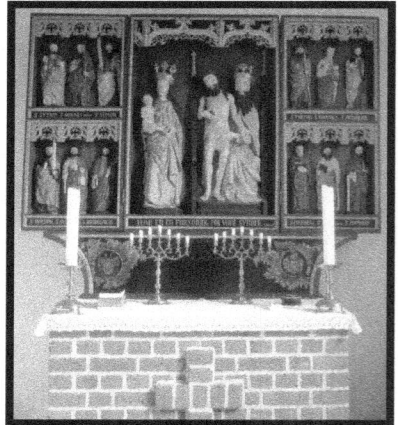

Surrounding the church is the community graveyard where people have been buried for centuries. My grandparents and many of my relatives, including my stillborn baby sister are resting there. The gravesites are taken care of by the relatives of the departed and most of the plots are really beautiful with flowers, low boxwood hedges and fine head stones. With time, when there is no longer anyone alive to care for the grave, the church will raze the area, remove the head stone and bury someone else there. Otherwise the graveyard would soon run out of room. That is the way it is done all over Europe.

I'm sorry to say that the church itself is perhaps almost ready for burial in Denmark, if not in Europe as a whole. But when I was growing up the church was important in people's lives for baptism, confirmation, weddings and funerals. Babies were baptized when they were a couple of months old. That is also when they were given a name. Up until then they were nameless. Can you imagine having a baby around for two months and just calling it "IT"?

We were confirmed the year we turned 14. Twice a week for six months we went to classes at the church to study the bible and church history. We also had to learn a lot of hymns by heart. Confirmation took place in the spring with all the boys dressed in dark suits and the girls in long white dresses. It was quite a celebration event. After the priest had talked to us for a little while, telling us that the best years of our lives were over and we were now young adults, we were served Holy Communion with real wine; no grape juice in the Lutheran Church.

Confirmation 1946. I am standing in the middle row, farthest to the left.

31

ACCORDING TO ME

Of course weddings were really a big deal in the church. Prior to the big day, four Sundays in a row, the nuptials would be announced. Traditionally this was done to allow for someone who objected to the union to come forward. The ceremony would begin with the Bride and Groom walking in together, the priest did what is normally done and pronounced the couple man and wife.

A big dinner party usually followed these great events with dancing till the wee hours of the morning. I often went home when the sun was high in the sky the next day. Of course in Denmark the summer sun rises early.

Funerals were of course more subdued. People came from all over the countryside, because everybody knew each other; they had lived there for most, if not all, of their lives. After the funeral service a light meal was served. People made speeches about how wonderful the departed had been, whether he had been or not. I went to my neighbor's departure and he had certainly not been very nice, but everyone who spoke tried to say something positive about him. It is customary to say good things about the dead.

Our priest, Pastor Lilleør, had come to Grimstrup church in 1932. He was a large, bald headed man with dark heavy eyebrows. I got to know him when I was quite young. He always came to the school at the end of the year to oversee the final tests. I'm not sure why, but that was the way they did things. He took a liking to me, probably because he was a good friend of my maternal grandparents. I liked him because he always gave me straight A's on all my tests. But there were many people who didn't have much use for him. I think they questioned his religious convictions. He was a good businessman and made a lot of money

in, among other things, the peat industry. During the Second World War he was also the leader of a group of freedom fighters. Meeting secretly in the forest, he would carry a submachine gun while pacing back and forth discussing plans for the next attack on the Nazis. Many people were suspicious of successful businessmen. Others felt that it was inappropriate for a pastor in the Lutheran church to be involved in the fighting. Consequently he would only have a half dozen people in church on Sundays. It must have been tough to give a sermon to so few, but he stuck it out until 1948, when he moved to another part of Denmark.

We attended church regularly, twice a year, Christmas and Easter. In our area that was fairly common, few people ever went to church, no matter who the pastor was at the time. But I was not without religious training. I was probably about four years old when my mother, as she was putting me to bed, began to teach me the Lord's Prayer. We repeated it together night after night until I knew it by heart. I prayed that prayer a lot growing up and it never did me a bit of harm.

JOBS

I couldn't wait till I was 14 years old when I would be out of school and could get a real job. When I was 12 years old, I was hired for the summer to work in a peat field. Peat consists of dead trees, leaves and grasses that have accumulated for thousands of years. It is usually found in swamps or bogs, forming a layer about five feet thick on average but could be deeper in some places. We used a special tool to cut and dig up the material. They would then shape it in something like blocks and let it dry. The peat was used as fuel for stoves for cooking and heating. After the war the peat business became commercialized and was a big business for a few years till all the peat was dug up and, as far as I know, the area is now useless swampland littered with large waterholes.

ACCORDING TO ME

The company I worked for had a machine that looked like an enormous meat grinder. Two men dug up the wet peat and loaded it into the top of the machine, which ground it up and pressed out the excess fluid. On the side of the machine was a rectangular opening through which the pressed peat came out like squared toothpaste. As it came out, a third man, using a large flat shovel, cut it into half meter lengths and loaded it onto a flatbed wagon. The wagon was equipped with very wide wooden wheels so that it would not dig in to the soft soil. Even the horse that pulled the wagon was specially equipped with something like a snowshoe so that it wouldn't sink in the bog. The peat was driven up to a drying field where it was unloaded by a forth man who used a large four pronged pitchfork. He laid the chunk of peat on the ground and then slapped it hard with the fork cutting it into smaller bricks.

We were three kids working at this place, driving horses from 7 am till 6 pm with an hour off for lunch. It was a very good job. We had a lot of fun and made relatively good money for our age. After laying in the sun for a few days the peat bricks were dry on one side and had to be turned to dry on the other side. Anxious to make even more money, I asked if I could have the job turning over the rows after hours. The peat was laid out in long rows. I used the same fork the man used to unload the wagons and I worked as long as I could see, which was until 10 pm. They paid me per row. It was one fantastic summer. I made more money than the common farm worker and that made me proud. It would be many years before I would be able to duplicate the income I had that year.

I never got paid for working at home. I didn't like that, so I went to work for our neighbors, Christian and Martha Poulsen. Their farm was a little larger than ours with the house and buildings built in a square around a large courtyard. The house had two separate apartments. Christian, Martha and their little daughter lived in one and his parents lived in the other. In Denmark, the houses are often connected to the barn. People do not want to go out in bad weather to care for the animals. The Poulsen's were wonderful to me. I had a lot of fun being there, which made the work easy. Christian would always make me laugh, especially at lunchtime. He would sit there and tell jokes and I would laugh so much that I couldn't eat, which meant that I would leave the table hungry. One day I decided that I wasn't going to laugh at him, I was going to concentrate on eating first. That worked quite well. I had found out that in order to eat a decent meal, I just had to ignore the comedian.

I arrived at their farm at 7 am and began mucking out the pigsties and behind the cows. The dung heap was just outside the barn. Wheeling the fully laden wheelbarrow out of the barn to the dung pile, I carefully maneuvered up the narrow boards to the top of the heap and dump the smelly load. As the year went on, the pile would get higher and higher and the boards would get steeper and steeper. I had to get a running start to get to the top. One morning we had frost and the boards were slick with rime. I had a full load of pig manure and, as I ran up the boards, my feet slipped on the ice. Falling, I put all of my weight in the wheelbarrow handles causing it to flip. There I lay at the bottom of a manure pile, and now it was Christian and Martha who had a good laugh!

I was only 13 years old when I began working for the Poulsens, but they let me do a lot of things that my Father was afraid to let me do at home. I handled the horses and plowed the fields with a single furrow plow, which you had to lift out of the ground every time you came to the end of the field, turning the horses around at the same time, to continue back the other way. Plowing a straight furrow was a skill and farmers scrutinized each other's work. One day, when I was plowing, Christian came out to inspect my work and he asked: "Are the furrows straight? It's important that they are straight." I probably didn't measure up to his expectations, but I still got to continue plowing. They had a 1929 Ford and Christian wanted to teach me to drive, but I had a little trouble keeping it in the middle of the narrow dirt road, and he quickly gave up on that idea.

AMERICA

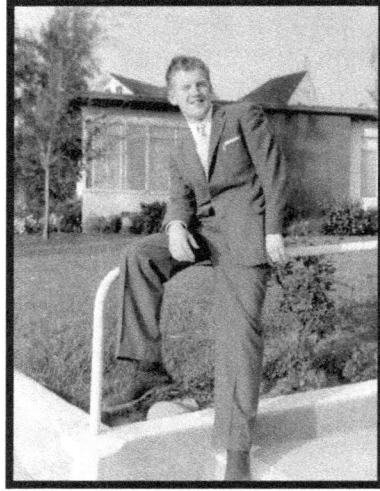

For years and years my dad had talked about going to America, but I didn't think that it would ever happen. I had begun to contemplate going over there sometime in the future. I detested farming; it was just a miserable existence to be out in the mud in all kinds of weather. I was sure that there was something else that I could do. Then all of a sudden, miracle of miracles, my parents decided to pull up the tent pegs and move to "The Land of Opportunities." It took a long time, three and a half years, to get through all the red tape. I told my mother, one day when we were working in the yard, that I didn't think we would ever get there. She replied that she was confident that we were destined for the good old US of A. "When we do arrive in our new country," she admonished, "have confidence in yourself, never be afraid to try new things and always do your best." I have tried to follow that sage counsel all my life.

With Uncle Søren's willingness to sponsor us and guarantee that we wouldn't be a burden on the U.S. government we

finally received our visas in 1951. We would travel to Fair
Oaks, California where Søren lived together with my aunt,
Esther, and their twin boys, Roy and Raymond, who were 16
years old, the same age as me. My parents were able to sell the
farm for a decent price and we started packing. According
to Danish law we were only allowed to take $50 per person
out of the country. That wasn't much to start out with in a
foreign country, where we didn't know the language and had
no jobs, but I didn't worry about that. I was just glad that we
were finally going to America.

In school I had been a little attracted to a girl named Ruth
who sat across the aisle from me. We were the same age and had
known each other almost all of our lives because our parents
were friends. I hadn't paid much attention to her when I was
younger but as I got older she began to catch my eye. It really
never developed into anything, but the other boys teased me
just the same. Just a few days before we were leaving, I ran into
Ruth. She suggested that we should be pen pals, to which I
gladly agreed. I really liked Ruth, but I never dreamt I could
have any kind of relationship with her.

We originally planned to travel to this great and magnificent
country by sea. We had booked passage on the good ship
"Batory," registered in Gdynia, Poland. But something
happened to our reservations, I don't know what, and we
decided instead to travel by air. Either mode would have been
fine by me, I just wanted to get there, but I was thrilled at the
prospect of flying in a big airplane all the way to America! Air
travel was still new and not many people flew in those days.
Although I had seen thousands of planes during the war and,
with the advent of air travel, a passenger planes could be seen
flying over our house every day at noon, I had never seen one
on the ground, let alone flown in one. Now we were going to
fly for many hours!

August 27, 1951 was the big day of departure. Most of our
belongings had been sent ahead by ship and would arrive in

ACCORDING TO ME

San Francisco two months later. Before leaving my childhood home, we all walked around the place to bid it goodbye. There were a lot of memories, some good, but there were many things that I wasn't going to miss. We went to our neighbors and thanked them for their friendship and support over the years. Lastly we said goodbye to my maternal grandparents and my mother's youngest brother, Eske, his wife Martha and their little boy, Henning.

Finally on our way, we took a taxi to Esbjerg where we boarded a train for Copenhagen. We spent the night at the home of an older man, Mr. Mortensen, who was my Aunt Ragna's father-in-law's brother. He lived in a beautiful house in an exclusive part of the city. I don't know if he was widowed or never married, but he had a live-in housekeeper, with whom he was on very formal terms. They always addressed each other by their last names, which I thought was a little strange, because she had been working for him for many years. But this was Copenhagen where people tended to be a little pretentious. Not to cast any aspersions on Mr. Mortensen, who very kindly took in our rather large family whom he didn't even know. We arrived at the airport the next day in plenty of time. Good thing we did, because when we got there my father realized that he had forgotten the tickets at the house. Getting the cabbie to drive him back, he retrieved the tickets and returned to the airport, still with ample time to check in. But I imagine that my father was rather stressed.

Awestruck, I gazed at the airplanes parked on the tarmac behind the terminal. They were taller than the buildings! The four-engine DC6s and DC7s were propeller planes and were much smaller than the big jets in use today. They carried 54 passengers at a speed slightly over 300 miles per hour. From Copenhagen we flew to Scotland for refueling, then to Newfoundland and finally to New York. The trip took 19 hours including layovers. Today we fly from Los Angeles to Copenhagen in 10 hours non-stop. Times have really changed.

I met some fascinating people on that flight. The Danish Prime Minister, Hans Hedtoft, was onboard and my mother was proud that she got to talk with him. She let him know that she didn't vote for him! There were also some Danish military officers, who were going to Texas for training. One of them was very accommodating, helping my father fill out the entry forms needed to enter the United States. For some reason I was temporarily deaf after we had landed in New York. I think it was caused by the atmospheric pressure coming down for landing. It was upsetting when people spoke to me, because I could barely hear them and, despite Mr. Bastholm's tutoring, I couldn't understand them.

New York City seemed to us an extraordinary place. Coming from what I consider a somewhat backward part of the world to this metropolis induced quite a culture chock. I'd heard about the skyscrapers, but couldn't really comprehend their grandeur before I saw them. They were absolutely astonishing. It was like passing through a gorge where the sun seldom reaches down to the street. Then there was the traffic. I had never seen so many cars; there were thousands of them. And the buses made strange sounds when they came to a stop. I had never heard air brakes before. Little things like that were very intriguing. Manhattan Island was like an anthill, with the millions of people living there running in all directions. It seemed like they were all in a big hurry. And to think just a few hundred years ago the Dutch colonists bought that island from the Indians for a few multi-colored beads!

After successfully passing through the immigration procedures, my dad hired a couple of taxis to take us to the Greyhound bus station, where we boarded a covered wagon (Greyhound bus) that same afternoon. It took a week to get to California, another magnificent experience! What better way to see this glorious country than to travel the open highways? Adventurous as I am, I loved every minute of it. I don't remember being tired, even though we must have been exhausted from that long-drawn-out flight, but we wanted to get to California as soon as possible, so we just pressed on.

I enjoyed riding the Greyhound bus. Driving out of New York, we crossed under the Hudson River through the Holland tunnel, coming up in New Jersey and were soon traveling through the countryside. The Eastern states are lush and green in the summertime because they get rain regularly, unlike the Western states, which dry up and turn brown from lack of moisture. We entered a big highway called "The Pennsylvania Turnpike," a name I thought sounded extraordinary. But then, at 16 years of age, I was mesmerized by everything I saw and heard. Pennsylvania has rolling hills with lots of deciduous trees. It was like driving through an arboretum.

Pulling into Chicago after a couple of days on the bus, my parents were totally exhausted and decided that we needed to find a hotel, so that we could get at least one good night's sleep. I would have been willing to stay on the bus, if that had been the program, but I admit it really felt good to crawl in between those nice white sheets, stretch out and sleep all night. It was an older hotel and the only thing I remember about it is that the lady who took us to the room had blue hair. I'd never seen anything like that in Denmark!

We ate breakfast the next morning at a drugstore. I remember that my father kept asking for more butter. We ate a lot of butter in Denmark. Walking towards the bus station, Jytte, my four-year-old little sister, tore herself away from my father and raced down the street. Always a rascal, she was used to running free in the country and didn't understand the dangers of city traffic. Luckily my father was able to catch her before she ran out into the street.

We were on the bus again. Although most of our fellow passengers ignored us, some were curious and tried to talk to us. My father was the only one who could speak enough English, however broken, to be able to hold a conversation. I knew a few words from the lessons I had received from Mr. Bastholm, but it didn't amount to much. One nice thing about taking a bus across the country is that it stops every two to three hours for meals and other physical needs. I have always thought that I preferred traveling by bus rather than taking a train. On a train you can never get off before your destination and I think the trip would be less exciting.

We rolled into Sacramento, the capital of California, on September 2, 1951. My dad had trouble using the phone to call a taxi but, with a little help from a bystander, he succeeded and we were soon on our way out to the beautiful little hamlet of Fair Oaks, where Uncle Søren and Aunt Esther lived.

Fair Oaks, at that time, was a wonderful, quiet community located just north of the American River and about 14 miles from Sacramento. I felt that if heaven isn't better than this, it's still going to be magnificent. My uncle and aunt lived on a small quiet road, in a modest, but adequate, white house with green trim. Compared to today, there was very little traffic anywhere. The house was built on five acres in the middle of an olive orchard. I love fruit and, arriving in the beginning of September, it was harvest season, so there were all kinds of fruit, peaches, apricots, grapes, etc.

Already on my first day, I was introduced to the antics of American kids. My cousin's friend showed up in his father's new car in the afternoon and the four of us went to the state fair in Sacramento. We must have been going about 70 miles per hour, when the driver and my cousin, Raymond, decided to switch seats without bothering to stop the car. It was a real eye opener for me. Arriving at the fair, we went straight to the carnival area and got on some crazy ride that spun us around in all kinds of ways. I wound up with a stiff neck that lasted several days. On the way home we stopped at a big vineyard to pick some delicious grapes.

A couple of days after we had arrived, Uncle Søren's brother-in-law, Barney, took me fishing on the river. In time we became very close and I consider him to be my uncle also. He had an old rustic cabin in the mountains, where he often invited me to come get away from it all, and do a little fishing. Barney worked for the county hospital as a painter, which was a very good and clean job, and he didn't have to work very hard.

I had gotten the impression that you could find gold on the streets of California, which, at one time, they actually did, but I didn't find any. So in order to get a little spending money, I went looking for a job. Not being able to speak the language made it complicated, but Uncle Søren had connections. He got me a job pulling weeds out of his neighbor's lawn. I was paid the princely sum of 65 cents an hour. I did that for three days, and decided that there had to be something better that I could do. I dug a hole by my uncle's driveway, where he was going to install a gas tank so that he could fuel his car and tractor. My uncle was a landscaper and used a tractor in his work. The soil was clay and hard like concrete and almost impossible to dig. I wasn't used to that. In Denmark it was easy to dig holes, something we often had to do either for postholes or to get down to the sand that we used around the farm.

GRIDLEY

Shortly after our arrival my dad found a job on a dairy farm, owned by the Machados family, in Gridley in Northern California and we all moved into a small cottage on the farm. Mrs. Machado had emigrated from Portugal with her husband many years before. She had a son and a daughter, Mary, who was spinster and lived with her mother. Her son, Manuel, was married and lived in town. He had no children, only a small dog. Manuel and his mother were wonderful, but we didn't care much for the daughter. She was often complaining about something and trying to take advantage of us by asking us to do extra work that we didn't get paid for. My father complained to Manuel about her one time, and Manuel told him not to pay any attention to her. Notwithstanding Mary's interference, I have pleasant memories from that time of my life.

Gridley was a very small town in the middle of the fertile Sacramento Valley. The dairy farm, where we lived, was located about three miles south of town, next to the Feather River. It had about 500 acres, half of which was pasture for the 72 cows that we had to milk twice daily. Manuel leased the rest of the acreage to a Japanese vegetable grower, who raised tomatoes. I had never seen so many tomatoes! An enormous plum orchard lay to the west of the farm, and across the road, on the north side, was a great peach orchard. Fruit lover that I am, I thought that I had died and gone to heaven. I was eating fruit and tomatoes all the time, which resulted in a terrible upset stomach that lasted the duration of the season. When the local fruit harvest was over, we bought boxes of oranges at the cannery, which we ate most of the winter.

We had a pleasant surprise one of the first nights we were on the farm. As we were sitting down to dinner we heard a knock on the door and wondered who it could be. Opening the door, we found an older couple standing on our doorstep. They asked if we were the Pedersens who had just arrived from Denmark and, when we told that we were, began to speak Danish. Einar and Elizabeth Vedam, both from Denmark, had lived in America many years. They had a poultry farm with thousands of chickens and sold eggs to people in the area. Einar was still working as an inspector in a cannery in town, but he retired shortly after we met them. It was great getting to know the Vedams who became our lifelong friends.

I made quite an impression on Manuel Machado the first day on the job. He had come to the farm to see how we were getting along and he liked to talk. Since my father was the only one who could speak English, I could only stand by and listen. Later, walking with Manuel out behind the very long barn, we came to a big tractor that he said he needed moved around to the front. I managed to convey my desire to drive it, and he consented. I climbed on and he started it up and showed me how to put it in gear. Driving that big monstrosity along the building went well until I rounded the corner. I made the turn just fine, but for some reason I couldn't turn the wheel back, so I just kept turning till I went right through the wall of the barn. I finally had sense enough to push in the clutch, and stopped just as the wreckage of the barn came level with the steering wheel. Manuel stared in astonishment, but he didn't say anything to me. Either he figured that I wouldn't understand what he said, or he was just too shocked to speak.

I had to help my father with the barn chores. Getting up at 3 o'clock in the morning, I would go out and gather the animals into the barn. Most of the cows were already in the corral waiting for us, but there would always be some stragglers out in the field that I would have to go out and chase them down. This could be a difficult task in the dark and, at least in my memory, often in the rain. When the cows were in their stalls, my dad could begin milking them, four at a time, with the milking machines. I carried the milk to the milk house where I poured it in to a cooler. From there it went into a holding tank from which it would later be pumped into a big tanker truck for transportation to the creamery in town.

When the cows had all been milked, it was my job to clean the barn, which was at least 150 feet long. Seventy cows, standing still in a barn, have nothing better to do than relieve themselves. First I shoveled up the abundance of dung, loaded up my wheelbarrow and drove it out. Then I took a long, one and a half inch, high-pressure hose and washed down the entire barn. It had to be spotless. The entire job took a little over four hours and then we would repeat the whole procedure in the afternoon. The winter of 51-52 we had a record amount of rain and the corral where the cows gathered was a real mud hole. Dragging their udders in the mire they soon developed mastitis. This eventually affected the milk and the creamery lowered the classification on it, which meant less money for the farmer. My father informed Manuel, who called the veterinarian. He prescribed some healing salve to apply to the cow teats, but it didn't help much. Manuel didn't seem overly concerned and there was nothing more my father could do.

Manuel Machado was a man who believed in second chances. Despite that appalling incident with the tractor, he still had confidence in me and asked me to take care of the small calves that were housed in another building a fair distance away from the barn. There was another tractor, at least as big as the one I drove through the wall, with one small wheel in front and a big scoop that could be raised up high. I drove it to the big barn, filled the scoop with hay and ran it over to the calf barn.

Part of my job taking care of the calves was to give them milk. First I had to teach them to drink out of a bucket. Letting them suck on my fingers, I used my other hand to shove their heads in to the bucket. If you've ever seen a calf nursing from its mother, you've seen how it gives her udders a good nudge when the milk doesn't come fast enough. Well, a calf drinking from a bucket does the same thing. I had to be sure to have a good hold on the bucket or it would go flying.

Manuel taught me how to drive in his big old GMC truck. Driving along a dirt road, I shifted in to third gear from second, but I did it with a little bit of a jerk. Manuel told me to put it back in second and do it again. He said that I should be able shift gear without him feeling it. It was good advice that I have tried to follow anytime I drive a car with manual transmission, which doesn't happen very often. In time he let me drive everything he had on the farm, including his new pick-up truck. There was also a small tractor, which connected to a manure spreader. I just had a ball going up and down the field throwing manure in all directions to fertilize the ground.

Although I didn't do any fishing, I liked walking along the river observing the flow of the water. We didn't have any rivers like this in Denmark. It was especially fascinating in October when the Salmon were running. I had never seen anything like it. The fish were so thick you could walk across their backs to the other side. Not really, but if you threw in a hook you could be sure to pull up a fish. Some people did just that, but I don't think they were very good to eat because they were half dead, on their way up the river to spawn and getting pretty beat up on the way. Their mouths become distorted when they enter the fresh water and they can no longer eat. When they reach their destination in the river, the females lay eggs and the males fertilize them. This is their ultimate task before they die. You find a lot of dead salmon lying along the river's edge in the late fall.

In February of 1952, six months after our arrival, I decided that I wanted to go to high school to improve my English skills. My mother questioned my rationale, insisting that the education I had received in Denmark was satisfactory. But I was adamant. Gridley's high school was small, only 300 students, and they were very nice to me. One boy showed me around the place and introduced me to his friends. Since I only had a rudimentary knowledge of the English language I was enrolled in the freshman class together with kids three years younger than me, but I didn't care. I was there to learn the language. My best subject was math since numbers are the same in any language.

One day I got in trouble and was sent to the principal's office. Needing to go home early, I was caught red-handed while writing my own note to be excused. This, of course, was not allowed and I was hauled off to talk to Mr. Guilford, the principal of the school. I explained that I had to go home to get the cows in for milking. I was sorry about writing the excuse, but even at home I would have to do it because I was the only one in the family who could write in English. Mr. Guilford let me go. I'm sure, given the size of the community, that he knew and understood my situation. Not many kids, if any, had to get up a 3am and work four hours, go to school all day, then go home and work another four hours. Getting to bed at 9 pm, I averaged about six hours sleep a night. Sometimes I fell asleep in class, partly because I was tired, but also because I didn't understand everything that the teacher said.

I have never been interested in sports, but I had to take PE in school so I tried a little of everything they offered like baseball and basketball, which I have never liked, and track, which was running and jumping hurdles. Hurdles are about 30 inches high and you jump over them with one leg first and the other following. I told the guys that I could jump over them with both feet together. That was a big mistake. Getting a running start, I jumped with my feet together, but I didn't clear the top of the hurdle and I tumbled over, fell on my shoulder and broke my collarbone. Writhing in pain, the coach took me to the emergency hospital where I laid on a stretcher for the longest time before somebody came to take care of me. I don't remember them taking any X-rays; they just bound me up real well with my arm tied to my body and sent me home. That was the end of my schooling in Gridley and the end of my work on the farm. My father had just been hired to work on a gold dredger in Folsom, Ca. He quit his milking job and, within a couple of weeks, we moved back to Fair Oaks and never worked on a farm again.

FAIR OAKS

I was glad to be back in Fair Oaks where I could hang out with my cousins. One evening I was riding around in Roy's Jeep when I noticed that the bandage had come loose and I felt a big bump on my shoulder. I showed it to my uncle and he thought that I had better see his doctor in town. The next day, after examining me, the doctor said that my injury was beyond his expertise and recommended that I see a specialist in Sacramento immediately. My father drove me to Sacramento where we located the office of the orthopedic surgeon. Dr. McNeal was a wonderful person and I will forever hold him in the highest regard. He determined that I needed surgery immediately if I was going regain normal function in my shoulder. My father worried about how he was going to pay for it, but Dr. McNeal told him not to worry about payment, that my well-being was more important. He operated that same night and repaired my broken collarbone by wrapping it in surgical wire and driving two long nails into the end of the bone, the ends sticking out of my shoulder about half an inch. I spent three days in the hospital before I was sent home. I had a little trouble sleeping on my left side with those nails sticking out. Six weeks later, after examining me for the last time and determining that I had healed well, the doctor grabbed an old pair of pliers, put a firm hand on my shoulder, took hold of the nails and just yanked them out one at the time, as if he was pulling them out of an old piece lumber. As far as I remember the whole ordeal didn't cost more than $165.00. That was a rock bottom bargain, even in those days.

I finished up the year at San Juan High School in Fair Oaks where my cousins also attended. I want to say right now that I was not an honor student and I was glad it was over. I was 17 years old and I knew the English language well enough that I didn't think I needed to go to school any more. I wanted to get a job and make some money. I have always been a hard worker and finding a job was never difficult. I began doing work in people's yards getting paid $1.25 per hour, which was fine. I didn't even have to pay taxes. Then I got a call from the city and was asked if I would like to work in the park doing landscape maintenance. They offered me $ 1.00 per hour, but I insisted on a dollar and a quarter and prevailed. I worked half days, five days a week. Later, I got a job cleaning up the beach at the river, where people gathered to swim and have bar-b-ques. With those two jobs, plus my other gardening jobs, I was working 10 – 12 hours a day and doing quite well economically. Of course, when my parents noticed that I was in the chips, they decided that, if I was going to be this industrious, I should begin paying for my room and board at home. That was reasonable and we determined that I should pay $ 75.00 per month.

I worked all summer in the park running a lawn mower, weeding and doing anything else that needed to be done. My boss was an older man, Mr. Swarosky. He was very nice to me and often invited me to his home, where I began to feel like part of the family. He and his wife were raising two teenage granddaughters but, although I was around them a lot, we didn't really hit it off. The Swarosky's were spiritists and believed that they could communicate with the dead. Thank goodness, I didn't get involved in that. They had lost a son sometime in the past. One day they showed me a picture of a tree and there among the leaves was something that looked like a face. They were convinced that this was the spirit of their dead son attempting to communicate with them or be near them.

PAINTING CAREER

One day, in the fall of 1952, Mr. Swarosky had me paint a stairway. I found that I enjoyed that kind of work. Time passed quickly when I had a paintbrush in my hand and I thought this could possible become my life's work. I knew that I wasn't going to be a park employee the rest of my life. One day I told Uncle Barney that I thought I had figured out what kind of work I would like do in the future. My father had just been hired at Crystal Creamery and we were moving to Sacramento. I asked Uncle Barney if he knew anybody in the Sacramento area who would hire me as an apprentice painter. He came to me a couple of days later and told me that he had located a painting firm, the Ted J. Cook Painting Co. They hired me, but in order to work for them I had to join the Painter's Union and, since I was under 18, I also had to obtain a work permit from a Sacramento high school. I thought that was strange, never having gone to school there, but I was able to get the paper work so that I could continue working. My union scale wage at the painting firm was only $1.05 per hour, and then they withheld taxes and other things. My parents were renting a nice house in Sacramento, but the rent was higher than in Fair Oaks, so I was now paying them $100 per month. Financially my new career was a loss, but I knew that in time it would all be worth it.

I must say that I started learning my new trade from the bottom. When I showed up the first day, there was another kid who was same the age as me. We were taken out to a new high school, still under construction. Handed paint buckets and small brushes with the handles cut off, we were sent up on the roof to paint the inside of the rain gutters. Looking back, it was rather ridiculous. I have never seen that done anywhere else, but some crazy architect insisted that the inside of the gutters had to be painted. Graduating from painting the inside of gutters, we were given the job of painting piles of lumber before it was installed in the new buildings. We worked primarily on schools still under construction, as many new schools were being built to accommodate the influx of population in California after the war. I painted boards for a year until I finally graduated to actually painting on buildings. It took a long time before I was allowed to do finish work, like applying enamel and varnish. When I was finally allowed to use these materials, I felt that I had really arrived.

I actually did quite well. The apprentice period was supposed to run for four years, but by the end of my third year I received my journeyman's card. I was now making very good money and was working as much overtime as the company would allow. I was also looking for work on my own, moonlighting on weekends and evenings if there wasn't any overtime available.

The first job I did on my own may have ended in disaster. I was painting a small bathroom for some people in our neighborhood. The bathroom was green and they wanted it painted the same color again. I decided to match the color myself. New at the trade, I really didn't know what I was doing. I had the white paint and a bunch of colors and I began mixing it, but I just couldn't get the right shade. Finally I gave up. The color I had made was way off, but I locked the door and painted the room. The people paid me and never complained.

Years later I became quite proficient at matching colors. One of my clients was a very nice, but demanding, lady. She wanted the glossy trim to exactly match the flat wall color. I managed to get close to a perfect match. Of course the sheen on one object and the lack of it on another is always going to look a little different, so I told her to stand right in front of a door jam, close her eyes so that she could barely see the color, and it would then look the same. That is how I convinced her that the color matched. Sometimes you have to use psychology with your customers.

Later, when we were living in Los Angeles, I was working for a painting company in charge of maintenance of a large apartment complex that offered their tenants a free paint job every four years. If they were willing to pay an extra fee they could even choose the color. We had begun working in a large apartment when our foreman brought up 10 gallons of the special color the lady had ordered. She took one look at the paint and exclaimed that it was not at all the color she had ordered and she wasn't going to have it in her apartment. The foreman told the coordinator, who had been working with the lady about the décor, and he took the paint with him down to his office and left it there for half an hour. Bringing it up again, he asked the lady what she thought about it now. She said that it was just right, and why didn't he bring that up in the first place. He had done absolutely nothing to it. We had a lot of laughs about that one.

According To Me

Returning to Denmark

I had been in the United States for nearly two years, had saved some money and thought it could be fun to go back to Denmark again for a visit. Ruth and I had been corresponding regularly and I thought it would be nice to see her again. I was, perhaps, too exuberant in my letters. She got nervous and wrote to me that we better quit writing to each other. This was upsetting and I decided to cancel my travel plans. My parents, however, encouraged me to go anyway. After all, there were a lot of other people to see over there. Following their advice, I prepared for the trip. Since I wasn't a U.S. citizen, I couldn't just buy a ticket, leave and expect to come back again. I had to go to the immigration office and request a reenter permit. When I applied I told the official that I was going to be gone for two months and that is what the permit stated. A few days before I was to leave I looked it over and it said that it would expire January 13,1954. I didn't know what that meant, so I called the official. He said that I had to be out of the country by that time and wished me a good trip. I bought a round trip ticket, Sacramento to New York, on the Greyhound bus, and a round trip ticket, New York to Copenhagen, on the Swedish Passenger ship "Kungsholm." From Copenhagen I would take the train to Esbjerg. It was quite a trip for a green 18 year old.

Saying goodbye to my parents and siblings, I boarded the bus heading for New York on December 1, 1953. Crossing the country took five days, 24 hours a day. As I've said before, it's a wonderful way to see the country. Maybe not the way I did it, five days straight, but I could have taken in a hotel at night and it would have been less tiresome. The bus stopped every two or three hours for food and bathrooms.

I have always liked boots and had bought a pair of engineer boots that had a strap over the ankle. I thought they were very sharp. On the bus I slipped them off for comfort. But after a couple of days without showers, my feet got to stinking so bad that I was embarrassed, and I had to keep them on the rest of the trip.

Arriving in New York City, I checked into Hotel Times Square, right in the middle of Manhattan. I was there four days and spent the time taking city tours and walking around looking at the sights. From the top of the Empire State building you can see the entire city and beyond. It was quite an experience being so high up in the world.

On December 9th I boarded the beautiful ship," Kungsholm," and began the eight day cruise across the Atlantic Ocean. The "Kungsholm" was brand new, on its maiden voyage, and was really delightful. I met three other young men, who were also going back to Denmark, and we really hit it

off. The food was unbelievable and plentiful. The dining room never seemed to close. We never went to bed early, dancing until late at night. Half way through the trip we hit a Mid-Atlantic storm. Amazingly I never got seasick, although I came close. The ship was rolling so much that, while passing through the corridors, I alternated between walking on the floor and walking on the wall! Trying to sleep in my bunk at night was something else. The ship was going up and down, front to back and side-to-side, and it felt like I was in a barrel rolling down a hill. Every now and then the rolling of the ship would lift the propellers out of the water. Spinning in the air, they made the whole ship shutter and reverberate. After a few days the sea smoothed out nicely and people began coming back to the dining room again, after literally being "under the weather."

Passing through the Danish waters I was filled with a feeling of nostalgia. After all, this is where I had spent most of my life up till that time. It was awe-inspiring to sail past Hamlet's castle on the coast by Ellsinore. As we entered Copenhagen's harbor some people on deck started singing the Danish national anthem. They had been gone for many years and became quite emotional having returned to the country of their birth.

After clearing immigration and customs, I took a taxi to the railway station, right across the street from Tivoli. There was a train leaving shortly for the west coast. I arrived in Esbjerg somewhere around 2 am and got a taxi to Grimstrup, where my maternal grandparents lived. I must have arrived there about 3 o'clock in the morning and my grandmother was a little confused, wondering if ships came in that time of night, not realizing that I had been on a train for several hours. They had recently retired and moved to a small house they had built across the road from the farm where they had toiled for so many years. It was a nice house with two bedrooms, but very primitive. They had no running water and no bathroom. In a small room adjoining the mudroom they had a bench with a hole in it and a bucket underneath that my grandfather would empty when necessary.

It was great to be home with family and friends. I enjoyed celebrity status, coming from the New World, and had arrived just in time to celebrate my birthday. My grandparents threw me a big party and I connected with people that I hadn't seen for a couple of years. I had definitely not been away from Denmark long enough to have forgotten the language, I still haven't after 58 years, but I had been influenced enough by English that I my sentence structure was not quite Danish and it didn't go unnoticed by my contemporaries, who were quick to tease and point out my mistakes. Christmas was just as I remembered it, with fantastic food, songs and gifts. We played a card game, Whist, which was the game of choice in those circles. Money was involved, but you could never lose or win more than a few crowns; a very friendly game. My grandfather and one of my uncles were very amusing. Every time we finished a hand, they analyzed every trick that had been played, what they did and what they should have done. It was really very entertaining.

A Christmas dance was being held in the old village hall in Roust. Spotting Ruth, I watched her from a distance for a while, hoping that she would make the first move, but she didn't. After a while I went over to her and asked her to dance and she said she would. We chatted as we were dancing, recapping what had happened over the past two years. She was attending college in Ribe, an old city about 25 miles south of Roust, studying to be a teacher. After a few more dances she asked me to come down to visit her when school began after the New Year. I promised that I would but didn't get around to it until the middle of January. It was a long way on a bicycle, which was the only mode of transportation I had available. Opening the door at my knock and finding me standing on her doorstep, she burst into tears. She thought that I hadn't come because I didn't want to see her again. I've always been a sucker for women's tears and I begged her forgiveness for not coming sooner. It was a rocky start but soon we were laughing and having a wonderful time together.

According To Me

Ribe is the oldest town in Denmark and there are lots of interesting places to visit. There was a very good bakery around the corner where we would go and buy baked goods to go with our coffee. Ruth also made the best sandwiches. With that kind of hospitality I was enticed to make that trip several times in the next couple of weeks, turning up in the afternoon and leaving late in the evening. One night we were walking around in the city, being especially affectionate, and I said something really crazy, "Let's get engaged." She said yes, and the next day we went to a jewelry store to buy a couple of plain gold rings. Now we belonged to each other.

I was a little apprehensive about how her parents would respond to our engagement. Ruth told me later that her mother burst out in tears, but her dad took it all in stride. I had always liked him, but her mother made me a little nervous. She had told me that I could not visit Ruth in Ribe. I understood why, but I went there anyway. I want to clarify this right now though; we never did anything together that we couldn't have done in front of her mother. I was invited to their home every Saturday and Sunday afternoon for dinner when Ruth was home and we would play cards until I had to go home to my grandparents. It was nice to be included in the family like that, but somehow I knew that there would never be a marriage, because there was no way that I would live in Denmark, and I didn't think that Ruth would leave her parents. They would do anything to keep her home. Even so, we sustained the charade as long as I was in Denmark.

The first week in February, Ruth, her father, her sister and I went to Esbjerg to see a travel agent to confirm my travel back to the U.S. The agent accepted my paper work and told me to come back in a couple of days. I had a premonition that something would go wrong, and when I went back to his office the agent gave me some devastating news. My re-enter permit had expired on January 13th, my resident visa was no longer valid, and I could not return to America. That is what the official in California had meant when he said I had to leave the country by the expiration date. Although I had understood him to mean that I had to leave the United States by that date, he meant that I had to leave Denmark. I was shocked. The agent told me to contact the American embassy in Copenhagen. I made an appointment and took a train the next day. At the embassy the representative told me that I would have to re-emigrate and, even though he could put me on a non-quota list, it would still take time to get through all the red tape and it would also be quite costly. I told him that I didn't care what it cost; just get me back to America as quickly as possible. Denmark was great to visit, but I sure didn't want to live there. I had to go through the entire process of getting an American sponsor, medical examinations, paperwork, etc. At home with my grandparents I waited, promptly filling out and returning any paperwork I was sent. Nevertheless, every cloud has a silver lining. I had more time to spend with Ruth, sneaking down to Ribe mid-week and visiting in her home on weekends.

Waiting for my visa to come through I eventually ran out of money and I began looking for a job. One of our old neighbors, Niels Bro, hired me as a farmhand. I had room and board plus 20 crowns per day, less than $3, a mere pittance. It was really hard work and I had grown soft. My back was so sore the first week that I couldn't straighten up and my hands were full of blisters and cracks. It got easier after that but I longed to go back to my Promised Land. Eventually God had mercy on me. On May 20, 1954, when I had been working on that wretched farm for three weeks, my documents came through and I was allowed to leave that appalling way of life.

All in all it had been a glorious trip. For five months I had lived a life of leisure, been treated like a celebrity, fallen in love and gotten engaged. Not wanting to admit that the romance was already cooling off, I fantasized that Ruth would come to America where we would live happily ever after. Deep down, though, I knew it would never be. Seeing me off at the train station in Esbjerg, she gave me a little hug and a book to read on my long journey and that was the last time I saw her. A few months later I received a big package in the mail. Enclosed was, not only the engagement ring, but also every gift I had given her over the six months that I was trapped in Denmark. She obviously wanted to wipe me out of her life completely. Of course I was hurt by her actions, but time heals all wounds. Today I'm convinced that it was in all probability best for both of us, especially for me.

It is impossible to describe the feeling of exhilaration I had when that train rolled out of the railroad yard in Esbjerg towards home, because that is what America had already become to me. My ship was sailing from Gothenburg and, having never been in Sweden before, it was exciting to experience a new country even if it was through the window of the train.

Boarding the "Kungsholm," the same ship on which I had crossed the Atlantic six months earlier, I recognized some of the crew, and the headwaiter remembered me as well. I was looking forward to eight heavenly days crossing the ocean. My roommates were three old men, a Dane and two Swedes. The Dane had never traveled out of Denmark before and was a quite uncertain about what to do. The Swedes were diametrically opposite of each other. One was very religious, always reading his Bible. The other was an unadulterated drunk. I never knew what he would do next, but he was undeniably entertaining.

I won't bore you with the details of the voyage, but there is one incident that I just have to share. They held a banquet the night before we docked in New York, the Captain's Dinner, a particularly nice affair. Later, at about 11 PM, the saintly Swede and the old Dane were asleep in their bottom bunks, and I was finishing up my packing, when the old drunken Swede came in on wobbly legs. Jubilant, he was telling me that he been up on the bridge helping the captain guide the ship. We were laughing about this when, all of a sudden, he lost his balance and fell into my open suitcase. Helping him up, I told him that

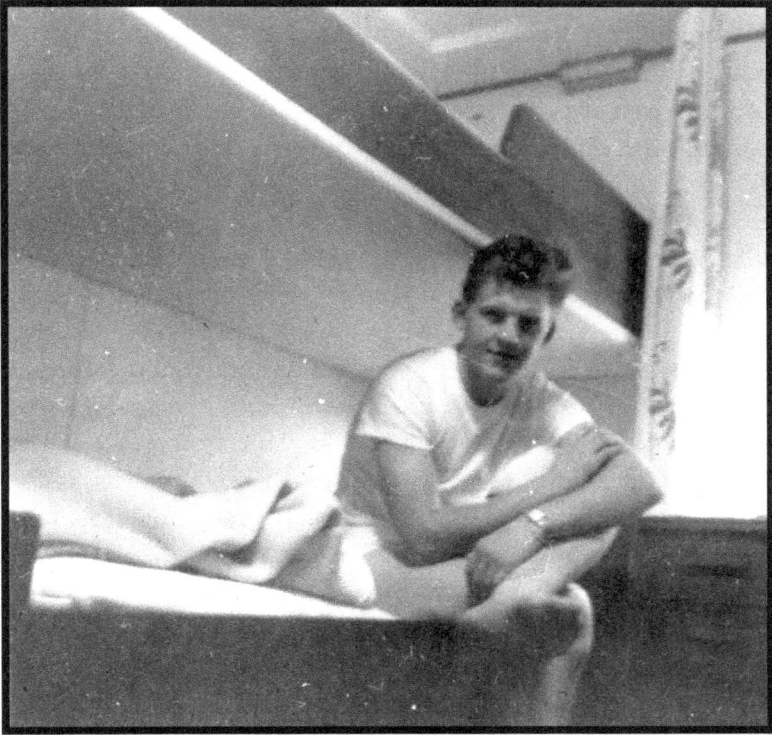

now would be an excellent time to hit the sack and I helped him undress and climb up on the top bunk. The next morning there was a terrible commotion that I somehow managed to sleep through, but they told me about it later. Waking up early, the old Swede had to go to the bathroom. He toppled out of the top bunk and, still quite intoxicated, got turned around and a bit disoriented. Instead of turning left towards the bathroom, he turned right, which placed him at the head of the bunk directly below his own where he took aim.

Opening his eyes to gaze into the barrel of a gun, the old Dane who had been sleeping in the lower bunk awoke just in the nick time to stop the inebriated Swede from emitting an amber stream right in his face. There must have been quite a hullabaloo and I'm so disappointed that I slept right through the vocal exchange.

ACCORDING TO ME

Standing on deck as we sailed into the New York harbor we marveled at the beautiful skyline with the Empire State Building towering over all the other skyscrapers. With at least one thousand passengers disembarking, there was a throng of people all passing through immigration at once. Some immigration officers seem to be drunk with power and can be very overbearing. The guy I came in contact with was a pockmarked, moon-faced jackass. He chewed me out because I had stayed away so long, possibly missing military service. Finally he stamped my entry visa and I was on my way. I almost kissed the ground when I got out on the street. Taking in a deep breath of air, I was heady with the knowledge that nothing could stop me from returning to California. Hailing a taxi I headed to the Greyhound station.

Just like my cross-country trip earlier, I rode non-stop, only getting off the bus for food and bathroom stops. Arriving in Sacramento early one morning, I called my father to tell him that I could really use a ride home. He came right down to the bus station and I hugged and kissed him, not because I really felt like it, but because it seemed the right thing to do. You see, even then I still had ambivalent feelings for him. I yearned for a relationship with him, but just didn't think that could ever be possible. It would be many years before that miracle would come to pass.

42ND STREET

You may have heard that while the kids were out, the parents moved so they couldn't find them. In this case it wasn't quite so bad, but my parents had moved. About a month before I came home they bought a very nice house in a fashionable part of Sacramento. It was a wonderful neighborhood and people were very friendly. The homes were beautifully maintained with manicured lawns, lots of flowers and every property had two huge trees, so that when you drove down the street in the summertime it was like passing through a great arbor.

I went back to work for the Cook Painting Company, who had promised to rehire me when I returned from my involuntary exile. It just so happened that they were doing a job at Mercy Hospital, two blocks from my house, which was great. I could snooze till 7:30 every morning and my mother would sometimes wake me up with breakfast in bed. I was really living the privileged life.

When I was 18 years old I had asked my father to sign for me so that I could get a driver's license, but he refused and I couldn't get it without his signature. I don't really know why he refused; maybe he was worried about liability exposure. I had to wait till I was 21 when I no longer needed his approval for anything. I never told anybody on the job that I didn't have a driver's license and every once in a while somebody would give me the keys to his car and send me to get something, like coffee and donuts. I must admit that I sometimes abused their confidence and drove too fast. My father, too, would often give me the keys to the car so that I could wash it and, as everyone knows, the best way to dry off the car is to take it for a spin afterwards. I would go flying down Howe Avenue at 80 miles an hour. Amazingly, the police never caught me; that might have gotten real interesting.

My brother and I always liked guns, but all we had was a BB gun. We hung a small moving target on a string in the garage and tried to hit it, succeeding once in a while. However, there was some collateral property damage. The back wall of the garage was covered with a piece of tin and the projectiles would ricochet through the open door and hit the windshield of my dad's car, which was parked under the carport in front of the garage. That windshield was peppered with chips, but my dad never figured out what caused it.

According To Me

My First Car

On my twenty-first birthday, finally of age, I went directly to the DMV and got my driver's license. The driving examiner, impressed with my driving skills, wanted to know where I had learned to drive. I told him that I had been driving on a farm, which, though not the whole truth, was not a lie either. From the DMV I went to the car dealer and put a down payment on a brand-new 1956 Chevrolet Impala hardtop. It was a beautiful two-toned, black and chartreuse, car. I had been saving my money ever since I returned from Denmark and was able to pay it off in six months. After that though, I could never save any money. It's amazing how much it costs to keep a car going, even though gas prices were low back then. It cost $4 to fill the tank. I've recently paid that much, and more, for one gallon! But I was driving all over California. I would go anywhere at the drop of a hat. One evening I was visiting a young couple, friends of mine. As we were talking the lady said that she would like to go see her parents in Santa Maria, California. I said, "Let's go! We can take my car." I went home and packed a few things and we set off on a 400-mile journey. I did this several times with different friends and saw a lot of California that way. I just loved to drive and still do.

DANISH LODGE

When we moved to Sacramento I joined the Danish Lodge. The lodge was part of an organization in California and Nevada called Dania. People who came from Denmark or were of Danish decent, or who were married to a Dane, were welcomed and encouraged to join and for several years it was a very successful society. Members paid a modest amount in dues and, if he/she got sick, would get a few dollars per week. It was kind of a medical insurance, which probably originated in the depression era. There were bi-weekly club meetings, segregated for men only and for women only. Every now and then we held potluck dinners and dancing, and in the summertime we had a picnic in a park. We were just like a big family. I got very involved in the club right from the beginning, going through the chairs, as they called it, and eventually became president one year. I don't think that I was more than 21 years old. I found out that just because you are president, even in a small club like that, it doesn't mean that you have a lot power. Older members, who have been there a long time, have the influence to stop you at every turn. Not that I really had an agenda that I was pushing. It was a good experience to become involved and it was a good education.

They had a few silly rules we had to adhere to. It you came late to the meeting the door would be locked. When you knocked on the door the sergeant-at-arms would open a peephole and ask for the password, which was changed every year, and if you knew it he would let you in. I don't know if he ever denied anyone entrance. At the meeting the president, the secretary and the treasurer sat on a platform at the end of the hall, with the members sitting in a ring lining the walls. The vice-president sat at a small desk in the middle of the floor and heaven help you if you walked between him and presidents podium during the meeting. It was silly and they took themselves too seriously, but I enjoyed getting together with the people even though most of them were old enough to be my father or grandfather.

ACCORDING TO ME

Every year a convention was held somewhere in California or Nevada. They would last about three days and the officers of the grand lodge would be installed with great pomp and circumstance. Veterans of the Danish Royal Guard in their uniforms, without the tall bearskin hat, would bring in the colors. Men, dressed in tuxes, and women, in the most colorful gowns, marched into the hall and up to the installing officer, who would solemnly give them the instructions for their respective offices to perform for the coming year. The new grand president would then take the podium and pontificate to the rest of the members that we had a great organization and admonished us to make every effort in support of it and pay the dues on time.

In April 1956 the convention was held in Solvang, a Danish settlement near Santa Barbara. My friend John, who had recently arrived from Denmark, and I decided to drive down there and take part in the great event. We had a grand time being there and taking in all the festivities. It was fun going to the various Danish restaurants and ordering authentic Danish foods. In a way it was like having a cake and eating it too. We could experience the Old Country for a short time without having to go there.

LOVE ON HIGHWAY 101

Sunday morning, April 22, 1956, would change my life forever. Of course I didn't know it at the time, but it would be the commencement of God blessing me greatly from then on. I say this even though I know He has also been blessing and protecting me all of my life prior to this. John and I were just leaving Solvang, on our way back to Sacramento. Stopping at the stop sign before turning on to the 101 highway, we noticed two girls in a Ford convertible go zooming by. We decided that we should take a better look at them and off we went. I must have wound my car up to at least 95 m.p.h. to catch up with them because they were really moving fast. I passed them

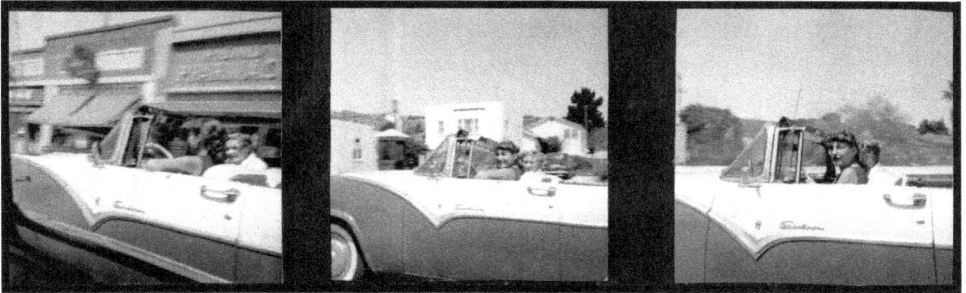

and then pulled over in front of them and slowed down so they would have to pass us. Then I passed them again and we repeated the procedure several times. As I was passing them, John took several pictures. We still have some of them. The girls are clear, but the landscape is all a blur. I suggested to John that the next time we passed them, he should ask them to stop for some refreshments some place up the road. But the girls ignored him and just looked straight ahead. They eventually drove in to a gas station. Passing by, I told John that I thought that we had invested too much time and effort in this adventure to quit now. I slammed on my brakes, threw the car in reverse and backed up the quarter mile back to the station. Now we had the girls cornered and we went over to talk to them and found out that their names were May-Britt and Melitta. Hearing that they both spoke with foreign accents, we found that we really had something in common. We told them where we were from and found out that May-Britt was from Sweden and Melitta was from Austria. They agreed to go with us someplace for coffee to get better acquainted. I talked May-Britt into getting into my car with me, and John jumped in with Melitta, who was driving her car. We drove up the road for quite a while and I tried to get May-Britt to talk, but she was very quiet, not at all sure about what she had gotten herself into. We had to drive about twenty miles before finding a coffee shop.

Well, the girls must have enjoyed our company because we were in that restaurant for four hours, just talking and drinking coffee. May-Britt and Melitta told us they were traveling around the western coastal states selling magazine subscriptions and were on their way to San Francisco. In those days every restaurant had jukeboxes and on the table was a little satellite with a list of music to choose from. I put a quarter in the slot and May-Britt picked a song called " Why do Fools Fall in Love?" I don't remember this, but she tells me that I said, "I wonder why they do?"

When it was finally time to leave we made a date with them, arranging to meet in San Francisco the following Wednesday evening. On the way back to Sacramento, John and I stopped off in Fresno for dinner, choosing a nightclub, where there was dancing and a comedian performing on stage. Enjoying ourselves, we didn't leave until the place closed at two in the morning and we still had a three-hour drive ahead of us. We got back to Sacramento in time for me to get an hour's sleep before going to work.

On Wednesday we were off again, this time to San Francisco, a 100-miles away, where we met May-Britt and Melitta at the hotel where they were staying. After some discussion, we decided to go to Bimbo's 385 in North Beach. John hooked up with Melitta and May-Britt became my date. Bimbo's was an excellent nightclub and John and I thought we could go there for a couple of drinks. We were seated at a very nice table with a good view of the stage. When the waiter arrived the girls ordered dinner. We were slightly shocked, because we had not intended to spend that kind of money and we couldn't afford to order dinner for ourselves. When the girls asked why we didn't eat, we said we had already eaten. Still, we had a wonderful time with them and it was almost three o'clock in the morning before we dropped them off at their hotel and were on our way home again. We had made no plans for a future rendezvous since they were leaving town in a couple of days, going north towards Canada, and we weren't going to chase them that far. They were a little rich for us anyway.

I was a real speed demon in those days and, driving back to Sacramento, I was doing between 90 and 100 miles per hour in the pouring rain. I could barely see the white line on the road. It's a wonder that I'm still alive. Once again I got one hour of sleep before having to get up and go to work. I could handle one late night, but not two in one week. I was so tired I couldn't wait for the day to end and went straight to bed when I got home.

I did get a card from May-Britt a few days later thanking me for the absolutely magnificent time she had with me in San Francisco. Those kind words softened the blow to my wallet and I thought more compassionately toward her. Then one night, about a month later, there was a knock on my parent's door, where I was still living. There, standing on my doorstep, were May-Britt and Melitta, who were now canvassing Sacramento attempting to sell their magazine subscriptions. They let me know the hotel in town where they were staying, just in case we wanted to see them again, which I certainly did. Now here is something funny. I had found out that May-Britt was slightly more than two years older than me, but that didn't bother me; I enjoyed her company. However, when John found out that Melitta was six years older than him, he dropped her like a hot potato. I didn't think it should really matter. We were like ships passing in the night and would probably never see them again, because they lived in Los Angeles. I had a half dozen dates with

ACCORDING TO ME

May-Britt during the week they were in Sacramento. I remember saying goodbye to her the last time in front of the old hotel, and can still see her beautiful face looking at me longingly as I drove away. It had been fun, but all good things come to an end.

I continued to live at home with my parents, although most people my age had moved out on their own. A friend of mine had a room in a boarding house. I was paying my parents $125.00 per month, which was very fair for all concerned. Still employed by the Cook Company I kept busy with lots of overtime. I was also moonlighting on my own, becoming very proficient at my trade. I'd come a long way since I painted that first bathroom. Now I knew what I was doing, for the most part.

Melitta came to visit me again one afternoon and asked me if I could help her with something very important. She had been married, but was now divorced and had two small children that she wanted to send over to Austria to her parents. She was wondering if I had some contacts in Copenhagen, who could help the kids transfer planes. As luck would have it, I actually did know somebody there and they did help the kids when they arrived. I don't know why the airlines didn't take care of them, but that is the way it was. When I asked her about May-Britt, she told me that she was driving to New York on her way back to Sweden. Then she told me that May-Britt was interested in me, which surprised me and lit a little flame in me. But how would I be able to contact her? Melitta suggested that I write her a letter and send it to the "Stockholm," the ship she would be sailing with. Getting home that night, I sat down and wrote a letter to her telling her about my meeting with Melitta and that I would like to stay in touch.

A few days earlier, May-Britt had been passing through Sacramento and tried to call me. My sister, Birgitta, had answered the phone and told her that she would go and get me, not realizing that I had just left on a trip to the mountains with my neighbor. Coming back to the phone, she told May-Britt that I was not there. May-Britt figured that was simply a lame excuse and that I actually didn't want to see her anymore. I had given her a picture of me that she always kept in a prominent place. After that phone call she buried it at the bottom of her suitcase. Telling herself that she would soon get over me, she drove on to New York. Boarding the ship on July 25, 1956, there was a message waiting for her at the purser's office. She couldn't imagine what it could be since few people knew how to get in touch with her, and was astonished when the clerk handed her a thick envelope. After reading my long epistle, she dug my picture up out of her suitcase and placed it on her nightstand.

The "Stockholm" left the New York Harbor early that evening and sailed out past Nantucket Island. At 11 PM May-Britt was getting ready for bed, standing by the sink brushing her teeth. Suddenly she was knocked to the floor by a terrific jolt. Pulling herself to her feet, she went out in the corridor, where there was a great commotion and she could smell smoke coming from somewhere. Up on deck she learned that they had collided with another ship, the Italian liner "Andrea Doria." It was the first evening of the voyage and passengers had not yet been informed of where the life preservers were kept or which life boat station they should report to in case of emergency. Losing all interest in sleep, she spent the night up on deck watching the commotion. After a while it became clear that while the "Stockholm" was going to stay afloat. The "Andrea Doria," however, was in mortal danger. Lifeboats were sent from the "Stockholm" to pick up about 500 survivors from the sinking vessel. Other ships arrived in the area to help in the rescue. Between 50 and 60 people were killed in the accident, primarily during the collision itself, but several were killed during the rescue operation. The next morning, at about 10 AM, eleven hours after the collision, the "Andrea Doria" sank into the depths. It took the "Stockholm" two days to limp back to New York again with at least 50 feet missing from her bow. May-Britt spent a few days with friends in New York and then, boarding a Norwegian ship, returned to Sweden.

According To Me

May-Britt wrote to me as soon as she arrived in Sweden, telling me about her adventure and her plans to return to America after two or three months. She was a very good letter writer. I would get a letter from her every other Thursday and would, of course, respond in kind. When three months had passed she wrote a letter telling me she had decided to stay in Sweden over Christmas and New Year's. In January I received a letter stating that she was going to stay a little longer so that she could go skiing with friends in Norway. Soon after that I got another letter saying that she had bought a little Volkswagen, and that she and a girlfriend were planning a trip through Europe. Driving through every free country in Europe (west of the iron curtain), except Greece, they traveled down to Tangiers, Morocco in northern Africa before turning around and heading home. I got letters and cards from all over the continent. In one of her letters she mentioned that she was a Christian, attended church and spent time in prayer. I didn't really understand the significance. I had been raised Lutheran, was baptized and confirmed in the church, and figured that was all there was. Later in life I learned a lot more about what being a Christian means and I have her to thank for leading me to a closer walk with the Lord.

Citizenship

I wanted to become a US citizen as soon as possible. One of the requirements for naturalization is that you reside in the country for a minimum of five years. I was concerned that my prolonged stay in Denmark would disqualify the two years I had been here prior to leaving, and that I would have to start all over. But fortunately it didn't become a problem. Another requirement for naturalization is that you attend citizenship classes, gaining a grasp of American history and an understanding of the three branches of government. George, a Greek man who talked me into buying a life insurance policy, was a very pleasant person. I told him that I had been here five years and was planning on taking citizenship classes. He told me that he taught classes a couple of nights a week at the high school. I enrolled in his class and found that he was a very good teacher. When I eventually took the test, I passed it with flying colors. One very exciting day in February 1957, I, together with a large group of other foreign nationals, was sworn in, becoming an American citizen. I celebrated by taking the day off work and just drove around town in my new car.

ARMY

I was getting bored with work and was looking for more excitement. I decided to enlist in the Army. The Air Force had been my first choice, but they wouldn't take me because I didn't have a High School diploma. I was inducted into the armed forces in Fort Ord, California on May 22,1957. I spent a few days getting fitted for uniforms (not that they fit all that well), having my head shaved and generally getting initiated into military life. At that time I made what could have been a terrible mistake. After visiting that villainous barber, I went over to one of those automatic photography booths, where, for a couple of quarters, you could have your picture taken. Not very good pictures, but they did show what you looked like. I sent one of those pictures to May-Britt. Apparently I looked so different from what she

remembered that she had nightmares about me. Luckily she kept writing to me.

After induction we were shipped off to Fort Carson, in Colorado. There were probably a few hundred recruits going there and, for some reason, I and eight other guys were told to dress in our Class A uniforms and board a Western Airline's Champagne flight, changing planes in Denver and continuing on to Colorado Springs. The other recruits were put on a DC3 with bucket seats (not like you find in cars, these were more like real buckets), and given box lunches. We had beautiful stewardesses serving us Champagne and good food. It was a great trip that took all day. This was the pre-jet era and planes only flew half as fast as they do today.

This luxury ended, however, as soon as we arrived at Fort Carson. Restricted to our barracks for four weeks, we couldn't even go across the road to the PX store. Boot camp is a test of endurance, where you are told when to get up, when to go to bed, and when to do everything in between. Awakened at 5am, we dressed hastily in our ill-fitting fatigue uniforms and were run ragged all day long. Every day a few of us would be assigned to KP duty. You had to report to the kitchen at 3 am and work until 11pm. The work was so terrible it made you wish you were a civilian again. The first time I was assigned KP I found it was everything it had been rumored to be, one of the worst days of my life. I was told to wash dishes and utensils, which was an all-day job. There were no dishwashers in those days; we were the dishwashers. After spending a whole day up to my elbows in the strong detergent, my hands were full of blisters that took over a week to heal. The next time I was assigned KP, I paid another guy $10.00 to do it for me. The army didn't care as long as there was a body to do the assignment.

One smart move I made when I arrived at that infamous place was to join the company choir at the chapel. It is not that I'm such an excellent a singer, but it got me out of a lot of misery laid on us by our drill sergeants. As choir members, we traveled all over the surrounding area singing at diverse functions. I saw so many rodeos that, after a while, I got bored with them. One night we were even invited to sing at the new Air Force Academy where General Maxwell Taylor, the Chief of Staff, was in the audience.

Once, during the two months of boot camp, all the different companies assembled and marched 25 miles to an area for bivouac. We each carried half of a pup tent. In the evening we paired up, buttoning our tent halves together and hanging it over a line strung between two poles forming a simple shelter where we could sleep. One day we were training warfare in a field and it was so awfully hot. All we had to drink in our canteens was water, enriched with salt tablets, which tasted terrible. A rumor began circulating that K Company had been given iced tea. We suspected that K Company was always treated nicer than the rest of us and thought that they were a bunch of sissies. We started hollering that we wanted iced tea, too, and eventually a truck brought out a bunch of five-gallon cans with the delectable libation. Lining up with our canteen cups, which our sergeant said would only be filled half full, I watched the sergeant pour tea for the soldiers. Getting an idea, I devised a plan that would get me a full cup of tea. When it was my turn at the well, I held my cup up tight against the lip of the can so that the sergeant had to push slightly on it to pour. When it was almost half full, I quickly lowered my cup so that he spilled it over. I learned a few new cuss words, but he didn't make me share it with somebody else. In the middle of bivouac someone came and told me to report back to the barracks and get cleaned up for choir duty. After living in the wilderness, using my steel helmet for a washbasin, I relished the shower and probably stood there for half an hour before I got dressed for the show. Somehow I survived and graduated from boot camp and was given a couple of weeks pass so I could go home.

I was glad to get out of that old hellhole, Fort Carson. Taking a city bus to the Greyhound bus station I caught the next bus back to Sacramento. I have spent a lot of time on Greyhound busses, crossing the country three and a half times, plus all the times I used them for transportation in California. After that two-month ordeal it was good to be back home and just relax until my leave was up and it was time to report for my next assignment at Fort Gordon near Augusta, Georgia, where I was going to study Morse code and learn to type.

I decided to drive my own car across the country, which, although it took longer because I had to sleep at night, was even better than taking the bus. The first day I drove to Barstow, California, on the edge of the Great American Desert, arriving around 2 o'clock in the afternoon. Not wanting to drive across the desert in the daytime in the middle of August, when temperatures reach 120 in the shade, I found a motel and, asking for a wake-up call at midnight, went to sleep. I got back in the car a little after midnight and by the time the sun was high in the sky, I was out of the desert. I really enjoyed driving through the south-eastern states, the landscape is so idyllic with rolling hills; I even saw a man working his field with a team of horses just like we used to do in Denmark.

Fort Gordon was a lot different than Fort Carson. There were no Drill Sergeants running us ragged 18 hours a day. We were there to study and it was really no different from a regular college. The climate was also different, much hotter and very humid. Every day it would rain for about 20 minutes. Afterwards you could see steam rising off the ground adding to the humidity.

I had been in Georgia for almost two months when May-Britt wrote that she would be returning to America in the late fall. It dawned on me that joining the army was, perhaps, a strategic mistake. School would soon be over and there was a good chance that I would be shipped off to a foreign country and would never see her again. I thought of joining the 101st Airborne, which wouldn't be shipping out for a couple of years, but first I needed to see a doctor about the problem in my groin. The extra strenuous training would probably be too much for me. I made an appointment with a doctor on base to see about an operation. He took one look at me and told me that my condition qualified me for a medical discharge. It didn't take me long to make up my mind about what to do next. I applied for release from the Army and within a couple of weeks I was a civilian again.

Instead of returning home to Sacramento I decided that I wanted to see Florida, maybe even get a job there for a while. I drove all the way out to Key West, seeing many of the sights on the way. Sitting in a parking lot, staring out at the ocean, I contemplated my options. I didn't know a soul in Florida and if I did find employment, I would also have to set up housekeeping, with all that that entails. I realized that I already had all of that waiting for me back in California. I started up my faithful Chevrolet and began my journey home. Keeping my speed at 70 mph, I drove long stretches at a time and I was back in Sacramento four days later.

Rehired at Cooks, life soon returned to normal. I've never regretted my four months in the Army. It was a good experience and I also got to see quite bit of the country.

LIFE CHANGES

May-Britt returned in late November settled down in San Francisco instead of Los Angeles, which she would have preferred. She explained to me later that San Francisco was close enough for me to come and see her. Sacramento would have been too close; she didn't want to appear too eager. That has never made any sense to me, but what can you do with a Swede? Just love her.

She had, of course, sent me the address where she lived. Never having driven in San Francisco, I didn't know how the streets were laid out. She lived a couple of blocks off Market Street. Missing the turn, I went around the block and somehow got lost. In San Francisco city blocks are not necessarily four sided, they could have three or even five sides. Eventually I did find my way back to Market Street and subsequently to where she lived.

It was wonderful to see my pen pal again. My feelings for her were different now, stronger. After a year and a half of corresponding, I felt I knew her quite well. After a long embrace and a passionate kiss, she brought me up to the apartment and introduced me to her friends from whom she was renting a room. May-Britt had first met Jan and Ragnhild Danielsson in Sweden, shortly before they immigrated to the United States. They had been in California for four months and were now living in the Mission district of San Francisco, a modest community that enjoyed the best climate in the city.

May-Britt had brought a package from Sweden that she needed to deliver to some people living in Vallejo and asked if I would mind driving her up there. When we got to Vallejo we stopped at a gas station to look at a city map. I took out my wallet to get a piece of paper to write down the directions and walked out to the car. Arriving at the house, I realized that my wallet was missing and we turned around immediately. As we pulled into the station the attendant came running out with my wallet in his hand. I put it in my pocket and we returned to the house with the package. After a short visit we drove back to San Francisco.

We planned to see a movie and had purchased the tickets ahead of time. Stopping at the candy counter on our way in, I took out my wallet to buy May-Britt some candy and discovered to my horror that it was empty. That "pleasant" gas station attendant had lifted the money before returning it to me. She had to pay for her own candy. Adding insult to injury, when I dropped her off at her apartment after the movie, I had to ask

to borrow $20 so that I would have something in case of emergency on the long journey home. It was not the way I had envisioned our first date after her prolonged absence, but at least it was memorable!

I drove to San Francisco every weekend to see her and we always had a wonderful time together. Parting is sweet sorrow and it was always a struggle to say good-bye when it was time for me to go home. We would sit at the bottom of the stairs that led up to her apartment for hours and talk before I could finally wrest myself away from her.

I never proposed to her in the customary manner, whatever that is, but one night in February, after sitting a long time at the bottom of the steps, I got up enough nerve to ask her, " If I bought you a ring, would you wear it?" To my utmost relief she, understanding what I was really asking, said yes! I was so exultant I barely noticed the drive home. I went to a jewelry store and bought an engagement and wedding ring. I was so poor that I had to buy them on time, but I wanted to put that ring on her finger as soon as possible. I had to wait until the next weekend to see her again and a week has never passed so slowly. The drive to San Francisco also seemed unending but I finally arrived and placed the ring on her finger on February 22, 1958.

For some reason 22 has become my favorite number. I met May-Britt on the 22nd, we happened to get engaged on the 22nd, I had even joined the Army on the 22nd. I told her that our wedding ceremony ought to be on the 22nd and so we studied the calendar to see when the most suitable 22nd would occur. It turned out to be November that year, nine months hence, a most favorable amount of time for our assessment phase, which is what an engagement really is.

Discussing where we would live in the future, I maintained that it would have to be Sacramento, because that was where I was working. May-Britt, however, wanted to live in San Francisco because she felt the heat in Sacramento was intolerable. I had finally persuaded May-Britt that Sacramento had its advantages, when we attended a picnic held by the Danish Lodge. People congratulated us and wished us well. A friend of mine asked where we were going to live after we tied the knot. May-Britt answered that we had to live in Sacramento because I claimed I would not be able to find work in San Francisco. Surely, he said, I could find a painter in San Francisco who would hire me. In fact, he knew a Danish painting contractor that I should contact. On my next visit to San Francisco we went to see the contractor, who said he would be happy to hire me. My goose was cooked. Sacramento was out. I had played my level best and lost. We would settle in San Francisco.

When we began to make plans for the wedding, my mother urged us to visit the pastor at the Lutheran church that she occasionally attended. Talking to the pastor, we learned that he did not allow kissing in the ceremony, so we decided to find another church. My mother felt that we could kiss as much as we wanted to afterwards, but we didn't agree. This was our wedding. We were paying for it and we were going to do it our way. We found another Lutheran church, with a pastor we liked much better, and we were married there on Saturday, November 22, 1958, which also happened to be the day after my parents 25th wedding anniversary.

❧ 50 Years ❦

1958

1968

1978

1988

1998

2008

After the wedding was over, the two of us went out for a nice dinner in the evening and drove back to San Francisco to the furnished apartment we had rented for May-Britt a month before. We had decided that we would never pay more than $80.00 per month in rent. This apartment rented for $65.00 and it really wasn't worth more than that. It had a small kitchen with no cabinets, a living room furnished with wicker furniture, and a small bedroom with a very small closet. The bathroom was located across a public hallway, where we often met other tenants coming or going. It was on the second floor of an old, three-story house, built up on top of a hill. We had to climb several flights of steps before we even got to the front door, but we didn't mind it, we were young and strong. Our landlords were an elderly couple, Mr. and Mrs. Jensen. Mr. Jensen was nearly deaf, but Mrs. Jensen could hear very well, often complaining that we were heavy footed and that our radio alarm clock woke her up in the morning. Meeting May-Britt at the front door, she would embark on an endless tirade of complaints. Needless to say, we soon began looking for another place.

Some friends told us about a small apartment behind the Covenant church, where we attended, that would soon become available. The couple that lived there had bought a house and would be moving at the end of the month. The rent was

The honeymoon is over

$70.00 per month and we jumped at the chance. To reach it you had to walk through a long corridor at the bottom of a four-story building, cross a courtyard and climb the stairs to the apartment that was built over a storage structure. It was a lot nicer than the little furnished unit we were living in and moving would get us away from Mrs. Jensen who was becoming nastier as time went on. It

81

was, however, unfurnished, so we had to find some furniture quickly. We'd spent all our savings on the wedding; in fact we had to pay the photographer over time. Although we were both frugal, we hadn't accumulated a lot of funds yet. We found a place where we could buy furniture on a 30-day no interest plan. We started with a bed and a refrigerator. Later we acquired a living room set and the rest of the accessories we needed and never paid interest for anything.

I was supposed to have had a job waiting from me when I moved to San Francisco after the wedding and was ready to start on Monday morning since we couldn't afford a honeymoon. Unfortunately the contractor called me on Sunday evening to tell me he didn't have any work for me since the job he had expected had fallen through. I woke up Monday morning wondering what I was going to do. Taking the phonebook with me, I pounded the streets looking up painting companies. I had no luck with the first four companies, but at the fifth one I hit pay dirt. I found the owner, Albert Hasbun, next door in a bar drinking coffee. After talking with him for a while, he decided to hire me. We got along famously and after a couple of weeks I was promoted to foreman. He even gave me a stack of business cards on which I was titled, "Superintendent." After a couple of months he bought two new Chevrolet pick-up trucks and gave me one to use as long as I worked for him. It was a wonderful job. Albert and I became great friends both on and off the job, getting together socially with our wives.

We had been married over a year and May-Britt had not become pregnant. Wondering if something was wrong, we went to a doctor who, noting my congenital condition, informed me that I was sterile. May-Britt was tremendously disappointed and cried bitter tears. The doctor suggested I undergo surgery to have the testis pulled down to where they belonged. Although he couldn't promise any improvement we decided to go ahead with the procedure. Along with the main problem I also had double hernias, which the surgeon repaired. It was an absolutely agonizing ordeal. I was given pain shots every three hours for three days and then sent home, where I was laid up for 6 weeks before I could go back to work. When I went back to the doctor to be tested, he told me that my sperm count was only 10% of normal and didn't give us much of a chance of ever having a child. This was especially discouraging after the agony I had endured, but we reconciled ourselves to our destiny. Life goes on.

San Francisco would be a great place to live if it wasn't for the wind and the fog. May-Britt spent a lot of time fixing her hair, but as soon we were out on the street it would all be ruined. Unhappy, she dreamed of moving to Los Angeles. I was hesitant but eventually conceded. I wasn't too crazy about the Bay Area either. In the spring of 1960, we began planning to move south.

LOS ANGELES

May-Britt was working in a small coffee shop on Montgomery Street in the financial district of San Francisco. Most of her customers were regulars and she got to know them fairly well, making good tips for good and friendly service. One morning one of her customers came in with his father-in-law. After greetings she told them that we were planning to move to Los Angeles to get out of this cold, foggy and windy city. The old man, Burr Moulthrup, told her that he had a house in Monterey Park, about 15 miles east of Los Angeles. He and his wife were going to move to Hawaii. They didn't want to sell it, but they also couldn't rent it because it was financed by a California Veteran's Loan. He told her that we could live there for free if we maintained the property and paid the utilities. It was a real deal. When she told me about it we both felt it was too good to be true. I told her to find out if he was really serious. We were, after all, perfect strangers. When her regular customer came in the next morning she asked him if his father-in-law was really serious about the house. He told her that he most certainly was and gave her his father-in-law's phone number. We called them the next day. They were very friendly and invited us to come down and see the house and get acquainted so we could see if we were compatible. If we took them up on their offer we would be living with them in the house for a couple months before they made the move to Hawaii. We arranged to meet with them the following week in Los Angeles. After a night at a hotel we arose early to take a drive around West LA and Santa Monica. Still very skeptical about the proposition, we wanted to check out the neighborhood before deciding our destiny. May-Britt had lived there before and was somewhat acquainted with the area.

In Monterey Park we turned onto the street where we might soon be living and were pleasantly surprised by the neighborhood. The Moulthrups lived in a neat little house with three bedrooms, one bath and a two-car garage on a quiet street with nicely maintained yards. The back yard had a big patio, lawn and a couple of big shade trees. We couldn't believe that we could have this for free. We got along famously with the Moulthrups and were accepted to live in their house with the understanding that it would be a trial period for six months. After that we would decide if the arrangement was working out to everybody's satisfaction.

Returning to San Francisco, we gave our employers and landlord notice that we were moving and started packing. I rented the biggest U-haul trailer I could find, 14 feet long, and hooked it behind the car with a bumper hitch. We loaded all our worldly belongings, spent the night with friends and got an early start the next morning driving south towards sunny Southern California. The trailer, fully loaded as it was, weighed at least as much as the car and I found that I had to drive very carefully. If I went over 45 miles per hour the trailer would begin to swerve from side to side and we were in danger of losing everything, including our lives. It got a little hairy driving down the hills through Ventura into Los Angeles. The trailer pushed down hard on the car, forcing the speed and soon began swaying from side to side. I knew better than to apply the brakes too hard, but with gentle pressure I got the monster under control again. We rolled into Monterey Park on June 16, 1960 and set up housekeeping together with the Moulthrups. They were always nice and we got along just fine, but we were glad when they finely left for Hawaii and we could have the place to ourselves.

A year later the Moulthrups returned to see if the house was still standing. They were pleased with the care of the property and they decided to build an addition to the house, adding another bathroom and a family room with a fireplace. It took about 6 months and turned out very nice. But now they asked us to pay rent. We had lived there for a year and a half rent-free and had gotten used to their generosity. Still the rent was only $75.00 per month, which was $5.00 under our resolute budget of $80.00.

PAINTING SKY SCRAPERS

Immediately after arriving in Los Angeles I found a job with a large painting firm. That first year I worked almost exclusively on industrial structures and tall buildings. I worked a lot with a deaf-mute, so we didn't carry on much of a conversation. He and I painted the outside of a 17 story building, 220 feet tall, in downtown Los Angeles. We had two baskets connected by a 24-foot long plank. Each basket contained a winch with a very long cable that was attached to a large hook we hung over the firewall on the roof of the building. Climbing into the baskets, we winched ourselves up to the top of the building and began painting from the roof down. Hanging 220 feet off the ground is exciting enough, but one day it got a little too exciting.

ACCORDING TO ME

Columns lined two sides of the building. Between the columns were windows, yet to be installed, and below each window was a pre-finished panel that had to be kept clean. A lot of time was wasted cleaning off the paint from the spray of the paint rollers. One day our foreman came up with a bright idea. We could wrap a sheet of plastic around the bottom of the scaffold and up to the railing. It did work better and we spent less time cleaning up. But when we came down to the twelfth story a gust of wind came through the building, catching the plastic like it was a sail, and swept us out about 15 feet away from the wall. My friend, unable to speak, began grunting big time. That was enough of that, we descended as quickly as possible and removed the dangerous plastic.

The painting company had a contract for the maintenance of about 5,000 upscale apartments in Park La Brea in West Los Angeles. A position on the crew was highly coveted but nearly impossible to attain since the same men had been working there for years. Once you were accepted, you didn't give it up easily. After a year of working on commercial and industrial buildings, I got my chance. A sudden influx of apartments came on line and they needed more people on the crew. Luckily, I was one of the men they sent over. I worked like a madman, as hard as I possibly could, and was given a permanent position. It was very clean and easy work, always indoors, never too hot or too cold. We worked together in pairs and we always had a lot of fun, which made the work much easier. We were eight regular painters and were almost like a little brotherhood, laughing at the other men who would sometimes come out to help because they couldn't paint a bathroom as fast as we could. I have seen a man spend an hour painting a bathroom, whereas the fastest guy on our crew could paint one in ten minutes. I spent two years on that job, but all things are only for a season, good or bad.

IT'S A......GIRL?

In the fall of 1960 we were the recipients of an improbable discovery. May-Britt had been feeling somewhat under the weather for quite a while and eventually went to the doctor for a check-up. To our great surprise, we found out that she was pregnant. We were overjoyed! My only concern was that she could lose the baby. I wouldn't let her do anything strenuous and we didn't take any trips. We had always gone to Sacramento, to my parents, for Christmas, but we cancelled. There was no way we were going to take any unnecessary risks.

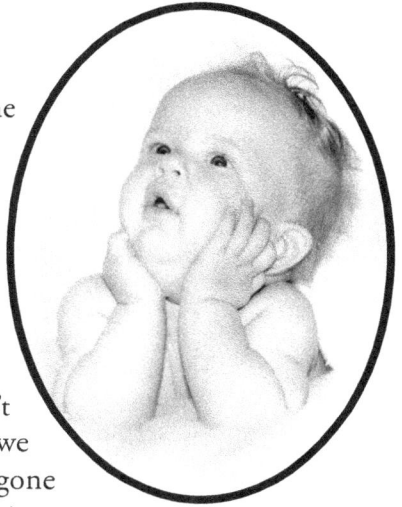

July 28, 1961 was an exciting day. I brought May-Britt to the hospital in the morning for delivery of our first child. I was so keyed up, I was becoming a father and I was confident that the baby would be a boy. I sat in the waiting room all day, only allowed an occasional visit to May-Britt to find out how she was coming along. Finally, at around seven o'clock in the evening, I heard my name called from the delivery room. Handing over a tightly wrapped bundle, the nurse said, "Here is your little girl."

"Is that what it is?" I replied.

I will admit I was disappointed. But what could I do? I now had a daughter and I didn't know what I would do with her. I was allowed in to see May-Britt, who was somewhat out of it. Apparently she was also under the impression that she had delivered a boy, because she asked if they had circumcised the baby yet. I told her that we had a little girl and that she was perfect, no alterations were necessary.

I went to the hospital several times over the next couple days to visit May-Britt and my new offspring. We decided to call her LaVonne Esther. We had heard the name, LaVonne, and thought it unusual, yet very nice. Esther was in honor of both her grandmothers. I was becoming more and more excited with the idea of having a new baby in the house. It was going to be a life altering experience for us, but it was going to be a lot of fun. On the third day I went to the hospital to pick up my little family. A nurse rolled May-Britt, with LaVonne in her arms, out to the curb in a wheelchair. I cannot describe my feeling as I drove them home to our little house in Monterey Park.

A dozen red concrete steps led up to the house. I took LaVonne in my arms and carried her up those steps and into the house. We have a movie of the event, so I guess I did it at least a couple of times for the camera. I don't remember if there was anybody there besides us, so May-Britt must have been the one taking the pictures. We brought LaVonne into the nursery and put her in her crib. Standing there, admiring what we had accomplished, she became very still and we, thinking that she had stopped breathing, were suddenly frantic. She hadn't, though. As new parents we were simply a little over anxious.

I was amazed at my new baby. When she cried she would kick her arms and legs propelling herself around in her crib. I had to go the hospital for something and I told the nurses that my 3-day-old baby was crawling. They just rolled their eyes and said something about "new fathers." Apparently I didn't have much credibility with them.

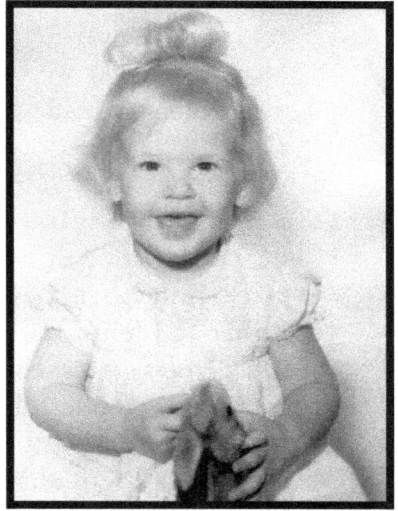

LaVonne grew to be a healthy and easy child. She seldom cried and we had a lot of fun with her. Sometimes, when I came home from work, she would be in her crib and would call "Daddy." When I answered, she would laugh. Then she would call, "Daddy," again. I would answer, and she would laugh. We did this several times before I went into her room and picked her up. Years later I'd drive her to school, leaving early so we had time to stop at a job site and at the donut shop. We'd talk about this and that, nothing really important, but it was time shared and, she tells me now, it is one of her most precious memories of growing up.

She went to college in San Diego and we let her have our 73' Buick, which was a big car. One day she was complaining about having to drive "that big boat." When her mother told her that she was welcome to leave it home and take the train, she said, "Oops!" Sometimes one can go a little too far to one's own detriment.

SAVED!

I told you before that my mother taught me the Lord's Prayer when I was just a little boy. I would pray that prayer often, adding a few lines of my own like," Make me a better Christian." Over the years I strayed far from the Lord and forgot about praying. Looking back, I think that the Holy Spirit has always been drawing me gently back.

When we got married, May-Britt wanted to go to church and, wanting to please her, I went with her and actually enjoyed it most of the time. When we had moved to Monterey Park, we began attending the Covenant church in Pasadena. I really liked the pastor, Pastor Arvid Carlson, a Swede. He often preached about the love that God has for the world, that He gave His one and only Son to be sacrificed for us, and after that God raised Him again from the dead. Whoever believes in Him, that person would not perish in hell, but have life eternal in Heaven with God the Father and Jesus, His Son. For many Sundays I sat listening to this message, and heard that we shouldn't wait too long to accept this wonderful gift, if we were to die it would be too late. Once you are in the grave, there is nothing you can do. He often had an altar call, urging people to accept Christ into their hearts before it's too late. Week after week I sat in the pew and felt that I should go forward, but I just couldn't get myself to do it. Finally one Sunday I couldn't resist the unseen force that pulled me up out of my seat and down to the altar. I prayed, with Pastor Carlson's help, for the Lord to forgive me and come into my heart. Needless to say, May-Britt was very happy with my decision to follow the Lord.

DOOLITTLE

At the end of 1963 the Moulthrop's refinanced the house and raised the rent to $90.00 per month. We started house hunting and found a similar house in Arcadia. Paying $14,800.00, our payments were $77.00 per month, 3 dollars below our $80 budget limit. The house had a big lot, which we split and had a new house built in the back. We rented out the front house for $100.00 per month, which helped with the payments on both houses, and moved into the new house in back. It was a great location. The yard was completely enclosed so we could let the children play without fear and solicitors never bothered us since nobody knew that there was a house back there! It was wonderful.

A SON!!

God has blessed us in so many ways. On September 12, 1964 Orla Jens arrived. I was beside myself with happiness. I had a son, an heir, who could carry on my name. Although there are an awful lot of Petersens around, there are not as many Pedersens. I jokingly maintain that Pedersen is of a higher class, almost blue blood. The day after he was born we were shocked to learn that there was something wrong with his blood and we didn't know if he would survive. Devastated, we cried and prayed and asked everybody we knew to pray for our little boy. After three blood transfusions in two days he was o.k., but the doctors warned that there could be some brain damage. For years we watched him carefully, looking for signs of retardation. Thankfully there were none and he went on to develop quite normally. Now the perfect family, we had a beautiful girl and a handsome boy.

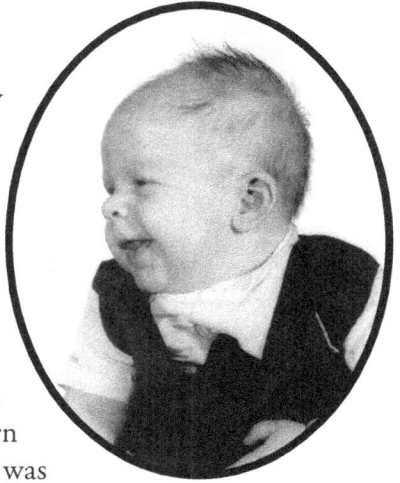

Orla Jens was also a very good and happy baby. As long as he was fed and dry, he was quite content. LaVonne was happy for her little brother and was like a little mother to him. He was very neat about himself, couldn't stand a dirty diaper. As soon as he had a messy one, he took it off and threw it into the bathroom. If he had known how to put on another one, I think he would have done that too.

91

ACCORDING TO ME

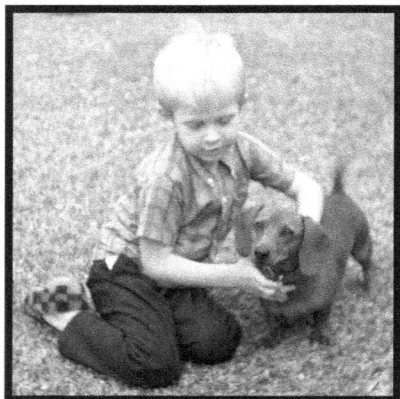

When he was still very young, we got a little Dachshund puppy that we named Flicka. Growing up together, she and Orla Jens developed a love/hate relationship. They played well together, Orla Jens running around with Flicka right there nipping at his heels, something she didn't do with the rest of us. But Orla Jens teased the poor dog unmerciful by pointing a stick like a gun at her. After a while, all he had to do was point a finger at her and she would go nuts. One night we were all sitting around a low coffee table. Orla Jens and Flicka were next to each other on the floor. I notice that the dog was kind of scowling at him and giving him the evil eye, as dogs sometimes do. All of a sudden she jumped up and nipped at him. I didn't do anything, he had been teasing the poor dog so much, and she was just getting even. But Flicka kept glaring at him and jumped up and bit him again, this time harder. I don't remember if he cried, but she had crossed the line, and I told Flicka to go to her bed and stay there. Humiliated, she slinked off ever so slowly.

We were a tidy little family, if I do say so myself. We went to church every Sunday, dressing up as we did in those days. Orla Jens had a little suit and tie like his dad. He looked like a real little gentleman. It was really wonderful times. But there were dark clouds on the horizon.

HEALED RELATIONSHIPS

My relationship with my father had always been strained. Uncle Barney, having noticed that I didn't get along with my father, told me about his relationship with his own father and that he felt bad that he never made amends with him before he died. He told me that he hoped I would not suffer the same fate.

For a while I had the bedroom next to my parents and I could hear him, through the wall, grumbling at my mother long into the night, which was very upsetting for me. Even after I was married and had moved to San Francisco, lying in bed at night I could still hear his angry voice in my head. It took months until the sound faded away.

When we moved to Los Angeles we would drive up to Sacramento a couple of times a year to visit. My father was still working nights at the creamery and we'd stop by to see what he was doing. Although I didn't really want to see him, I felt obligated, afraid that he would take it out on my mother if I ignored him. That's the way our relationship was for many years until sometime in the 1970's.

We had been visiting for a couple of days and we were leaving to go home after lunch. I remember that things were a little uneasy during the morning, but we survived it without anything really unpleasant happening. As we were leaving, I hugged my mother first and thanked her for the time we had spent there. When I hugged my father and said goodbye, I told him that I wished that we could have a better relationship. I

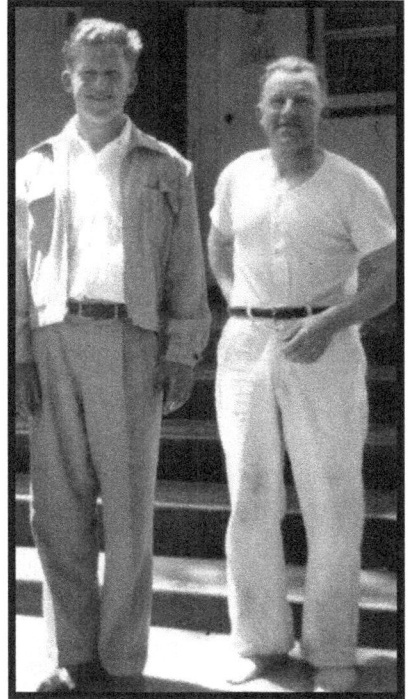

93

don't know what happened next, but I totally lost it. I started crying my heart out and fell on the floor. They carried me to a couch and I laid there crying, for I don't know how many minutes, until I gained control of myself. Something had happened that I couldn't explain. As time went on, I noticed that my feelings for my father had changed. I didn't see him as the ogre I had always thought he was. He still had his faults, but my eyes had also been opened concerning my mother, and she was no angel either. She always considered herself better than my father; that she was of a finer stock than him. She was often belittling his pedigree and I think that bruised his self-esteem, which caused him to react so violently.

What had happened was like a catharsis, a sudden purging of my soul. The animosity that I had felt towards my father for so many years was replaced by a new love for him, which continued to grow till he died in May of 1987. It was wonderful to have that relationship with him and I'm so thankful to the Lord that the rift was healed before it was too late. The last few years of his life he was in and out of the hospital due to heart problems. Whenever we visited him there, I was usually the last to leave his bedside so that I could pray with him before I left him. He had accepted Christ as his personal savior several years before and appreciated my prayers. I still miss him even though he has been gone for over 20 years. He was very interested in what I was doing and I enjoyed taking him around and showing him the jobsites.

When Orla Jens was born, I was the happiest guy around. I had a son that would fill my life with pleasure. The first years of his life I was really proud of him, but then I began to become more and more critical. He could never quite measure up to my expectations and I was often disgusted with him. After a while he really couldn't do anything that would please me.

When he was eight years old we enrolled him in Boys Christian League where they played several different ball sports. Orla Jens didn't enjoy it and it seemed to me like he just wasn't cut out for playing ball. The last night of the season there was a little celebration with all the boys parading across the stage to receive a ribbon for their efforts during the summer. Orla Jens got several ribbons, but I didn't think he deserved any of them and I didn't congratulate him or hug him or anything. All these years later I still feel very guilty about how I treated him. A picture, taken that night, along with his three ribbons hangs on the wall by my desk, a constant reminder of the many years of fellowship we lost because I failed to recognize and appreciate what a precious gift I had in him.

Our relationship didn't improve as the years went along. As he got into his teens, he would work with me on my construction jobs and most of the time things would go well, but there was always an underlying disapproval of him. I wanted a good relationship with him, but somehow I couldn't get there. One day we had been working together on a job and I had blown up at him over his performance. Parking the car in the garage when we came home, I was really upset with him and with myself. Asking him to stay in the car for a minute,

I told him that I was really sorry and frustrated with the lack of love between us and I wanted to pray that we could achieve it. I prayed a short prayer for us there in the car, but nothing changed between us.

A few more years passed and he was in his early 20's. May-Britt, trying to ease the situation under which she, too, was suffering, decided that he should move out of the house and found a little studio apartment for him. But my feelings didn't change. Although he had done well in college, graduating with honors, I wasn't able to appreciate it and didn't think that he would ever amount to anything.

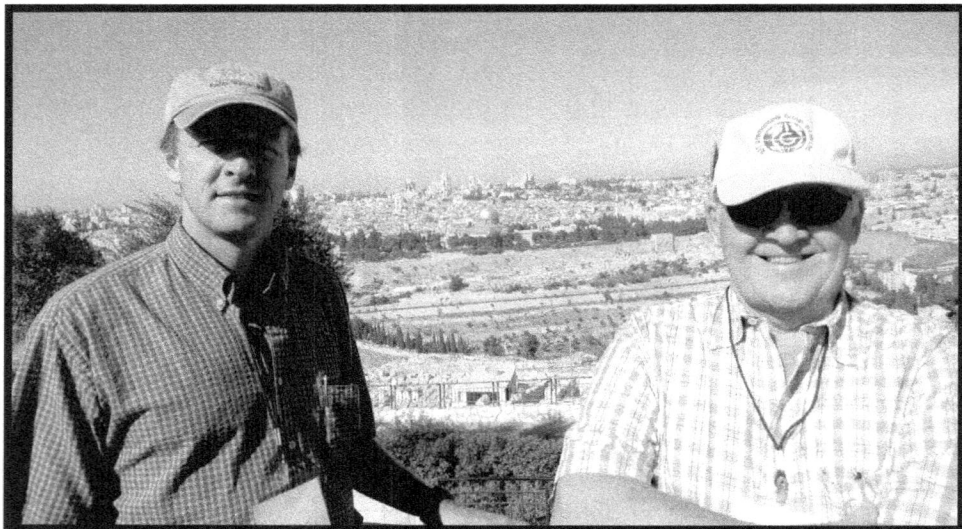

Finally one day May-Britt told me that she had come to the end of her rope, she couldn't handle the split in the family anymore and she wanted us to go to counseling. She had already made an appointment with a Christian counselor. I have always loved May-Britt more than anything in the world and I was sorry to have hurt her all those years with my animosity toward Orla Jens. Besides, I figured that counseling couldn't hurt, so I agreed to go along with her.

It was an amazing experience. I'd always been skeptical of psychologists and counselors, but I was about to have my eyes opened. I cannot remember the details of the first sessions with the counselor, except that she was understanding and appreciated my wish to make things better, even if I didn't believe it could be. The first couple of times May-Britt and I met with her alone. She opened each session by saying a short prayer and then asked us questions for about 50 minutes. I don't remember what we talked about, except that it was obviously about my relationship with Orla Jens. After a couple of sessions, she told us to bring Orla Jens with us the next time. After an hour discussing all of our feelings, Orla Jens and I were told to go home and write a letter to each other about our feelings and wishes. I went home and wrote a long letter to him asking him to forgive me for all the years of harassment and that I longed for a loving relationship with him. He had written more or less the same to me. When we met again at the counselor's office, she had us read the letters to each other. It was tough, reading the letters out loud, but also very meaningful. Afterwards we all hugged and cried and prayed together.

For me it was almost like my experience with my father. No one will convince me the time for miracles has past. Our relationship was healed almost instantaneously and the animosity I had felt for years was replaced with a deep love and appreciation for my son. We are now the best of friends and enjoy each other's company.

We took up sailing and joined the Harbor Island Sail Club in San Diego. As members we could use the 14-foot sailboats, free of charge, or rent at half price any of the many larger vessels available. Sometimes we would each take a 14-footer, racing each other around the bay. It was a lot of fun. Sometimes we keeled the boat over too far and water would slop over the railing. We'd have to bail it out at the same time as we were handling the sails and watching out for traffic.

ACCORDING TO ME

One day, while sailing together on the San Diego Bay, I talked to him about my treatment of him as he was growing up. I told him that I, too, had grown up in a dysfunctional family. Dysfunctional problems seem to continue from generation to generation. I don't know anything about my parents' childhoods. My mother claimed that she was never spanked when she was a child, I am not sure that I believe her, but she sure beat the tar out of me on a regular basis. So I begged him to stop this evil cycle in our family and treat his children with loving care and to spend time with them. When my kids were growing up I didn't spend much time with them. I was always working and getting involved in projects that didn't include the family. If I could do it all over I would change all that. I'm not sorry for being strict with my children or driving them to develop a strong work ethic, but I still bear a lot of guilt for not showing enough love and giving them quality time.

I am so very happy to say that Orla Jens is an exemplary father to his children, spending lots of time with them, teaching them to become good citizens and guiding them towards a godly life.

Jens with his wife, Darla, and daughters, Lydia and Mallory. Hiking the Colorado Trail with Frosty the Llama, August 2010.

CAREER MOVES

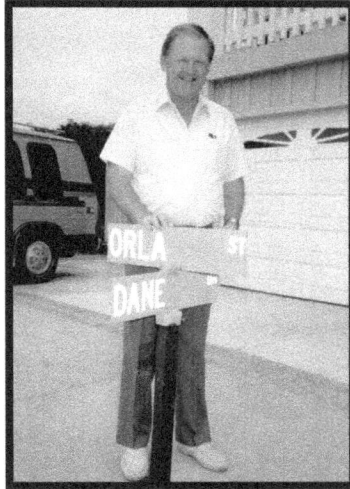

May-Britt has been a Godsend to me, not only as a wonderful, loving wife and exemplary mother, but also because she has a great business sense. Not that every venture was a success. A few months after we settled in Los Angeles, she suggested that we should invest in rental properties. We didn't have much money, but we went looking anyway. We answered an ad in Inglewood and met with a real estate lady. She showed us four old units. There was a duplex in front, an apartment attached to the garage and a small building at the rear of the property containing one room and a bath. After some negotiation we bought the property for $21,000 with the seller carrying $3,000 on a second trust deed. Borrowing $800 from a friend who trusted us, we acquired the property with virtually no money.

That property was a real learning experience for us. I have always told people who wanted to break into property ownership to start easy till they learn what it is all about. Things you've never anticipated can go wrong, which is what happened to us.

ACCORDING TO ME

From the very beginning the sewer pipes kept plugging up. I would unplug them with a water hose, but that would only last a couple of weeks. Finally, I had a roto-rooter plumber come and he solved that problem by clearing all the roots that had grown into the pipes. Another time I hired a guy that was moonlighting as a plumber on weekends to come and fix a problem in one of the units. He showed up on Saturday morning, hung over, with a broken arm from a bar fight he had been in the night before. I wound up doing the work myself, while he sat and watched me. After that I decided that I would only hire a professional if I got into trouble trying to fix the problems myself. As it turned out, I could handle most of it and I don't remember hiring anyone to do anything for several years.

We held onto this property for a couple of years and then put it on the market. It fell out of escrow three times. The first two buyers simply backed out, but the third time around nearly ended in disaster. A young couple made an acceptable offer on it, but then questioned why there were four units on a property that was only zoned for two. When it was brought to the attention of the city I thought we were going to loose two of the units. There was a meeting and it was determined that three of the units were acceptable because they had been there for a long time. The little unit in the back, however, could only be rented in conjunction with one of the other units. So I told the lady who lived there that, as far as anybody else was concerned, she was now renting it together with the people in the garage unit. That worked, and we sold it for the fourth time. All went well until we had a termite inspection. The inspector said that the wood floors on the duplex were so close to the ground that he couldn't get under the building to inspect it and, consequently, couldn't issue a guarantee against termites. I thought we were going to lose another sale, but then I suggested that we fumigate the whole building. That was acceptable and we were finally rid of that nightmare.

It seemed to me that being a real estate agent would be a better profession than painting. Agents wore a suit and tie and never got dirty, which appealed to me. I went to a small real estate office near our home and inquired about how to become an agent. The broker told me that first I needed to pass the test and then he could sponsor me. I was given a stack of books and began studying. I passed the test, got my real estate license and was ready to hit the streets to find property to list. The task wasn't as easy as it seemed. I did get a couple of listings, but they never sold. I also sat at open houses, but that wasn't very successful either. One Sunday afternoon I was sitting in an open house in a nicer part of Monterey Park. I was showing the house to an oriental couple when my broker showed up. After the couple left, my broker told me that the next time a non-white couple wanted to see the house I should very politely refer them to the office and he would show them something which would be more suitable. Interestingly enough, Orientals are now the majority in Monterey Park and the surrounding communities.

Long before we were married, May-Britt had invested $2,500 in what was supposed to be an up and coming development in Riverside. The development petered out and the lots were only worth half of the purchase value, if you could find a buyer, which was doubtful. Feeling terrible having brought this problem into our marriage, she scoured the classified ads to see if there could be a solution for her predicament. One day in early 1962 she spied an ad that offered property for sale or trade. Calling the number, she was invited to come to the office to see what they had to offer. We went there that same day bringing LaVonne with us and placed her in an infant seat on the desk between Fred Shubin, the seller, and us. He told us that he owned 11 apartments in Downey, with an asking price of $62,000. When we saw them, we were a little disappointed. The three triplexes and one duplex had once been the upper story of military housing that had been lifted and moved onto the property. They were in a very poor condition and needed a lot of work. May-Britt and I determined that there was no way the property was worth anywhere near the asking price. When I called Fred later, I told him that we had inspected the property but didn't want to insult him by making an offer on it. He claimed that he would never be offended by any offer, so I told him that all we could offer was $48,000, and we had two lots in Riverside worth $3,000 that we wanted to use for the down payment. Fred asked us to come back to the office for further discussion. He told us that we could have the property for the price we had offered, but he wasn't interested in the lots that we so desperately wanted to unload. Instead, we could have the property with no down payment. We figured there wasn't much to lose in the deal, but we were still stuck with the Riverside property.

There were some vacancies, which was fine because that gave us a chance to make the necessary repairs. Still working for the painting company and taking all the overtime they would give me, we worked on the apartments in our spare time. There were many nights that we worked till long after midnight to get the unit completed. Once the apartment was fixed up it was easy to rent since a big aerospace factory in the neighborhood had just received an enormous contract and was hiring a lot of new people who needed housing.

We offered a young couple a cut in the rent if they would manage the property and collect the rents. They were very responsible and worked out quite well but, unfortunately, soon moved away. In the meantime another young couple, David and Jeanette Crocker, recently arrived from Michigan, were now renting one of the units. We liked them right away and offered them the job, which they gladly accepted. David was not working and was looking for any kind of employment. They would become lifelong friends.

Fred Shubin called about a year later offering us another building. It was a two-story, ten unit apartment house in East Los Angeles. Although only four years old, it was in bad shape, with broken doors and holes in the walls. We offered him $45,000 and insisted that he take the Riverside property in exchange for $3,000 off the purchase price. This time he agreed, revealing years later that he could never locate the property and that it was eventually lost in bankruptcy. We worked very diligently fixing up these units and sold them eight months later making a $12,000 profit. That was more money than we had ever seen and we congratulated each other on our good fortune.

I had been working at the Park La Brea apartments for two years and, for the first time in my life, had taken two weeks' vacation. By this time we owned several properties and it was really getting to be too much to keep up with the maintenance on top of a full time job. May-Britt and I had been working on an apartment all day and in the evening went out for dinner. I told her that I was thinking about not going back to work and she encouraged me to quit. The next day I called my boss, thanked him for the job and told him that I wouldn't be coming back. I had always wanted to have my own business, so I studied for my California State Contractors license, passed the test, and started my own painting company. At first I advertised in the local paper, but soon found that it wasn't necessary as I was getting enough work through referrals.

We bought several properties from Fred Shubin and accumulated a fairly good size portfolio of real estate. By the mid-60s we owned between 30-40 apartments. We were doing well when, all of a sudden, thousands of apartments became available and rental income took a nosedive. For months we had several vacancies and were losing lots of money. We decided that we had to do something soon, or we would lose the property. Then we hit on the idea to furnish the vacant units. Every Thursday and Saturday May-Britt would scan the furniture ads in the paper, check out and buy what we needed and arrange for me to pick up the items in my pick-up truck after work. We were able to rent the furnished units for more money and the furniture paid for it self, since we had no more vacancies.

ACCORDING TO ME

ORLA'S CONSTRUCTION

In the late 1960's we bought a house built on a large lot. We were able to split the lot into three smaller parcels. Leaving the original house intact on the front lot, we commissioned a building company to build two small houses on the back lots and sold them. Watching the development we found that building houses didn't look very difficult and decided to try it ourselves. We purchased a small lot in Monrovia and had a plan drawn for a very small house. Only 940 square feet, it was arranged very efficiently with three bedrooms and two full bathrooms, a small living room, dinette and a very small kitchen. It had an eye level oven and cook top over the dishwasher. I built it in five weeks and sold it very quickly, making a fine profit.

We were off and running. I had found a new profession. The painter's trade had established me well, but I was now a builder and would never be a painting contractor again. We found a triangular lot next to the freeway. It was so small that we had to build a triangular house. There was no room for a garage, only a single carport.

FRED SHUBIN PARTNERSHIP

Shortly after I changed careers Fred Shubin contacted us and proposed that we get together on some real estate deals. We had always liked him and we formed an informal partnership, buying property adjacent to the freeways from the State of California. Some of those properties had older houses that we renovated and then resold. Others were vacant lots. We relocated houses from properties we owned elsewhere to the vacant lots, renovated them and sold them. I did the work and Fred was in charge of sales. It was quite a profitable venture.

GHOSTS?

We had lived in our new house on Doolittle for four years and had been quite happy. But May-Britt wanted something bigger and better and convinced me that we could afford to move up in the world. So we bought a house on a nice quiet street that was within city limits and in a better school district. The property had an enormous backyard with a big walnut tree that the kids could climb. The house itself was on a raised wood floor, with floor to ceiling glass windows in all the living areas. I don't know that I believe in ghosts or haunted houses, but there was something eerie about that place. The neighbors told us that the former owners had done horrible things to each other, fighting and swearing. The husband had once thrown his wife through the big glass window into the fishpond in the atrium. From the day we moved in, until we moved out four years later, May-Britt was unhappy. It was like a dark cloud hanging over her head and she complained about everything in the place. Thankfully none of the houses we have lived in since then have had similar problems.

WINNIE WAY

Some of the streets in Arcadia had properties with very deep lots that were larger than people wanted to maintain. The lots were so deep that developers could purchase the backyards backing up to each other, put a street through the middle and still have adequate lots on both sides. We decided to buy one of the better lots on one of those new streets and, in 1972, built a very nice house with a three-car garage and a swimming pool in the backyard. It was wonderful to live there. The climate in that area is perfect almost all year round and we practically lived on the large covered patio. In the 15 years we lived there, I wore out three grills preparing hundreds of medium rare steaks.

Bank Relations

I was now building more and more houses. I had even moved several houses from one end of the county to the other, placing them on vacant lots that I owned. There was a limit to how many houses I could build out of pocket and needed to establish a relationship with a bank to obtain loans. I began working with First City Bank in Rosemead, Ca. and did business with them for quite a few years. The first time I approached them for a loan they looked favorably on my plans and told me to bring them a cost breakdown. I asked the bank officer what exactly they required on a cost breakdown. She told me that I had to list the price for all the different contractors and materials that were entailed in constructing the house. I actually had no idea what each item cost, but I knew that I could build a house for $10.00 per square foot. I multiplied the square footage of the house by ten and, adding a few percentages, came up with a bottom line. Then I worked backwards to itemize the calculation. This worked wonderfully. The bank was satisfied and I was always able to build the houses for less than the amount of the loan and would have enough money left over to invest in another building lot. It worked great for many years and I developed a wonderful working relationship with the bank personnel.

Lakeview Pines Mobiel Home Park

We were also acquiring apartment buildings in better areas. For a period of time we had over 100 units. We thought it might be interesting to buy a mobile home park. Thinking that Big Bear Lake, located in the San Bernardino Mountains, would be a likely area, we attended an open house held by some acquaintances of mine. Meeting a real estate agent at a the party we told him we were in the market for a mobile home park and he told us that he had just recently sold one right

down by the lake. A month later he called and told us that the people that had bought the park didn't want it anymore. If we were interested, it was available. I went back to First City Bank and told my friend and loan officer, Gary Eggen, that I wanted to find out what they really thought of me. He asked me what I meant by that. I told him that I wanted to borrow $85,000, with only my good name for collateral, for a down payment on a mobile home park. He said he would present it to the board. After talking to him I kind of put it out of my mind and forgot about it. Visiting the bank a few days later, Gary approached me and said that I was approved for the loan. "What loan?" I asked. He laughed and said that I could have the $85,000 I had asked for. To make a long story short, we bought the park. With 75 spots for mobile homes, mostly occupied, a house and a cabin, it was a good investment. It also gave us a vacation spot for skiing, a sport we had yet to embrace, but thought would be an activity we could do as a family.

According To Me

English Oaks

In Arcadia, along Foothill Blvd, there were many old and large estates that were quickly be bought up by developers who tore down the existing house, subdivided the lot, put in a cul-de-sac and built upscale homes. I was really anxious to get my hands on one of those properties and asked my favorite realtor, Marlene, to keep her eyes open. One day she called me and said that there were two smaller estates available adjacent to each other, maybe I could put them together? I made offers on the properties on the condition that I would be able to do that. The offer was accepted and I contacted a civil engineer to draw up plans for the project. He designed a double ball cul-de-sac with 11 lots around it. It was beautiful and my bank thought so, also and awarded me the loan. I had my project. It was so exciting to start digging in the dirt and develop a little neighborhood. All went well and I began building houses there that would to sell for $235,000 to $250,000. It was in 1979-80 and the interest rate was beginning to go through the roof. I sold the first three houses to buyers that paid 18% on their loans. After that the sales came to a complete standstill. Not wanting the bank to get nervous, I needed to come up with ideas quickly. I told my realtor that if she could procure buyers who could give me 40% down, I would carry the loans at 12.5%. That turned out be a fantastic solution to my problem. We sold all of the houses and I carried these wonderful first loans for years. I was able to pay off the construction loan to the bank.

VALLEY KNOWLLS

A few of years later a friend of mine from the bank, Dane Haas, called and told me that he was now working with another bank. After getting through all the good-natured comments, he told me that his new bank did joint ventures with builders and asked me if I was interested. If I could propose a project valued between a minimum of 3 million and a maximum of 17 million, the bank would carry the financing and I would do the developing. It sounded almost too good to be true and I said that this was the opportunity I had been waiting for all my life. Dane and I spent the next couple of months driving all over Southern California searching for a suitable piece of property. I also let my realtors in Arcadia know that I desired a substantial piece of land zoned for residential use. In time one of them contacted me and told me that they thought that they had found something that could fit my purpose, 67 acres located in San Marcos about 30 miles north of San Diego. It already had a tentative plan for 199 houses plus a pool and community hall. In August 1985, after negotiating with the seller for a long time, he finally accepted my offer of $2,400,000. I made a nonrefundable deposit of $25,000 into escrow, which I was to close in 9 months. If I were unable to close by that time, I would be charged $2,500 the first month, $5,000 the following month and so on, becoming more expensive as time went by.

ACCORDING TO ME

I had just opened escrow when I called Dane and told him that we had a project. "That is fantastic!" he exclaimed. Twenty minutes later he called me back with some ghastly information. Due to new government regulations the bank could no longer enter into joint ventures, but, he promised, they would still give me a very favorable loan. Shocked, I racked my brain for a solution. If I didn't come up with something soon I would lose my $25,000 deposit. May-Britt and I discussed our options and, after a few days, decided that we could do the engineering and then sell the package to another developer. I contacted the engineer in San Marcos who had done the engineering for the tentative plan and told him to go ahead and design the final plan.

After a while though, the challenge didn't seem quite as insurmountable as it had at first. If we refinanced some of the properties we owned, we might be able to pay for the land. Then it would be possible to get financing for the rest of the development. With that in mind we began exploring the possibilities. I had already done some developing, the little eleven home cul-de-sac in Arcadia, and felt confident that I could even handle a larger project. The real hurdle was convincing the bank of my abilities.

Complying with city regulations, I hired a consultant to represent me. I needed a $ 3,000,000 bond for streets, storm sewers and everything pertaining to the offsite not included in the house lots. The bonding companies I contacted practically slammed the door in my face as soon as they heard that an eleven-home cul-de-sac was the extent of my developing experience. An acquaintance of mine, who sold car insurance, claimed that he could find a bonding company, but I didn't really believe him. Finally, as a last resort, I contacted him. Amazingly, he did find a bond company that, for some reason, had enough confidence in me to sell me the bond. Of course, I had to leave nearly every property we owned as collateral.

Financing the building phases was my next challenge. I planned to build the project in six phases, starting with 40 homes including a 4-house model complex. Every bank I contacted turned me down. Eventually, I contacted a loan broker in Temple City who wanted 1% on any loan he acquired for me, which, by this time, I was happy to pay. He hooked me up with Great American Bank in San Diego, which turned out to be a godsend. They structured a loan, promising to lend me $7,500,000, including a land draw in the amount of $900,000 to help to pay off the land. Agreeing to everything that I wanted to do, with some modification, they would allow me to build the model complex plus 16 houses. Once I had sold half of those units they would allow me to build out the remaining 20 of the first phase.

When the papers had been drawn up and signed, the finance director, Frank Orosco, asked me to come to the bank later in the week for instructions on how they wanted the cost breakdown to be structured. This was a big difference from the somewhat arbitrary breakdowns I had produced for First City Bank. Each line item on the document demanded minute calculation. There were cost breakdowns for each model, plus an aggregate cost breakdown for the whole project with line items for every entity involved. Not just for the houses, but also for the miles of streets, sewers, storm drains big enough to drive a small car through, and everything else pertaining to a big development that is being built from scratch. On the appointed day I drove down to San Diego. For some reason I couldn't park in the building and had to find a parking space a few blocks away. It was a very hot day and I arrived at the bank sweating profusely, partly from the exertion, but mostly because I was nervous about what I was getting myself into. Never in my wildest dreams had I ever contemplated being in this situation. I was about to enter on to a sea of uncertainty, crossing the Rubicon, and there was no turning back. If I could pull it off I would be the largest developer in San Marcos, at least for a while.

According To Me

Entering the office, I was offered a cup of coffee, shown to a seat in a brand new, upholstered chair and told that Frank would be right with me. I was so nervous that, when he came in, I spilled the coffee all over that beautiful new chair and myself. Embarrassed over my clumsiness, and still jittery and sweating, I sat in that conference room together with several bank associates and listened as Frank explained the intricacies of filling out a draw request for funds, including with it the necessary copies of bills, material and labor releases from the various contractors. If all the t's weren't crossed and all the i's weren't dotted, no funds would be disbursed.

I soon made friends at Great American. One of the ladies, who I at first only spoke to on the phone, had a rather heavy accent that I thought could be oriental. However, when I later met her in person, I discovered she was Swedish! Kristin Rumar and I became immediate friends and she was a tremendous help guiding me through the all the red tape involved in doing business with the new bank.

Over a year had passed since I opened escrow and the extension penalties were mounting up now to over $20,000 monthly and gaining. But I now had nearly all my ducks in a row and was almost ready to get started with construction. I told the bank that, although I didn't have any permits yet, I needed the $900,000 land draw so I could close escrow. They approved my request and I closed escrow. Suddenly, I was $7,500,000 deeper in debt.

I had given the excavation contract to a young man named Pat, who would become one of my closest confidantes and a very dear friend. I told him that I had closed the escrow on the property and was only waiting for the City of San Marcos to approve my grading plan before I could give him the signal to begin moving more than a million yards of rocks and dirt around on the project. Pat was chomping at the bit and pleaded with me to get started. I told him that I couldn't get a money draw from the bank before I had my grading permit, and I didn't expect to get that until the last week in November. He told me "No problem!" He wouldn't present me with a bill until the middle of December if I let him begin right away. Being a gambler of sorts, I gave him the go-ahead and he started moving dirt on November 16, 1986.

The equipment that appeared on the property was mind-boggling. One enormous bulldozer, weighing 75 tons, three twin-engine earthmovers able to carry 40 yards and go 40 miles an hour, and many more pieces of equipment shaved 40 feet off of two hills and raised a few valleys by 12 feet. My main concern was the cost, $18,000 per day, enough to keep me awake at night. I waited anxiously for the city to approve my plan but, due to the Thanksgiving holiday, the meeting was postponed until the first Monday in December. It was getting a little tight. Bills were piling up quicker than I had ever experienced before and I was beginning to wonder about my future.

On the Friday before the City Council meeting my engineer called me and told me to go to the city hall and get the agenda. My name would be at the top of the consent agenda, the first item of business that would just be a formality, and then I would be good to go.

I drove to the city hall, picked up the agenda, and scanned it for my name. It wasn't there. Panic mounting, I drove home and fell on my knees with my face in the sofa, a position I would assume many times in the future, and prayed fervently for the Lord to help me in my dilemma. I could see myself being ruined before I had even gotten started. Just as I finished praying, my engineer called me and, before I could tell her anything, told me that my project would be on a special consent agenda. On Monday evening, at the City Council meeting, it was just a formality, a rubber stamp, and I had my permit. Once again, in great relief, I fell on my knees, thanking the Lord for bringing me through a deep, dark valley.

We bought a house with an oversized 3-car garage across the street from the entrance to the project. It was really handy living practically on site, keeping an eye on things. May-Britt was still living in our home in Arcadia. On Friday afternoon I would climb into my truck and drive the 110 miles back to Arcadia, spend the weekend with her, and return Sunday night, drinking cokes to keep me awake on the two hour commute.

I set up the office, such as it was, in the family room. To begin with, all I had was a tiny desk and a copy machine. I worked that way for several months, without any office or field help. I later converted a portion of the garage into a nice 20' x 20' office, still leaving room for a two-car garage in compliance with city ordinance. I then brought my big 4' x 7' desk down from Arcadia. Doing all the supervision, office work, paying bills and preparing fund requests for the bank was tough to handle on my on my own. It was a wonderful release when Friday afternoon came around so I could go back to my wonderful wife in Arcadia for a short respite from the enormous challenge I had taken on.

Mondays were always chaotic, with all kinds of problems to handle. Tuesdays weren't much better. Wednesdays were a little easier, and by the time Friday rolled around things were going fairly smooth. I could never figure out what happened over the weekend, when nobody was there, that could create such a nightmare every Monday. But that was the pattern throughout the duration of the project, even when we were more or less living in the house full time.

I could have used a shrink in those days, because the project was really nerve-racking and often overwhelming. Instead, I found solace by going down to the bank and chatting with the girls, with whom I had developed a very good relationship. After spending a short time chatting with Kristin, my Swedish loan officer, I felt like I could go back and carry on with the tasks at hand. I showed up there a few times just to chat, but most of the time I had a legitimate reason. Filling out the fund requests was complicated and I had to redo the forms several times before they would release the money. It was quite exasperating. Occasionally Frank would invite me to lunch at a nice Spanish style restaurant across the street from the bank. We became better acquainted, and I was always straight with him, keeping him informed about how the development was coming along. Of course the bank had its inspectors out to make sure that the work was done according to the plan.

An architect acquaintance of mine in Arcadia designed the four models. Ranging in size from 1,200 to 1,500 square feet, there were three three-bedroom homes and one four-bedroom home. Each model had three available front elevations but, even with 12 dissimilar facades, they still looked like cookie cutter houses. We hit the market just perfect. Real estate was on the way up after a severe recession in the early eighties and interest rates came down from the astronomical heights of 24 % to a more workable rate of 7 – 8 percent.

It was quite an education to come into a strange city and become, for a time, the largest developer. It took a long time for me to get used to the bureaucracy and for the bureaucrats to get used to me. One neighbor did not like me at all. If anybody began work a minute before 7 am, he or his daughter would call the city and complain. He was successful in getting the city to take me to court, and I was fined.

It was Pat's fault; I just couldn't keep him from starting early. I pleaded with Pat to keep better control of his people and he promised that he would, but it seemed that he didn't have complete control either. The company he contracted with to maintain the equipment came after hours to service them and that caused problems. I don't remember how much I was fined that time but, after a while, it all worked out with the city and things began to run a lot smoother.

One night I heard a blast in front of my house. I thought it was a car backfiring and didn't think anything about it. Going out to get the paper the next morning, I saw some splintered pieces of wood lying by the front door. Entering the house and walking into the front room, I saw there was a hole in the window. Somebody had shot at the house with a large caliber weapon. The bullet came through the front window, penetrated the adjacent wall, splintering the wood on the outside of the house near the front door. I called the Sheriff and made a report, but nothing came of it. Although I have my suspicions about who did it, there was never any evidence for a conviction.

Getting the first houses, including the model complex, built took longer than I anticipated. I had trouble with various contractors doing their jobs to satisfaction. I had to fire one and she took me to arbitration court. Since I can't remember the outcome, it couldn't have been too bad. I probably paid her off and got rid of her.

Once the models were built, they had to be decorated and furnished. I found a decorator who really did a good job for me, but it was expensive. It cost $100,000 to do the four models, each in a different style and all beautiful. We named each model, from the smallest to the largest, Gothenburg, Oslo, Copenhagen and, the largest four-bedroom, Stockholm, in honor of all the marvelous Swedes.

Once the project was well underway and I had weeded out the less desirable contractors, things proceeded smoothly. The first two superintendents that I hired didn't work out very well. I managed to convince the first one to quit, and had to fire the second one. I finely hired Richard Rimestead, who was able to supervise the entire project and made things a lot easier for me.

I didn't have a secretary for the first six months and the paperwork and telephone calls were quickly becoming overwhelming. Pat said I couldn't continue like that, I needed help in the office. I told him I had never had a secretary and wasn't sure how to work with one. He found a secretary and spent half a day with her setting up my files and showing her, and me, how to run an office efficiently. She didn't last very long, but I found another girl, Terry, who was absolutely perfect for me. She took over everything that I would let her do. At the end of the week she would lay a pile of checks on my desk for me to sign for the bills that were due. She took it upon herself to inspect the houses before the buyers moved in, minimizing complaints later.

By the time I finished the first phase of 40 houses and the second phase of 29 houses, I had developed a very good relationship with the bank. When I set up the loan for the third phase, Frank told me that I didn't need to go through the effort of submitting all the paperwork in order to draw funds for the project. All I had to do now was call them and tell them the amount of funds I required transferred to my account and they would accommodate me, as long I didn't exceed a line item amount. It seemed they would do anything for me. One day I called Kris Rumar and told her that I was starting a big phase of 44 houses and needed 5 million dollars. She told me to come down and fill out a loan application. I asked her to fill it out for me, because it was too cumbersome, and she did. All I had to do was sign it. Unfortunately the Great American Bank succumbed in the purges of Savings and Loans that occurred between 1989 and 1991. But before they went under, they had extended to me a credit line of a million dollars on my signature alone.

To this day I believe that there was a divine intervention in this project. So many things fell into place and, despite my limited experience, I was able to achieve my objective. Getting the large bond was a miracle, and Kristin told me that Great American Bank, who really didn't know me or what I was capable of, had never granted a loan like this for anyone.

Thinking back, I marvel at how the development proceeded. At one time I had 87 houses under construction at once. One phase of 44 was almost finished and I began construction on 43 additional. House prices in California rose steadily. The houses from the first phase sold for between $105 - 118,000. By the time we reached the sixth phase, three years later, prices were as high as $170,000. House sales were brisk, sometimes selling 12 – 14 in a weekend. Of course, half of them fell out of escrow due to buyer's credit problems or regrets. By the time I finished the project, we had, on the average, sold every house twice. It was really remarkable.

As we entered 1990 a recession hit again and house sales came to a screeching halt. Luckily I only had six houses left unsold. I rented them for a while and eventually they, too, sold. It was a great relief. After three years filled with restless nights, I was exhausted but God had sustained me. I felt His support many times. Sleepless nights, I would leave my bed and go down in the family room and fall on my face in a sofa, crying out to the Lord to give me strength and peace. Usually when I arose from my knees I felt better about my circumstances. I am sorry to say that, as the project wore on, I found myself moving away from the Lord. The feeling of closeness I'd experienced when I began the development was gone. I had not rejected the Lord, I simply forgot about Him. Later, I made some bad financial mistakes and lost a lot of money and I often wonder if it would have made a difference had I stayed closer to the Lord. I have since asked the Lord to forgive me for my backsliding and I feel that He has. I have peace in my soul.

CHAMBER OF COMMERCE

I joined the San Marcos Chamber of Commerce when we bought the property for the development. It was the fastest way to get acquainted with the business community, which was very important since I was moving into a strange city. People were friendly and seemed as glad to get to know me, as I was to get to know them. The monthly Chamber mixers were well attended. Sometimes hundreds of people would show up for a cocktail and hors d'oeuvres and to network, getting to know other business people to broaden their connections.

After I had been a member for about a year, I was asked to sit on the chamber board. They may have been impressed by the fact that I was the biggest developer in town, at least for a while. I became acquainted with some of the interactions between the chamber and government. Once a year board members traveled to Sacramento and meet with chamber representatives from all over the state. There would be speeches by the governor and several other politicians.

The third weekend in September we held our own conference, usually in Palm Springs, where we discussed ideas about how to improve the business community, something that became progressively harder as the country slipped into another recession.

By 1992 the recession was in full swing. Except for the rental properties that we still owned and that May-Britt handled, I was not doing any business. The house market hit bottom, nothing was selling or being built. I went to my office in San Marcos almost every day, just to piddle around and spend time.

Then I was asked to be president of the chamber for the year, which turned out to be eighteen months since there was some delay in replacing me. I was amazed how busy I became as president. Sometimes I had three meetings per day, which was a bit tiresome. I was also invited to events that most people didn't get the opportunity to experience.

One day I was invited to Camp Pendleton Marine Base for lunch. Able to bring two guests, I invited Orla Jens and Darla to accompany me. There was more brass than I have seen anywhere before or since, former and present marine commandants, several four-star generals, and oodles of lesser officers. After walking around looking at a lot of war equipment we were ushered into a big tent for lunch. We were served a package of MRE, meals ready to eat, just like what the marines get on the battlefield. I'm sure it was nourishing, but I wouldn't want to live on it.

When the lunch was over we were all loaded on to buses and driven to a bluff overlooking the ocean. Sitting on bleachers we watched as several commando units exhibited what they had been trained to do in diverse situations in some future campaign. We observed a Harrier Jump Jet fly over in front of us, slow down and hover over one spot. Turning around on its own axis, it took off like a regular jet fighter. Hostage rescue commandoes jumped from helicopters a couple of miles out in the ocean, and paddled to land in an inflatable boat. The announcer was telling us to imagine that what was happening was in the darkness of night. When the commandoes entered the perimeter of the area where the hostages were kept, they shot the three guards, blew open the door to the building rescuing the hostages inside. In the meantime, a big twin-engine helicopter landed nearby to ferry them away. There must not have been room for the commandoes in the helicopter, because they attached themselves to a long cable hanging down from the helicopter, which flew out over the ocean with six marines hanging on the line like a bunch of grapes on a vine.

My visit at Pendleton was probably the highlight of my tenure as president of the Chamber. But a close second would have to be the Installation Banquet, installing my successor and honoring me for a job well done. The numerous awards I received that night, coming from the United States Congress all the way down through and including the City of San Marcos, are now covering most of a wall in my office.

MOVING TO THE ROCKIES

Focus on the Family moved to Colorado Springs in 1990, taking with them several of our friends as well as May-Britt's nephew, Dwight and his family. Sometime in the spring of 1993

Orla Jens and Darla went to Colorado Springs to visit Dwight and some other friends. While they were there, Orla Jens went to a real estate meeting. As a real estate broker in California where business was slow, he was interested in the conditions in Colorado. At the meeting there was an offering of 30 home lots by the Resolution Trust Commission, the organization that killed all the savings and loans in the country and were now in competition with the real estate business. Orla Jens called and asked if I would be interested in making a bid on the lots. I told him that I wasn't interested in doing anything in Colorado but would be happy to go there and write the trip off as a business expense. The auction was held in early May. Orla Jens, May-Britt and I flew to Colorado Springs a couple of days early so we could acquaint ourselves with the project and the area.

The lots were scattered over a relatively large area on the slopes of the majestic Cheyenne Mountain at the southern end of town. With an elevation between 6,500 and 6,800 feet, each lot had a fantastic view over the high plains to the east and Pike's Peak to the west. We viewed a few of the houses being offered for sale in the area, and were amazed at the size of them. In the Broadmoor Bluffs area, where the lots were located, houses averaged about 5,000 sq. feet with full basements, more than twice the size most of the houses in California!

Driving around trying to locate the various lots, we grew more and more excited about the prospect of acquiring them and moving to Colorado to build houses. The day before the auction we stood on one of the lots and prayed for the Lord's blessing in the project. We had decided that we would bid $775,000 and if we got them it would be a positive answer from the Lord. Orla Jens submitted the bid that afternoon and we waited till the next afternoon to hear the outcome. When he called to inquire about the result he was told that we had been overbid. Happy in California and content to be going back, I really didn't mind but May-Britt and Orla Jens were distraught and almost in tears as we flew home to the Golden State.

ACCORDING TO ME

But God works in mysterious ways and His timing is not ours. A couple of weeks later the Colorado Springs broker, Bob Garner, called Orla Jens and told him that the people who had overbid us decided that they didn't want the lots and that we could have them for the price we had offered. Excited, we told him that we would take them, and motions were set in gear to acquire the properties.

May-Britt and I flew up to look for a place to live for the first year or so, while we were getting organized in a new location. At first we were looking at homes in the northern part of the city, near our friends the Davis'. Fortunately we also looked in an area called Lower Skyway, which was close to downtown and to our newly acquired property. We found a small house in a quiet neighborhood. It was 1,300 square feet with three small bedrooms and two bathrooms. It had no basement, which is unusual, but it did have a crawlspace we could use for storage. Orla Jens and I moved to Colorado first. If things worked out in Colorado, the ladies would come later. Darla was studying for her Masters Degree in San Diego and May-Britt still had the rental properties to manage in California.

On November 1, 1993, Orla Jens and I left wonderful, warm California for our new life in the Rocky Mountains, where there would be snow and ice six months of the year. We had skied in the California Mountains many times, but had never actually lived in a winter climate, so this was going to be a new experience. I drove a rental truck filled with household goods and pulled Orla Jens' minivan. He followed in my El Camino pickup. Arriving at our new home at about 3 pm the following day, we unloaded the truck and set up the beds. I let him have the master bedroom, took one of the smaller bedrooms for myself, and set up our office in the third bedroom with a computer, copy machine, etc.

We met with the architect the following day. Bob Garner had recommended Chuck Englund, and May-Britt and I had met with him during the summer. Showing him some of our ideas

122

for the houses we wanted to build, we also asked for the names of contractors we would need to get started with construction. Chuck was very helpful and soon had the plans ready to hand over to his structural engineer. In no time at all we had submitted the finished plans to the city and had our permits for the first two houses.

Everything was new for me in Colorado Springs. In California all the lots were on a level plane. If they weren't, we leveled them out with dirt. In Colorado our lots were on fairly steep slopes and we had to build according to the terrain. It didn't take long to learn, although I did lean on Chuck's shoulders quite a bit for the first couple of houses. I had also never built a house with a basement before. In California we simply dug a trench 12 inches wide and 12 inches deep and poured the foundation. In Colorado, where most of the houses have basements, we had to first determine the depth of the basement by measuring from a predetermined point, like the curb at the street, and then stake out the area for the footprint of the house. We then had to measure five feet around the perimeter of the house for over digging, so people would be able to set up the forms for the foundation, which were usually four to ten feet high, depending on the slope of the terrain. In a couple of cases, the foundation wall was over 16 feet high.

Another thing that was different was the haphazard way the various underground lines for TV, telephone and even electrical was installed. On the first lot we found every line with a bulldozer, cutting off the neighbor's electrical wires while grading for the sidewalk. I called the city and they came out and repaired it before the neighbor knew anything about it.

Building houses was something new for Orla Jens, but he took to it like a duck to water. He really enjoyed learning to read the blueprints and figuring out how the house was to fit on the lot. I had him meet the inspectors and walk with them so he could understand their corrections. We took great pride in having the fewest corrections possible. I will never forget how excited Orla Jens was one day when we had final inspection on a house and the inspector, finding no corrections, signed it off. "Almost as good as having sex!" he exclaimed. By this time we had developed a good relationship with the inspector, who we'd heard had told somebody in town that we were among the best builders in Colorado Springs.

STAR RANCH

Darla finished her Master's program and moved up to Colorado and she and Orla Jens bought a house. May-Britt eventually joined me in Colorado Springs and we had been living in our little house for over a year when we decided to build a house for ourselves. We chose one of the lots, located on Star Ranch Road, and drew up plans with the help of a young designer. Our beautiful 6,200 sq.ft., three level house had a view of the mountains and the plains. Twice as big as anything we'd had in California, it had six bedrooms and six bathrooms. May-Britt wanted a second toilet on the main level, across from the powder room, for everyday use, but I nixed it. I reminded her that we had both grown up without any bathrooms in Sweden and Denmark.

BROADMORE RESORT

I figured that we would live out our days on Star Ranch Road, but fate has a sense of humor. The Broadmoor Company began developing a large area just west of us higher up the mountain. It was going to be a gated community and lot prices were upwards of $150,000 with million dollar homes. I thought, at first, that nobody would buy anything at that price. One night we were at a party where we met one of our neighbors, who had bought two lots and thought that it was a great deal. He was going to build a house for himself on one of them and wanted to sell the other. A few days later he invited us up to look it over. The price was $225,000, which we thought was a little high, but we realized the value was there and told him that we'd give it serious consideration. A few days later we were driving around the area and decided to go into the sales office to find out what they had to offer. When we told the salesman what we were looking for, he told us that he had a real sleeper for sale across the street from the office. The lot was a half acre and may have been used for a parking lot in the past, because there wasn't a tree on the building area, but had lots of beautiful pine trees and scrub oak on the west end. It had a 360-degree un-obscured view of the plains and mountains and for $250,000 it was a much better buy than the lots down the street where the houses are built so close together that I call it the ghetto.

We bought the lot and, getting together with our designer again, we drew up plans for the biggest house we have ever owned, 8,200 square feet plus a 30 by 45 foot garage. All of our previous garages have been too small, but not this one. Although the house is bigger than the house we had on Star Ranch, it only has five bedrooms, but it's loaded with storage space and the only things I store in the garage, are cars.

RETIREMENT

Orla Jens and I continued to work together for eight years and developed a wonderful working relationship, but all good things come to an end. Over the Christmas holidays, 2002, I called him into my office. He sat down and I told him, "I quit." It was fun to see

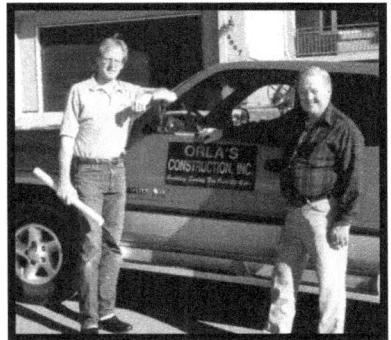

his quizzical, somewhat concerned expression. I told him that I wasn't dead yet and I would help him, if he needed me. He hasn't needed me for anything. He is a much better builder than I am, anyhow. I dissolved my corporation and he instituted his own, which, to my great pleasure, he called "Orla Homes."

I have now been retired for several years and have never missed the struggles of doing business. In fact I don't have time to work; I'm too busy traveling all over the world. That is my interest now and I hope to continue doing it a few more years.

WHY I STILL PICK UP PENNIES

When I was a young boy in school, I read a story that made a lasting impression on me. There was a young man, who was very poor. So poor, that he didn't know where his next meal would come from. One day he was walking on the road and he saw a potato lying there. He picked it up and took it home, where he dug a small hole in the ground and planted it. In time he watched some leaves appear and, as he watered it, it continued to grow into a big beautiful plant. In autumn, the leaves withered and he dug up the root. Attached were many new potatoes, which he saved till the next spring, when he planted them all in the ground. He continued doing this for many years and in time he had hundreds of acres of potatoes, which he exported all over the world. One day he was walking down the same road where he had found that first potato. He saw another potato lying at the side of the road. Giving it a swift kick, he smashed it in many pieces. From that day forward his life was plagued with bad luck and was soon poorer than when he had begun. You see, that first potato he picked up on the road so many years ago, was his good fortune. By kicking the last potato, he had kicked his good fortune in the face, and it left him.

Moral of the story: "Don't let wealth go to your head."

DEPUTY PEDERSEN

L iving on Doolittle we became friends with Don and
Ruth Stiver who lived down the street with their three
children. The youngest, Pam, was about the same age
as LaVonne. Don was a sergeant with the Los Angeles Sheriff
Department. I had heard about the reserve program and told
him that I would like to explore becoming a reserve officer. He
invited me to ride along with him in his patrol car and I enjoyed
the excitement immensely. I went to the Sheriff's Academy
and signed up for the program to become a deputy. Classes
were all day Sunday and Monday evenings for six months. It
was mostly theoretical, but did include some physical training
not unlike what I had experienced in army boot camp. It was
so tough that half of the guys dropped out, not being able to
handle the verbal abuse and invectives heaped upon them by
the drill instructors.

There were many amusing incidents at the academy, but
the story I'm going to tell now has got to be the funniest. In
the beginning we wore uniforms and leather, but no weapons.

ACCORDING TO ME

After three months we were told to purchase a 38-caliber revolver before the next meeting. I always rode to the academy together with another cadet who lived nearby. Jaus was a real hotshot who thought he knew it all. On Sunday, during our lunch break, a salesman from the Peace Officer store came by trying to sell some extra equipment that he claimed would be handy out in the treacherous world. Jaus purchased a quick loading device and was playing with it, loading and unloading his revolver. Immediately after lunch we formed up in three platoons for armed inspection. Our weapons were, of course, supposed to be unloaded. Our drill instructor, Deputy Mays, was a retired marine who acted as though he was still in the Marine Corps, and was one of the most abusive instructors at the academy. He was standing right in front of Jaus, when he shouted, "Order arms!" We all pulled our weapons and opened the cylinders. Jaus, who had inadvertently holstered his gun loaded, opened his and six bullets fell on his shoes and bounced onto Mays's feet. All hell broke loose. Mays screamed at Jaus, who was trying in vain to apologize. That evening I waited in the car for two hours after class while Jaus got raked over by Deputy Mays.

Jaus and I both survived the rigors of the academy and became legitimate peace officers. Jaus' career was short lived, however. One night while he and his partner were on patrol, they pulled a car over for a minor infraction. Jaus approached the female driver and asked for her driver's license. She handed him a business card with our captain's name on it. Jaus tore it to pieces and threw on the ground. "I asked you for your driver's license," he sneered. We found out later that she was the captain's girlfriend and when she reported in great detail how badly she had been treated by one of his intrepid officers, Jaus was immediately relieved of his hard earned six-pointed badge.

At one of our monthly meetings, we were asked to volunteer for role-playing one evening at the academy. Regular officers in the field were called in for special training to make them aware of the dangers of their jobs. Officers have a tendency to become careless in the routine of the day, especially patrolling traffic. Pulling people over for speeding or running stop signs doesn't seem very hazardous, but we were there to teach them the errors of their ways.

We were several volunteers, all reserve deputies, that showed up at the academy. As part of the exercise we were going to reenact an event called the "Maywood Caper," an actual crime that had taken place sometime earlier. A couple of patrol officers had received a call on their radio to be on the alert for a suspicious vehicle described as a dirty white van or camper. As they were patrolling the area, they observed said vehicle and pulled it over. Usually, when motorists are pulled over by the police, they stay in the car and wait for the officer to approach. But in the Maywood Caper the occupants of the vehicle opened the doors, while others hung out of the windows hollering and screaming and acting rather crazed. The officers, not quite sure what to make of the situation, stayed behind the open doors of the patrol car. Meanwhile another vehicle quietly rolled up behind them unnoticed and two people got out quietly and, sneaking up behind the officers, shot them. The two vehicles hurriedly left the scene, leaving the two dead officers lying there.

I'm still bothered by what happened at the academy that night. The regular officers were only told that they were to handle any suspicious vehicles. We, the volunteer reserves, were to play the part of the "bad guys" and several of the guys were asked to get into an old camper. I was paired with another guy and told to park my car in the shadows of building, out of sight. We were the shooters and were each issued a 38-caliber revolver with the barrel plugged, strictly for shooting blanks.

We sat there waiting, and after a while the old camper came rolling down the road, chased by the sheriff's vehicle, red lights flashing and siren blaring. When the camper pulled over to the side the passengers hung out the windows and doors acting crazy, screaming and hollering and cursing. This wasn't normal behavior and the responding deputies didn't quite know how to handle the situation. Knowing that they were being watched and evaluated they wanted to go by the book. Taking cover behind the open doors of the radio car, they waited and watched the idiots in the camper. Meanwhile, my buddy and I came out of hiding and rolled up behind them, parking about 50 feet away. The two deputies, engaged in what was happening in front of them, never noticed. Quietly getting out of our car, we snuck up behind them and shot them in the back, ending the exercise.

We did this with 12 different units, out of which we shot ten. Only twice did the officers notice us coming and asked us what we were doing, which is what they were expected to do. No matter what the situation, they were to be continually aware of their surroundings. Later that evening, at a meeting we were not invited to, their performance was analyzed and critiqued. I wish I could have been a fly on the wall. It still bothers me that it was so easy to kill the sheriff deputies. It's not something that happens often, thank God, but I wish it never happened.

I served the sheriff's department for twelve years, going out in a patrol car a couple of times per month, and getting involved in many other police events, such as directing traffic for the Rose Parade. I even had the thrilling opportunity to ride in a small patrol helicopter as an observer, operating the light, and one time was involved with Mountain Rescue. Although there was occasionally some excitement, most rides were pretty uneventful. I'd come home and complain to May-Britt that nothing ever happened when I was on patrol because she sat home and prayed for me. I'm glad she was praying though and, except for a case of food poisoning that resulted in rather embarrassing straits that I'd rather not go into, I was never in mortal danger.

THE WILD BLUE YONDER

For years airplanes had fascinated me. A friend of mine owned an airplane and had taken me on several trips around the country. The idea of being able to fly myself was enticing. One of our neighbors on Magna Vista ran a flight school at the El Monte airport about three miles away. In those days achieving a pilot's license was fairly inexpensive. I could rent a small two-seater Cessna 150, including fuel, for $8.00 per hour. In 1970 May-Britt reluctantly consented to me becoming a pilot and I began flight training. On the average it took about 40 hours of flying time to achieve the license, and it was recommended that you fly at least a couple of hours every week in order to not lose your touch. That wasn't possible for me; sometimes a month went by before I could work in a session. Consequently it took me over a year and about 90 hours before I passed my flight test. An older man administered my final test. After about 45 minutes he told me to land the plane, I had passed the test. But I had a laugh when we came into the office and he told the people there that he was going to go straight to the bar.

ACCORDING TO ME

I loved flying and decided to fly to Sacramento in the little Cessna 150 to visit my parents. That was the last time I rented that plane for a long distance flight. It was slow, flying only 100 miles per hour, and I had to land and refuel on the way. After bouncing all over the sky for a few hours, in seats that were only four inches off the floor, I was pretty uncomfortable.

After that trip I decided to check out a Cessna 172, which had four seats and was much more comfortable and roomier. I took LaVonne and Orla Jens with me several times, flying locally. One time I decided to take Orla Jens to the Salton Sea near the Mexican border for a fly-in fishing trip. We landed on a gravel strip and fished for Corvina, but we didn't have any luck. We got back in the airplane and flew around the lake. I decided to let Orla Jens take the controls and let him fly the airplane. He was so short that he couldn't see over the cowling, so I showed him how to fly with the instruments, which he did quite well and was probably in control for about a half hour.

Another time I decided to take LaVonne and her friend Sheri along with me to Sacramento to spend the weekend with the family. This time I checked out a bigger and faster airplane, a 182 Cessna. Nearing the city of Chowchilla, in central California, I noticed that we were getting low on fuel. I spotted a small airstrip and decided to land and refuel. It was crop duster's airport and I looked around awhile before I found a man in one of the hangars and told him that I needed gas. He was happy to oblige. Filling up, I realized that I had had plenty of fuel. I had simply gotten a little nervous looking at the needles. But it was getting a little late in the day and would be dark by the time we arrived in Sacramento. I wasn't certified to fly in the dark. I told the man my problem and he recommended a motel down the road a ways and offered me his truck for transportation. "Just bring it back in the morning," he said, "when you're ready to take off."

The girls found the whole adventure terribly exciting. An emergency landing! What fun! And in Chowchilla of all places! The motel had a swimming pool and we all donned our swimming suits and played in the water for a long time. After a while I went back to our room, but the girls discovered that if they stood on the chairs they could look over the wall at the traffic going by. They began to wave and holler at people in their cars. It was quite embarrassing and I had a hard time to get my young charges to settle down. The next morning we brought the truck back, parked in the designated area and took off for Sacramento, where we all had a wonderful time. On Sunday afternoon we were even invited to a Danish lodge picnic where there was lots of food and drinks. There was also a swimming pool but Sheri, being Mormon, couldn't go swimming on a Sunday. Monday morning we took off, winging our way back to Southern California and made it home without any mishaps. These are cherished memories.

THE NORTH DAKOTA ADVENTURE

I had been flying for a while and was getting bored of flying just to keep up my hours. I was itching to use my new skills for something more meaningful. My best friend, Ken Norheim, had two brothers living in North Dakota. One in Jamestown and one on the old family farm about 20 miles north of Jamestown in a little area called Kensal. For years Ken had been fighting an insidious disease, Granuloma, which was eating him up from the inside. Not one to just lay down and die, Ken wanted to live life to the fullest and to the best of his ability. I suggested that we fly up to North Dakota and visit his brothers. He had a high school reunion that he really wanted to attend and felt that he was strong enough to make the trip. So, getting permission from our wives, we made our plans.

I checked out a Cessna 182, a very comfortable four-seater airplane that would fly about 160 miles per hour. On June 30, 1975 we took off from El Monte airport and set our route towards Las Vegas. From there we changed course to Salt Lake City.

ACCORDING TO ME

The Granuloma had attacked his throat and he could no longer orally ingest food or drink. Instead he had a feeding tube going into his stomach. It was quite a contraption consisting of two tubes inserted directly in to his stomach, a little above his navel. The larger tube, the size of a quarter inch hose, was used to pour liquids and medications. Attached to it was a smaller tube that had a balloon on the end of it. The balloon was inflated inside the stomach in order to hold the tubes in place. Ken had had some trouble with stomach acids leaking out and burning the skin around the hole. Ingeniously he found that the cap from a baby bottle would fit perfectly over the tubes and clamp tightly to the skin giving some protection. He put a little cork in the end of the feeding tube, so that the stomach contents wouldn't leak out. I admired Ken immensely. I have never seen anybody suffer so much and still not give up on life. As we were flying Ken would pull his tube out of his shirt and tell me to hold the plane steady while he poured medicine through the funnel he had attached to the tube to keep from spilling.

All went well, we landed in Salt Lake in the afternoon and decided to stay overnight there because Ken was weary. We rented a car and drove to a hotel. After checking in I called my friends, Bill and Debbie Ritchie, who lived in the area and asked if we could come and visit them. They invited us to their house for dinner. On the way to their house we stopped at a liquor store and bought a bottle of wine for the table. Sitting at the table, poor Ken could only watch us eat. He had some kind of formula that he poured into his tube, a poor substitute for a glorious meal. He decided that, since we all had a glass of wine, he wanted to try it too. We went out to the kitchen where he got out his trusty tube and funnel and poured in a glass of wine. He smiled and said, "That was pretty good."

After breakfast the next morning we set of on the second leg of our trip. We crossed the Wasatch mountain range, east of Salt Lake City, and then flew out over the high plains of Wyoming. We were flying at 9,500 feet elevation but we were

134

still only 1,500 feet above the ground. The first 150 miles we flew over terrain that was so mountainous and rough, I was chillingly aware that, if there was an emergency, we would not be able to set down and we would be waking up in Glory. But we made it as smooth as silk all the way to Rapid City, where we landed for fuel. There was a moderate crosswind at the airport but I was up to the challenge. I came in fast with one wing high and set down on the right main gear and then the left and we were safely on the ground.

Flying up over the Dakotas we observed part of the breadbasket of America with its great grain fields laid out like an enormous checkerboard. Jamestown came into view just as we had planned, which meant that we had stayed on course. Ken's brother, Jim, worked at the airport, so he met us and took us to his home where his wife and daughter were waiting. We spent the night there and the next day drove out to the farm in Kensal where his other brother, Leonard, lived.

It was a village with only two blocks of street. One block was paved the other was gravel. The police chief of the little hamlet was a big woman, who ran the town like a top sergeant. I was told that it was absolutely illegal to make a u-turn in the middle of one of those blocks. She would issue a citation and you would have to appear in front of her father, the judge, who would levy the appropriate fine.

Leonard was in the process in preparing the fields for seeding and let me do some disking with a very large tractor. The enclosed cab had all the comforts of home with air-conditioning, a radio and a cassette player. It had rained a lot that year and there were several wet spots that I was told to avoid so that I would not get bogged down. Since there was so much water standing around everywhere, it was an ideal breeding place for mosquitoes. I have never seen so many bugs in my life as I did in North Dakota. I was also amazed at how hot it was, over 100 degrees. It was hard to believe that in only a few months it would be 40 below!

135

ACCORDING TO ME

The reunion was held at the school on the fourth of July. Since the graduating classes had been rather small, all students who had ever attended were invited. The oldest person who came was an 81-year-old lady. There was dinner and dancing and Ken, enjoying himself immensely, led his old girlfriends around the dance floor.

Norwegians, Danes and Poles had settled the area around Jamestown, North Dakota. Pictures of graduates dating back several decades hung in the school hallway. I amused myself by reading the names of former students that, except for the Polish decendents, bore the same names as the kids I had gone to school with in Denmark.

We were scheduled to return to California the morning after the reunion, although Ken had overexerted himself at the party and didn't feel very well. Nonetheless, we still had to go home. We climbed into the airplane. I did the preflight and we took off down the runway. As we were climbing out over the fields, the engine backfired so severely that it almost stopped the propeller. Ken wanted to fly out over the old farm and take some pictures. I decided we would give it a try. If the engine stopped all together I could simply set down on a road. Well, it backfired all the way out there and back, till I landed again at the airport. It was a Sunday morning and there were no mechanics to be had. We did find a couple of crop duster pilots in the hangar who, while not really mechanics, tried to help us. They decided that there was a problem with the mixture control cable and installed another one. We thought it would solve the problem. But as I headed for the runway the mixture control started coming out of the control panel. I taxied back to the hangar and showed the guys my problem. They fixed it with a clothes pin and a rubber band. That was too much of a barnstormer tactic for me. I called the rental place in El Monte and told them what was going on. He suggested kinking the casing around the cable, which I did, and it held. Problem solved, we were finally on our way.

136

We were flying at a fairly low altitude towards Rapid City. Approaching the Black Hills of South Dakota we had to climb up to an altitude of 9,500 feet. At 7,000 feet the engine backfired again and I told Ken that we were going to have to put down in Rapid City and get a mechanic out to fix the airplane. We landed and taxied to the parking place. Pulling on the mixture control to kill the engine, I pulled the cable all the way out of the control panel. (Normally you only pull it out about 3 inches.) The engine didn't die, however, and I had to turn off the fuel valve. It took over a minute for the engine to finally stop.

Since it was Sunday afternoon there were no mechanics available and no one would be coming in until 9:30 the next morning. It was late and really messed up our schedule. We took a taxi into town and checked into a YMCA hostel. Ken was having an awful time with his feeding tube and I felt that I should help him, but there was nothing I could do. I had to fly all the way to California the next day, so I went to sleep to get rested up for a tough day.

FBI agents occupied the fourth floor of the hostel. We found out the next morning that the Indians were on the warpath and were told to fly way around the Black Hills because there could be some shooting at us. Man, nothing like being in the Wild West! Wisely, we heeded the recommendation.

The mechanic showed up the next morning and reattached the troubling cable that our well-meaning friends at the hangar had messed up. We were finally on our way, but we had a long way to go. There were no more mishaps with the airplane as we winged our way back. We landed at the airport in Rock Springs for refueling. With an elevation over 7,000 feet, the air is hot and thin so there is less lift and it takes longer to build up speed for takeoff. The runway was long ending at a steep cliff. It seemed to me that I used the entire runway and just kind of dropping off the end of it.

ACCORDING TO ME

We continued on to our next refueling stop, which was at a small airport near Las Vegas. It had a short runway built on a moderately severe slope with buildings at the high end. As I was refueling I conferred with the attendant about which direction I should take off. The wind was coming down the runway blowing out over the desert, which was not ideal, but I didn't like to have to climb over the buildings. I decided to go with wind, downhill, so that I would be able to use more of the runway. When I got to the end I yanked the airplane off the ground. I was still losing altitude but the ground was falling away faster. It took a while for us to gain altitude so that I could get my radio bearings. Ken told me to just follow the highway and it would take us straight to Los Angeles. But as I was flying along the road, I noticed we were also following the Colorado River. As far as I knew, it didn't go to L.A. When we finally reached an altitude where I could begin reading the radio beam I changed course for home. By that time we had gone so far south we ended up flying through a restricted zone. Apparently we passed undetected since I never heard anything afterwards. We made it back to El Monte airport, landing for the last time just before dark. It had been a marvelous trip, even though the last day had been demanding. It was an event Ken would talk about for the rest of his life. He lived another 10 years with that debilitating, ghastly disease.

ROTARY INTERNATIONAL

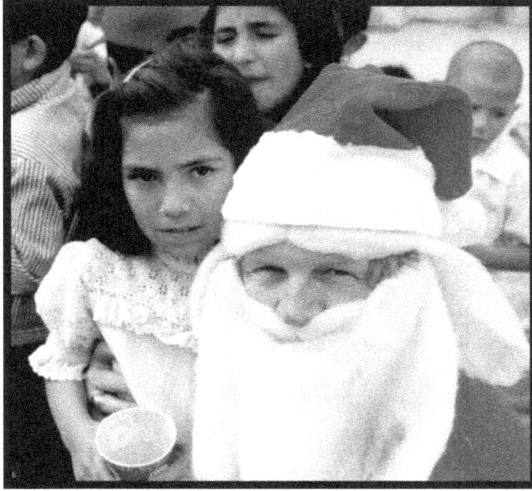

I had heard about the Rotary Club and the Lions Club and other service organizations that we had in our area and I was interested in joining one. They met weekly for lunch and usually had interesting and inspiring speakers. Dick Day, a life insurance salesman who periodically contacted me to impress upon me the importance of having life insurance, belonged to the Arcadia Rotary Club and was, at that time, president of the club. The Rotary Club is an elite international service organization with 1.2 million members in 32,000 clubs. I asked him questions about what was involved in being a member and he told me that the most important rule, as a member of the Rotary Club, was mandatory weekly attendance. If a member missed four meetings in a row, he could be expelled from the club. I had no problem with that and he agreed to sponsor me. After a long period of time, during which I was thoroughly investigated and vetted for eligibility, I was, in 1973, invited to join the Arcadia Rotary Club. I was now rubbing shoulders with many of the movers and shakers in the city and it felt good. I don't know how much it helped me in my business, but it certainly didn't hurt.

I dutifully attended the meetings every week and, if I missed, I tried to make up for it by attending a meeting at one of the neighboring clubs. But that was all I did for the first four years. I was what they called a knife and forker, who only came to eat lunch but never got involved in any of the many projects that Rotary had locally and internationally. I began to feel guilty and told Dick, my sponsor, that I felt that I should get more involved. The next thing I knew, I was invited to sit on the board. All of a sudden I was one of the "Big Shots." You might say I had arrived! It was fun to be on the board with the other men discussing what kinds of projects we could start.

Rotary has four project categories:

Club service – Includes projects which help further the club, like building membership. Rotary has stringent criteria for members. A proposed member has to be in business, or representing a business, and there can only be one of each category. For instance, there cannot be more than one homebuilder, one dentist and so on.

International service - There is no limit to the projects a club can get involved in internationally. There is so much to do in the world, everything from bringing food and clothing across the border to Mexico to building hospitals in India.

Vocational service - Includes helping kids learn to read better in school or supporting a local Boy Scout troupe, etc.

Community service – Includes projects that improve the city or community, like planting trees in a park, cleaning up a house for an indigent person or constructing a building for after-school clubs.

Since I was a builder, it was decided that I should help finish up a small building that we had begun to build at one of the schools. The 1,500 square foot building, with a hall, kitchenette and toilets, was a meeting place for scout troupes and other groups, and we were proud to provide it for the community.

Rotary is arranged in districts with about 50 – 60 clubs, headed by a governor. Our district governor was present at one of our board meetings. Being that I was rather new, I didn't contribute much to the meeting.

The Danish Exchange

Rotary International has a program called Group Study Exchange (GSE) where five promising young people, between 25 and 35 years of age, visit a foreign country to observe the culture, business, legal systems, etc. A Governor's Representative, a Rotarian who preferably speaks the language of the receiving country, leads each group. Several GSE teams, primarily from Asian countries, had come to visit our area. When the discussion turned to international service I spoke up, mentioning that I had not seen any GSE teams coming from Europe. To my great surprise the Governor told us that our district had a GSE team going to Denmark and that they needed a leader for the group. When I told him that I was born in Denmark and still spoke the language he offered me the job on the spot! It was difficult for me to get away for the five week, all-expenses-paid tour, but it was too good of an opportunity to pass up. Besides, my motto has always been, "Don't let business get in the way of pleasure."

We left for Denmark in early April 1978. The five men in the group and I had spent months going through orientation and getting acquainted with each other. We all had identical three-piece suits, a kind of uniform, with an extra pair of pants of a different color and reversible vests to match whichever pant we were wearing.

Delayed several hours, we arrived in Copenhagen around midnight, missing our connection and nobody was there to meet us. The airline put us up in a hotel and, after checking into our rooms, we caught a couple of taxis into Copenhagen. We had jetlag and didn't feel like sleeping so we spent a couple

of hours in the "Ratskeller," a nightclub, drinking beer and singing old songs.

I don't remember how our hosts contacted us the next morning, but someone came and took us to the airport where we caught a flight to Odense, on the Island of Fyn. The director of a small agricultural college met us and took us to his school where we were to stay for three days. One of the professors told us about the political structure in Denmark and we spent half a day with a judge who explained Danish jurisprudence. They treated us like visiting potentates, serving us delicious meals with traditional Danish foods and meeting our every need.

From Odence we traveled to Fredericia, an industrial city on the east coast of Jylland. Someone mentioned that Queen Margrete was going to be there to dedicate a new conference hall. I asked if we could possibly be there to observe the festivities, and it was arranged. When the Queen entered the building, we were so close to her we could have touched her. In fact, one of my guys tried to pin a Pasadena Tournament of Roses emblem on her, but was promptly pushed away by security.

Fredericia was a fun city. I've not experienced anything quite like it before or since. Every morning we met at the Danish Bank and then were taken out to visit the various factories in town. Four factory visits were planned every day. Arriving at the first one around 9:30 am, we were led into the conference room where we were told about the operations for that particular production. Several kinds of libations, soda, beer and liquor, and glasses stood in the middle of the table and we were invited to help ourselves. After a short lecture, we were taken on a tour of the manufacturing plant, ending up, after about an hour, at the conference room for a final drink before we said goodbye to our host. Then we were off to the next location, where the program repeated itself all over again.

At lunchtime, between factory visits, we were treated to some of the most delectable meals. The Danes spent a bundle on us, trying to outdo each other by offering us the finest gastronomic experiences achievable. We were served the finest food the Danish kitchen had to offer, plus all the drinks we desired. After lunch, feeling pretty good and well rounded, we visited two more factories. At the end of the afternoon we were poured into the cars and taken back to our host families, where we were served fine dinners every night.

Our third week was spent in a rural community where we observed farming, dairy production and even a fish hatchery. The food was always wonderful, but there wasn't much drinking. For the first time on the trip I was expected to translate for my group. My Danish is unsophisticated, at best, and I have forgotten more than I care to admit. Agriculture had advanced in many ways since I had lived in Denmark and I was unfamiliar with some of the terminology, but I managed to muddle through.

We spent the fourth week near the German border where, once again, our visits to industries were interspersed with parties, food and drink. It was interesting to experience the culture in this part of Denmark. In 1864 it fell under German rule and was not returned to Denmark until 1920, after WWI. They were involved in four wars with Germany in 80 years. Denmark was not involved in WWI, but this area, then a part of Germany, lost 6,000 people. Many people still remembered those times and there was a lot of hostility towards Germany, though not so much hostility that they wouldn't cross the border. Many of our excursions that week were to churches and castles across the border. In fact, we practically became rumrunners! Liquor was cheaper across the border, but Danes had to spend three days in Germany in order to bring two bottles back over the border. As American tourists, we could cross the border as many times as we wanted. Our hosts didn't miss that opportunity and we went across that border twice every day for a week and brought 12 bottles back each time.

Our final week, spent in the city of Nyborg on the island of Fyn, was relatively relaxing. The most interesting place we visited was the Lindø ship works, where they build jumbo oil tankers. We spent the last day in Copenhagen touring Tivoli before flying home to our families.

ROTARY AMIGOS

The new president of the club contacted me and said that, since I had been to Denmark with the GSE team, I was now an expert in International Service and that would be my function on the board. He told me to get a team together and suggested a new member, Dick Martinez, who was Hispanic and probably spoke Spanish. He thought that we could do some kind of a project in Mexico.

I called Dick and asked him if he would like to help me with an international project, to which he eagerly agreed. We set up a lunch meeting together with two other members, Jim Hanrahan and Lyle Cunningham. We agreed unanimously that Tijuana, Mexico would be a great place to investigate for possible projects. Dick contacted some of the members of the

144

largest Rotary club in Tijuana, who were very excited for us to come down and promised to show us around.

A couple of weeks later May-Britt and I, Dick and Katie Martinez, and Jim and Borinka Hanrahan drove the 150 miles to Tijuana where we met with our counterparts from the Tijuana club, Armando Meza and Alexandro Villalvaso, with whom we would become great friends. After lunch they took us out and showed us several orphanages. We decided that our Rotary club would try to help one of them, Casa Esperansa, home to about 80 children, varying in age from infants to teenagers.

Too late for us to return home, the Mexican Rotarians had arranged for us to stay at the Azteca Hotel. However, when we came to the hotel later in the afternoon, our rooms had been given to somebody else. Alex and Armando talked to the personnel and they decided to give us suites on the sixth floor, overlooking the city. Very nice, we thought, until we were ready to crawl in bed and a terrible racket thundered through the ceiling. Two great dance halls were on the floor above us and, since it was Saturday night, the Mexicans were celebrating by dancing the Cucaracha until the wee hours of the morning. Borinka, going out of her mind, demanded that Jim to do something. He called the front desk and asked if anything could be done about the noise, but the guy on the other end told Jim that he didn't understand English. Resourceful, Jim called back and, in his high school Spanish, asked when the dancing was going to stop. The man on the other end answered in English that it would be soon. Somehow we all survived the ordeal.

At the next Rotary lunch meeting we told the members that we had a very wonderful international project and all were invited to come paint and clean an orphanage for needy little kids. A month later, twenty-four of us went down with paint and cleaning supplies and worked all day Saturday. Some painted the kitchen and others did repair work on some deferred maintenance. That night we stayed in a different hotel and slept well.

ACCORDING TO ME

One of the other orphanages we had visited, Lazaro Cardenas, in a town south of Tijuana, had 120 children and was really run down. Mr. and Mrs. Krause, the directors, told us that they really needed a new kitchen, dining room and some new toilets. I told him, however, that our club only had the resources for smaller projects, like what we had done at the other orphanage.

God, however, has unfathomable resources. One night the club president called and told me that the Santa Anita Race Track had 28,000 t-shirts to donate if we wanted them. I didn't know what I was going to do that many t-shirts, but I said I would take them anyway. Twenty-eight thousand t-shirts is a big truckload and a lot to store. Luckily my flooring contractor had a big warehouse and was willing to house them for a while, and, eventually, he found a buyer who paid $9,500. I announced to the club that we now had the funds to do a real project in Mexico. Dick Martinez and I became co-organizers for the Mexican project that we named, Rotary Amigos, a project that would exceed everyone's expectations.

Nick Pokerjac, a retired real estate developer and a fellow Rotarian, called me one day and told me that he had a big portable restroom with three toilets. He said that he wanted to take it down to the orphanage to improve living conditions for the kids. There was no sewage system to hook this thing up to so I talked to another member in the club, whose business was manufacturing septic tanks. He promised to donate one and would even bring it down there on his big crane truck.

One weekend we had an entire entourage heading for Mexico with all this equipment. We hired a local man with a backhoe to excavate the hole for the tank and dig two ditches out to the slope of the hill where we laid perforated pipes in a bed of gravel. The ground was hard clay,

so there was no percolation and the water ran out to the edge of the hill. Years later, when we came to visit, the hillside was burnt brown by the sun, except for two green stripes where the pipes emptied out. Everything went according to plan until we hooked the toilets up to the water supply. There was so little water that it took forever to fill the tanks between flushes. Nick Pokerjac had an idea. He had an old 7,500-gallon water tank that he could bring down. The first weekend in December a group of us went down to Tijuana and helped Nick install the water tank. It took several days to fill the tank, but then there would be plenty of water for everything.

While we were there we organized a Christmas Party for the kids. We had brought enough hotdogs and buns with all the fixings for a wiener fry. I dressed up like Santa Claus and Dick Martinez took pictures with a Polaroid camera. Every child received a picture of him/herself sitting on Santa's knee. That is how traditions are born. Since then, the Arcadia Rotary club has held Christmas parties for children in Mexico every year on the first weekend of December. At first we held them at the orphanages, but later the Tijuana Rotarians organized the Christmas parties out in the communities, turning them

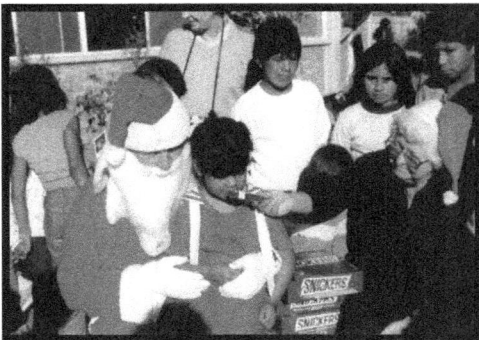

into much bigger events with 1,000 children in attendance. By the time each child had had a turn on Santa's knee I was almost blinded by the camera flashes. When I left California, Dick Martinez continued the project and has been stalwart in continuing the tradition.

147

According To Me

We still had $9,500 earmarked for international service. We asked the Tijuana Rotarians if they were interested in a joint project building a kitchen and dining room at the Krause's orphanage. They accepted the challenge with great eagerness and their architect drew up plans for a nice building that included a 2,200 square feet dining room, a large kitchen and toilets for boys and girls. It became a wonderful project with us supplying most of the funds and the Mexicans providing the labor and some of the materials. When the building was almost completed, we organized groups of Arcadia Rotarians to go down on weekends to do the painting. Several weekends in a row we drove to Mexico with paint supplies on Friday night, worked all day Saturday, had an enjoyable evening on the town, and went home on Sunday morning.

Normally we contacted our friends in Tijuana and arrange for them to meet us at a restaurant on the American side of the border. That way they could help us enter Mexico without any trouble. One weekend, I had two club members with me going down to work on the building, my truck packed with paint, drop cloths and ladders. Halfway down, I realized that I had not made arrangements for the Mexicans to meet us and I worried about how we were going to get across the border. I imagined that we would be turned around at the border and sent home again. Not mentioning anything to my travel partners about my concerns, I prayed earnestly for the Lord to smooth our border crossing. Amazingly, when we reached the border, the Mexican border guard just waved me through, as though he was a traffic cop, and we continued without incident to our destination.

One day at a lunch meeting, I sat next to one of the doctors in the club, Dr. McBane, and asked him what he thought of the possibility of organizing a medical clinic at the Krause's orphanage. He thought that was a wonderful idea and said that he would contact his son, who spoke Spanish, to come along with him. A few weeks later, on a Friday evening, we went down to Tijuana with two doctors, two dentists, seven nurses and several club members. We were invited to dinner at the home of one of the Mexican Rotarians. We didn't arrive before 10pm, which was ok since Mexicans eat late dinners – maybe not that late, though. We didn't get to bed until the wee hours and had to get up early the next morning. Saturday, fevered activity reigned in the new dining room. Hanging bed sheets, we partitioned off examination rooms where all 120 children were given a complete physical and vaccinated for DPT and Polio. The two dentists were pulling bad teeth all day long. Dr. Art Major, with whom I later became good friends, said that if we did this again he would try to get USC's mobile dental unit, which would have the necessary equipment. We did set up another medical clinic in Tijuana, but weren't able to get the mobile unit.

Our family dentist, who was also a member of our church, had moved to a new office and bought all new equipment. One day he called the pastor and asked if he could donate his old equipment to the church. The pastor told him to give it to me. I called Art and asked him if he thought we could use the equipment to create a mobile dental unit. Excited, he said it was absolutely possible. Together we dismantled the old office and stored the equipment in one of the church's storage rooms. I found an old travel trailer for $500. It took awhile to get everything assembled but when we were ready it had two chairs and all the equipment necessary. Art and I decided to take it down to Tijuana on Friday night and try it out the next day. I called him and told him that I had a problem. We'd had the trailer for a couple of years but never registered the license. I was worried that the Highway Patrol would pull us over on the way down there. Art said not to worry; he could take the license plate off of his horse trailer and exchange it until we crossed the border. In Mexico they weren't concerned about expired American license plates.

ACCORDING TO ME

The Mobile Dentil Unit was a great success. Art and I went down to Mexico every couple of months, providing dental care for the poverty-stricken people in the villages. As long we could get water and electricity we were in business. I, of course did not do dentistry, but I knew how to keep the equipment going so that Art could spend all his time doing his work.

Dick Martinez and I had made friends with the Rotarians in Ensenada. They heard about what Art and I were doing and the kept asking us to come to Ensenada and relive some misery there. The next time we were going to Mexico I called my friend Carlos Carall and told him we were going to bring the unit to Ensanada on the weekend and asked him to please set up a place for us to work. When I called to confirm, he told me that he had arranged for us to work on the inmates at the Ensenada jail. The jail, which is now a museum, was a 100-year-old adobe building in the center of town right in the middle of the shopping area. Little more than a dungeon, (we were later given a grand tour) I would never want to experience Mexican hospitality in that place! When Art and I arrived late one Friday night, we parked the trailer right in front of the door to the jail and went to bed in a nearby hotel. We figured that parking in front of the jail would be the safest place in town.

Early the next morning we were back and told the guards that as soon as we had the unit hooked up to power and water, we would be ready to accept patients. I usually hooked the long heavy cable to the best possible power source, which was right behind the meter. When I removed the glass meter the entire jail went dark, but the power came back on once I had hooked up the cable. When all was ready, two guards with carbines stationed themselves on the sidewalk at either end of the trailer and three others, with 45s in their belts, paced back and forth on the street. A Mexican dentist showed up that morning, joining Art in the trailer, and then the guards brought out the prisoners, two at a time. Their teeth were in terrible shape, some had only rotten stumps in their mouths and must have been living in agony from the toothaches. Doing what they could, Art and the other dentist worried about dry sockets and other complications, but were told that a local dentist would come back and take over their care.

Art and I went to Mexico every two months for a couple of years, providing dental care any place we could get power and water, sometimes way out in the countryside. It was always a lot of fun and at night we would take in some of the Mexican nightlife. It ended, though, when Art moved out of the area and I wasn't able to recruit another dentist for the project. We gave the trailer to the Ensenada Rotarians to use however they deemed necessary.

Armando Meza called me one night and invited me down to Tijuana for a big Rotary Banquet the following Wednesday night. I told him it was too far to drive for just one evening in the middle of the week, but Armando wouldn't take no for an answer. "You must come," he said. Well, since he put it that way, I figured that I better go.

The banquet, held in the biggest hotel in Tijuana, was attended by most of the big shots in Tijuana. Finding my friends, I sat down with them at their table and watched the festivities. The Rotary International president that year was from Monterey, Mexico. He was introduced and came up on stage and began speaking. Everything was in Spanish, which I don't understand. I heard my name mentioned, but thought I was mistaken. One of my friends nudged me and told me to go up on the stage to the president. Handing me a plaque, the president praised me for the work I had been doing in Tijuana. I was so overcome I did not know what to say, so I just said thank you.

When the banquet was over it was late and, as I said goodbye to Armando and Alex, Alex insisted that I accompany him home for a nightcap. I didn't get out of there until 2:30 in the morning. I drove to Agua Caliente Boulevard, which is a divided highway, and I had to make a u-turn at the traffic light. Waiting for what seemed like forever for the green arrow, I finally lost my patience and blew the red light. There was no other traffic, but I had no sooner made the turn when I saw a Tijuana police car behind me, red lights flashing. "Oh Boy," I thought, "I'm in deep trouble. I'm being arrested in the middle of the night by Mexican cops. This is not going to end well."

Pulling over to the side of the road, I got out of my car and walked back to the officers. They were two young guys and one of them asked me if I spoke Spanish. I said, "no," and asked if he spoke English, which he didn't. We stood there looking at each other for a while. Not sure what to do, I figured that they would want to see my driver's license and pulled out my badge holder where I keep my license. Seeing the badge, the first officer asked me what it was. I told him that it was a Los Angeles Sheriff's badge. He told me that I was free to go. I got back in my car, wiped the sweat off my brow and went home.

I was elected president of the Arcadia Rotary Club for the year 1986 – 87, but since I moved to San Marcos that year, I sadly tendered my resignation from the organization. I had been a member for 13 wonderful years and had lots of fun and meaningful experiences, but there is a time for every season.

When I moved to San Marcos I joined the Chamber of Commerce and the San Marcos Rotary Club. I thought it would be the quickest way to get to know people in my new surroundings, which was important for someone in my business. I was soon on the board of the Rotary Club and three years later I became president of the club. It was a much smaller club and I wasn't able to get an international project off the ground, although a small team of us did go to Mexico to do some work on an orphanage 130 miles south of the border.

The Rotary club uses fines as sort of a fundraiser, but each club has different policies. In the Arcadia club we were always fined $10.00 for our birthdays and $20.00 for other things, like buying a new car, getting in the local paper, etc. In the San Marcos club the members pledged how much money they wanted to be fined for the year, which, during my tenure, was anywhere from $50.00 to $300.00. As president, it was my responsibility to make sure that I collected these pledges by coming up with semi-legitimate fines for each member. I was not supposed to fine them the whole amount at once, but was supposed to recognize them several times during the year. There was one member, a doctor, who always came in too late for me to fine him. He had pledged $300.00. I had fined him for a total of $125.00 over the year, but I needed to collect the rest. One day I saw him come in a little earlier than usual and, approaching him, asked him if it was ok to fine him for the balance of the pledge. He said that would be fine. I went back to the podium and made up some grandiose story about him and fined him $175.00. Once I fined someone $10.00. He claimed that he was paid up, but I told him that he had not pledged enough. I don't know if he actually paid the fine.

One day a group of my friends from the Arcadia Rotary showed up at one of the meetings I was presiding over. Dick Martinez came over, told me that they were taking over the meeting for the day, sat me on a chair in the middle of the room and proceeded to roast me to the amusement of all present. May-Britt and our son, Orla Jens, were there, forewarned by Dick I assume. Orla Jens had a video camera with him and filmed the whole ordeal. Good thing, as it turned out. I had been having trouble with my gavel disappearing from time to time, but I could never catch the culprit. Viewing the footage that Orla Jens had taken, I saw an arm reach over, grab the gavel and put it away. I recognized the arm and knew whom it belonged to and, at the next meeting, the gavel thief got what he had coming to him with a hefty fine.

A demotion dinner was always held in honor of the outgoing president. When my term was over, several people, including my loving wife, roasted me. She got up and revealed all kinds of personal things about me, the thought of which still embarrasses me to this day!

AROUND THE
WORLD IN *Almost* 80
YEARS!

F or as long as I can remember I have dreamt of traveling the world. When I was a small child my mother read the comic strips in a monthly magazine out loud to me. I remember a couple of young adventurers, Bob and Frank, who traveled all over the globe and had all kinds of astonishing experiences. When I got older I read about people referred to as globetrotters. I envied them and pictured myself in their shoes, but wondered if I would ever be able to do the things that they were doing.

Although I never prayed to be able to travel the world, the Lord knew the desire of my heart and has fulfilled that desire to a significantly higher degree than I could ever have anticipated. At this writing I have traveled through all 50 states and have visited 50 countries around the world. Mostly I've traveled as a tourist, but I have also been on nine missionary trips to third world countries.

USA

My first great journey was of course coming to America. As a child, I went on short school excursions in Denmark, never going far. One time I had an opportunity to go on a 200-mile trip to Copenhagen, but the ruling powers decided it was just too far and too expensive. I think we would have had to stay a couple of nights, and the expenditure couldn't be justified.

When I came to America I'd go anywhere at the drop of a hat. Before I had a car I traveled around northern California with our neighbor, Dick Dewey. He was a few years older than me, but any time he asked me to go somewhere, be it San Francisco, the mountains or Carmel, I was ready. We always traveled on weekends so it wouldn't interfere with work. Our employers would not have appreciated us not showing up for work as expected. Later, when I had my own business, I developed a motto: "Never let business interfere with pleasure."

The first real long-distance trip I took after coming back to America was in the summer of '55. Hans and Manny, friends of my parents, were planning a trip to Calgary, in Alberta, Canada, to visit Hans' brother. I mentioned that I would love to go on a trip like that, so they invited me along. It was an extraordinary trip that became quite unforgettable.

The drive to Calgary was relatively uneventful, passing through beautiful and ever changing scenery. Arriving in Calgary I asked Hans to take me to Didsbury where my

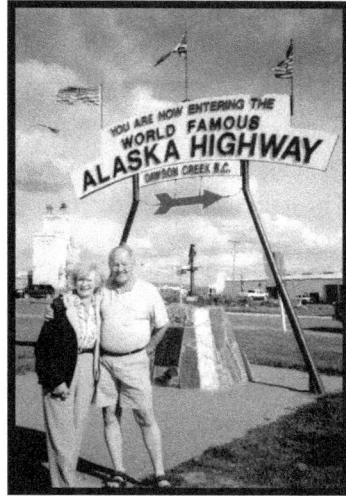

155

dad's old friends, Ole and Vagny, lived on a farm with their two young girls. I spent two nights getting acquainted with them and had an excellent time. They let me drive their huge farm equipment harvesting a grain field. I love operating large machinery, but my temporary job came to an abrupt end when a hot and humid day turned cold and it started to rain.

Hans came the next day and picked me up and we went back to Calgary. The following day we began our journey home. The trip was progressing nicely, south through the Canadian plains towards Montana. We crossed the border into Glacier National Park and came to a small town with a gas station, a coffee shop, a bar and a small motel. Stopping at the station we told the attendant to fill up the tank. In those days there were full service stations. They filled your tank, checked the oil and tires and clean the windshield. As we were walking into the coffee shop, I turned and asked the attendant to clean the bugs off the front window. I watched, a little astounded, as he squirted gas on the window to clean it. I told Hans about it, but he wasn't overly concerned. Perhaps he had done the same thing.

Finished with our refreshments, we went back to the car again. Hans asked the attendant to check the oil level. Finding it was low, he inserted the gas dispenser in to the oil spout and proceeded to pump in two quarts. Hans hollered, wondering what in the world he was doing. The attendant answered calmly that he had changed the pump to oil. Figuring that anything was possible in America, Hans accepted that explanation.

When he turned the ignition, however, there was a loud explosion. Fire and smoke billowed out of the engine compartment. Jumping out of the car, I grabbed my passport out of the glove compartment and my suitcase out of the backseat. People rushed out of the coffee shop and bar to see what was happening. Somebody pushed the car out near the road, away from the gas pumps. Puddles of gas, left there after the attendant's window washing, had caught fire. Somebody

asked Hans if he had gotten his belongings out of the car. Hans answered that they didn't have a suitcase, all of their clothes were lying loose in the trunk, but he had no desire to approach the car and retrieve them. The man asked Hans to give him the key and ran over to the car, opened the trunk and threw all the contents out for Hans to pick up. Just as he finished and moved away to a safe distance, the 18-gallon gas tank blew up and spread fire over a 100-foot diameter. Somebody called the fire department, but by the time they arrived the car was totally burned out. A tow truck was summoned but, on its arrival, they decided that the car was a total loss and not worth towing. The driver graciously offered to drive Hans and his family to the nearest town, West Glacier.

There was no room for me in the tow truck so I had to hitchhike, which was no problem. I stood by the burned out car looking forlorn and was picked up by the first vehicle that came by. Feeling sorry for me, the kind man and his son offered to drive all the way to West Glacier so I could connect with my friends. He was a very enthusiastic driver. Doing, I'm sure, 70 – 80 miles per hour on those mountain roads, he carried on a running conversation with me, pointing out the sights along the road. There was Devil's Elbow, where several motorists had met their maker and several cars lie crushed in the abyss. I'm sure we rounded that hairpin curve doing 60 mph, but we lived to tell about it. It was the kind of experience that brings sinners to their knees, and I was glad when he finally dropped me off in town. The next day we took the train home.

ACCORDING TO ME

ARIZONA

Although May-Britt and I both love to travel, we were so busy getting established those first few years of our marriage that we didn't take any trips. It was first in 1966 that we decided to take a week's vacation in Arizona. We left the children with our au pair, Grete, a Danish girl who took excellent care of them.

It was May and there was still snow on the rim of the Grand Canyon. One of the wonders of the world, this enormous hole in the ground has to be experienced firsthand. We took a ride on an airplane and the pilot flew way down below the rim of the canyon. It was very bumpy and I hit my head on the ceiling moving across to another seat. Flying below the rim is now illegal as it is so dangerous, but it was quite an experience. Driving down to Phoenix the temperature increased dramatically. Pitching our tent at a campground it was 102 degrees, in the shade. It was our first real vacation together and we'd had a wonderful time, but it was nice to be home with the kids again.

In 1968 we booked a two-week charter trip to Hawaii with a reasonably priced tour group. The Moulthrups, the couple whose house we had lived in when we first moved to Los Angeles, had a house not far from Waikiki Beach and had often spoken of how wonderful it was on the islands. We had wanted to visit ever since. The Hawaiian Islands are truly a paradise on earth where people live seemingly easy, lives, wearing grass skirts and eating the fruit off the land. The main fruit is pineapple and coconuts, but many other kinds of fruit are grown on the islands.

One day we visited the Polynesian Culture Center on the northern end of Oahu. It is an all day tour and truly worth seeing. The performers tell the story about how the islands came into being and how the Polynesian people sailed thousands of miles in flimsy outriggers crossing the Pacific Ocean before landing on these shores. In the evening we had a magnificent dinner and show, again reenacting the history of Hawaii.

ODESSA CRUISE

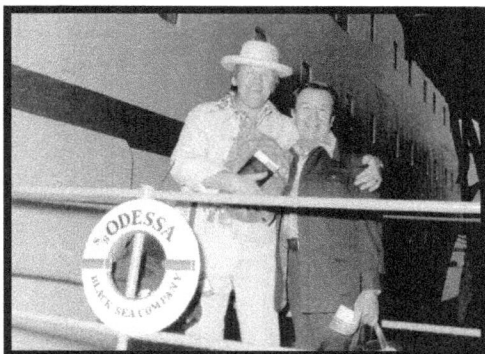

We had been in partnership with Fred Shubin for several years and decided that we would use some of our profits for traveling. In late January 1974 Fred and I, along with a dozen Russian-Americans from East Los Angeles area, boarded a Russian cruise ship, the Odessa, which sailed out of New Orleans into and around the Gulf of Mexico. May-Britt doesn't like cruises and opted to stay home.

During the 70's there was a thaw in the cold war that existed between America and Russia. The cruise line took advantage of this newfound familiarity and launched its beautiful, brand new ship in the Gulf. After we boarded and located our designated cabin, Fred and I began investigating our environment. I was surprised to see that the deck chairs were all made in Denmark. The inflatable life rafts, which were actually in barrels, were made in Esbjerg, the harbor city not far from where I use to live in Denmark. We missed the tour of the ship the following day, but in the evening at a party in one of the staterooms we met the captain who invited our group to tour the bridge the next day. It was fascinating. The officer showed us the instruments that controlled the ship. Everything was computer controlled, something that was new and intriguing for us. They simply fed the destination into the ship's computer and it drew up the route and steered the ship on autopilot. The screen showed the distance, estimated time of arrival and the amount of fuel needed. I mentioned to the captain that I had noticed all the accouterments on board were made in Denmark. He explained that the ship was built in Denmark originally for a cruise line in England. When it was finished, the English line reneged on the contract. Denmark then put the ship up for sale on the open World Market and the Russians picked it up.

We had a marvelous time onboard. The entire crew was Russian and few spoke English, but since many of the people in our group spoke Russian, we received special treatment. In the dining room we were served dishes nobody else got, real Russian cuisine, like borsht and caviar.

One day Fred and I were walking through a corridor, we came upon a young lady polishing the brass railing. Fred patted her on the back and said something to her in Russian. She stiffened up and responded to him, "You do not speak to ladies like that."

Fred was really astonished and asked what he had said that was so terrible. She told him that he had called her a streetwalker or a prostitute. Of course Fred began to apologize profusely and said that that was what they used to call young girls when he was a kid but, obviously, the language had changed.

The weather was terrible most of the week we were in the Gulf. We did get off in Belize for half a day and walked around town. We also took a tour bus out to see an old pyramid.

Upon returning to New Orleans, Fred and I were standing in customs line when he decided to go to the men's room. While he was gone, one of the people in our group came and asked if we could take a couple of liquor bottles through, since he knew that we didn't drink. I told him that I would be happy to and put one bottle in my bag and one in Fred's bag. When Fred returned I neglected to tell him. When the customs officer asked me if I had anything to declare I answered, "No, I just have one bottle of booze with me."

Fred was next. When the officer asked him if he had anything to declare, Fred said no. The officer asked him to open his bag and there was the bottle. The officer said, "What is this?" Fred looked like he was ready to go through the floor and answered, "I don't know." Incredulous, the customs officer asked, "If that was a bomb, would you have said you didn't know?"

I was about to split a gut laughing, but decided that I had better come to Fred's rescue. So I told the officer what I had done without Fred's knowledge. My explanation was accepted and Fred was gracious enough to see the humor in the situation.

We arrived just in time for the Mardi Gras. It has to be one of the craziest experiences that I have ever had. There were a million extra people in town for the celebration. Two parades were going simultaneously twice a day on Canal Street with people dressed up in the gaudiest outfits, riding the floats and throwing beads to all the spectators. I came home with a whole sack full of them. Sirens screamed continuously adding to the chaos, but it wasn't emergency vehicles. It was tow trucks! They were towing cars away left and right all day long. Fred and I took a city tour and I mentioned to the guide that I was impressed with all the cars being towed away. He told me that he had watched a tow truck hooking up a car to be towed and another car waiting so he could take his place. I don't know how New Orleans is normally, but during Mardi Gras it is a different world.

GREAT AMERICAN RACE

The Great American Race is a cross-country race involving over 100 vintage cars, at least 50 years old, the oldest dating from 1908. All of the cars were, of course, in working order and most of them made all the way to the finish line, but some had to be trucked home again. Unlike most races, the object was not to arrive first at the finish line but, rather, to arrive precisely on time. The route, which changed every year, was carefully mapped out to include the most challenging back roads of America, with speed and time calculated down to the last second.

I first became involved in the race in 1995 when Lindsey Spathie from Focus on the Family called me and invited me to

join their team. Focus was in the race, not as competitors, but for the publicity. They could not win any of the cash prizes. Lindsey explained that I could volunteer to join the team on a leg of the race lasting anywhere from one day to two weeks. It sounded like fun, so I told him that I would volunteer for three days.

That year the race ran from Tacoma, Washington to Montreal, Canada. Focus had borrowed a 1934 Ford Roadster with a rumble seat. I joined the team in Rapid City, South Dakota. We were four big men taking turns driving and I spent most of the time crammed into the rumble seat with one of the other guys. It was raining and the wind was blowing hard, but I wore a rain poncho and stayed quite warm. When Lindsey finally let me drive, I found out that it wasn't that easy.

Every morning the navigator is handed the map for the day along with a long list of instructions of exactly how fast to drive on every stretch of road. This is an exercise in precision and you have to follow the instructions "to a T." The cars are released from the starting gate at one-minute intervals, accelerating as quickly as possible to 50 mph. The navigator gives the driver instructions like, "hold this speed" or "drop down to 35 mph now." Coming to a stop sign, the navigator will count the seconds and then tell the driver to accelerate to a certain speed. We drove for hours at a time. Around 10 a.m. we'd stop for a much needed pit-stop. Then we'd break for a one hour lunch in a city enroute, where we were treated to a fantastic meal and lavished upon with gifts and mementos from the area. We had another quick pit-stop in the afternoon and usually arrived at the day's final destination anytime between 5:30 and 7:00 p.m.

Along the route we passed checkpoints where we were clocked and our time compared to a pre-determined schedule. The object was to pass the checkpoints at the exact second stipulated in the instructions we had been given. If we were successful we would be given an Ace sticker to put on the car and our achievements announced over a loudspeaker by a man we called, "Motor Mouth." Driving through the welcome arch at the end of the day, we were hailed by crowds of people who had come to join in the fun and show off their own vintage vehicles. Every evening was a festival!

We had a great time and I went on to volunteer for races for the next seven years. Each year was a different route. One year it started in Boston and finished in Los Angeles. Another year it started somewhere on the West Coast and finished in Florida. One year the route was shorter, going from Detroit, Michigan to Florida. Then I had the great honor to start the race driving two laps around the Michigan International Raceway and a couple of days later drove a lap around the Indianapolis Speedway.

My years in the Great Race brought me through many wonderful and, sometimes, less traveled parts of the United States. Eventually I became quite proficient at keeping the exact speed and was able to relax and enjoy myself. My partner and I usually achieved "Ace" every day. One day we tied for best time of the day, but the other car was older so they were given the ultimate prize. Darn it!

ACCORDING TO ME

ROAD TRIPS

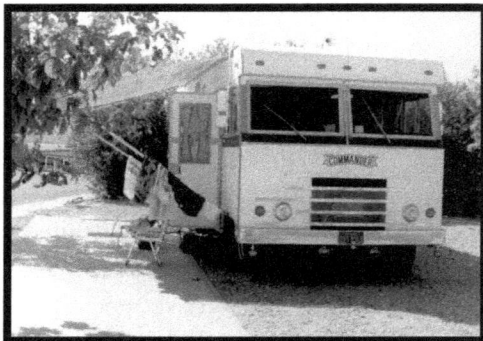

In 1980 we decided to try something new and daring, a road trip....with teenagers! I had a friend who had a motor home that I could borrow so we decided to take a trip to Arizona and the Grand Canyon. Not only did we have our two kids, now in their upper teens, we also invited our Brazilian exchange student, John, his friend from Wyoming, Jill, and our youth pastor's son, David, to come along. We were, perhaps, a little apprehensive about taking five teenagers, two of whom we barely knew, on a long trip in close quarters, but they were all great kids and we melted together like one big family. The motor home had six beds so John, who was the smallest, had to sleep on the floor, but he didn't complain.

Our first stop was at Lake Powell where we had booked a houseboat for a couple of days. We had rented a houseboat on the American River a couple of years previous to this and had enjoyed ourselves immensely and were looking forward to exploring the many coves and canyons of this desert lake. Loading up the houseboat with provisions we crossed the lake and anchored in a small cove for the night. The next morning, after breakfast, I turned the key in the ignition only to hear the awful grinding of the start motor burning up. We were stuck. There was a CB radio on board but we were unable to reach anybody. We waited, hoping that someone would venture into the cove and be able to help us or at least get help, but no one came. It wasn't a bad situation. We were in a beautiful place, the sun was shining, and the kids had fun with each other playing in the water and laying on deck. But as the afternoon wore on we began to feel a little desperate. Desperate people do desperate things. All five of the kids were strong swimmers so I told them to jump in and grab the line I had tied to the railing and tow us back to the marina. They were amazing! Like mermaids, or Neptune, they swam and pulled, good naturedly taking turns and laughing. With the optimism of youth they had no doubt that they would be able to pull us across the lake. I stood on deck shouting encouragement and, very slowly, we did eventually move out to the middle of the lake where we could hail a passing boat. The owner of the houseboat was contacted and came out to rescue us. Since our boat was out of commission and there were no other houseboats to rent, we rented a ski boat as a consolation and enjoyed a couple of days on the lake waterskiing and exploring.

After that we made a wide circle, driving through Zion National Park and stopping off at the Grand Canyon. We spent one night by Lake Havasu and the London Bridge before heading home. Despite our mishap, we were all satisfied with the adventure. Like a friend of mine used to say, "It wasn't a total loss, we had fun."

ACCORDING TO ME

THE ALASKA ESCAPADE

Although we had had a great time in the motor home, road trips were never May-Britt's favorite means of travel and twenty-four years passed before she was ever enticed into trying it again. In 2004 LaVonne and Stefan talked us into joining them on a trip to Kodiak, Alaska. They had made the trip once before with their five children and had so much fun they wanted to do it again. Only this time they wanted to make a detour from Colorado Springs and drive over southern California to spend a week at Disneyland. That was a little "over the top" for us and we said that we would meet them in Santa Rosa, California, a town north of San Francisco.

We bought a used 24' motor home with a double bed in the rear and another double bed over the cab. LaVonne and Stefan had a Dodge Van and a tent. At the appointed time we met them in Santa Rosa and continued on together along highway 101 through the great Redwoods and into Oregon where we turned east on Highway 5. Driving through Washington, we crossed the border into British Columbia, Canada and followed the road up through the majestic Rockies to Dawson Creek, where the famous Alaska Highway begins. From there it was pretty much straight on to Alaska.

166

Our grandkids took turns riding with us in the motor home. Sitting at the table playing games, or just talking, it was a unique opportunity to visit with, and get to know them. Nicolas, the middle child, had to go to the bathroom and walked to the back to the toilet. I called back to him that he would have to sit down like a girl so that there wouldn't be any misses on the floor or the walls. Daunted, he came back to the table but, unable to hold it much longer, he went back to the bathroom and sat on the toilet.

We passed through some beautiful country and stayed in some wonderful campgrounds where I would have liked to spend a couple of days, but we had a ferry to catch in Homer and couldn't spare the time. Our old motor home ran well the entire trip. When we arrived on Kodiak it was raining and it kept raining for eight of the nine days we were on the island. The sun came out on our last day revealing the stunning beauty of the snowcapped mountains, lush green vegetation and sparkling, blue ocean. Despite the weather, we had a wonderful time meeting LaVonne and Stefan's many friends and seeing many of the places they had often talked about. They treated us to a dinner cruise aboard the Harbor Master's boat, with Harbor Master, Marty, and his wife, Marion, acting as host and hostess and serving us the delicious meal they had prepared.

We left the motor home on Kodiak for LaVonne and Stefan to sell, and boarded a plane to Anchorage and then on to Colorado.

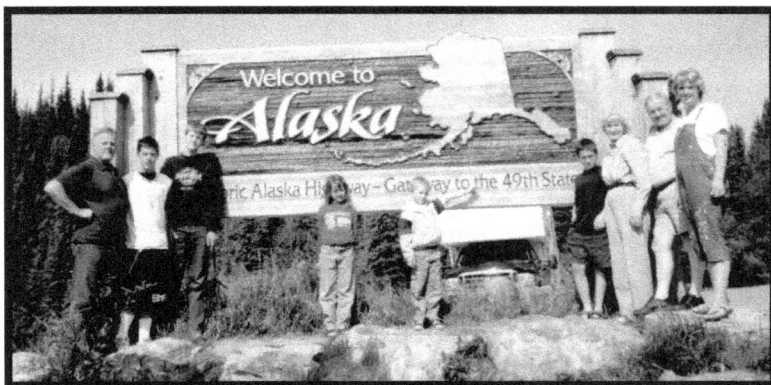

ACCORDING TO ME

OUR LAST MOTOR HOME

Looking through our pictures from our Alaska adventure we realized what a thoroughly enjoyable trip it had been and decided to take more road trips. We bought a travel trailer to pull behind our pickup truck but had only owned it a few months when we got a call from my brother-in-law Bill. Since my sister, Jytte, had died in 2003, he no longer wanted to use the motor home that they had so enjoyed together. We ended up trading. He took our trailer and we took his 1998, 38 foot diesel pusher, Class "A," which was the size of a bus and luxuriously outfitted. It was beautiful. We also got his tow vehicle, a 1998 Ford explorer.

We were invited to a wedding in September 2005. Our grand nephew from Sweden was marrying an American girl from North Carolina. It was the perfect opportunity to try our new rig and experience traveling in style. We invited May-Britt's sister, Solveig, to join us.

We planned to spend a month traveling to and from the wedding, stopping at places along the way. We had heard about Branson, Missouri, a town nestled in the beautiful Ozark Mountains that boasted over 100 wholesome shows suitable for families. We stayed there for five days, taking in several shows. After a few days Solveig suggested that we contact a realtor to take us around and show us some of the houses that were for sale in town. I was reluctant to waste anyone's time when weren't interested in buying, but the women were insistent. I called a real estate office and made an appointment with a young lady, who showed us a few houses. May-Britt fell in love with the last house she showed us, a 3300 square foot home on an acre lot with a full walk-out basement and wide front porch where we could sit in our rocking chairs and watch the people go to work. On a whim, we placed an offer on the house, it was accepted and we are now the proud owners of a house in the Ozarks.

Our one and only real road trip with our luxurious motor home was a great success. We reached North Carolina and witnessed a beautiful wedding and then headed home, stopping in Maryville, Tennessee to visit with our daughter-in-law's parents, Dan and Ginger Williams, who have become very dear friends.

With a second home in Branson we no longer had a real need for a motor home and eventually we sold it to friends who use it in their ministry. Three or four times a year we drive the 800 miles to Branson to spend five or six weeks in our country home. Orla Jens and Darla bought a vacation condo nearby and come down a once a year with their ski boat to play on the three large lakes in the area, teaching daughters, Lydia and Mallory, all manner of water sports. We join them occasionally, but most of the time we just sit in our rocking chairs, reading and drinking coffee on the front porch, a thoroughly enjoyable occupation.

According To Me

EUROPE

RETURNING TO SCANDINAVIA

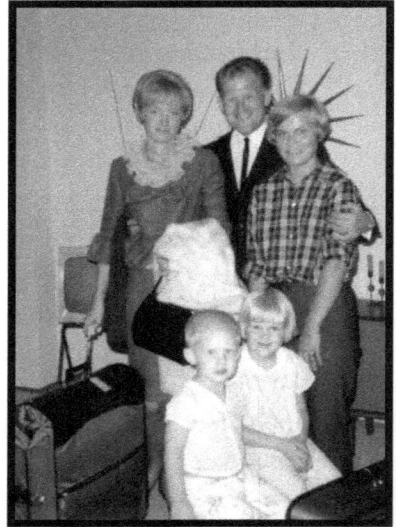

Throughout the years we had many au pair girls living with us. Most of them came from Scandinavia or Germany and all of them were good, trustworthy girls. Although it was hard to leave the children while we traveled, we felt they were too young to appreciate new countries and cultures. In 1967, when we decided to revisit our homelands, we were confident that our new au pair, Margitta, was quite capable of caring for them in our absence.

We had become acquainted with a missionary couple that was home on furlough from Germany. They were about to return to Germany, to Darmstadt, a town just south of Frankfurt, and invited us to come and visit them. We gladly accepted their invitation and stayed with them for a week. Being that they were not yet settled in their new position, they were able to show us around the area. We spent a day touring the medieval walled city of Rothenberg, and later visited Heidelberg with its magnificent castle.

Saying goodbye to our friends we took the train to Denmark, where I hadn't been for 13 years. My uncle Eske picked us up at the railroad station in Esbjerg and brought us to the old family farm that he had inherited. We spent about a week there visiting my relatives. One of my cousins took us to the little city of Varde. Feeling nostalgic I bought a red wiener with bread from a wagon on the square just like I used to do when I lived there. Looking

170

back I realize now that it must have been tedious for May-Britt, who had to sit for hours listening to me jabber with my relatives, not understanding anything we said in our rural dialect, but I didn't sufficiently consider her feelings at the time.

After a week in Denmark we went to Sweden. Arriving at a hotel in Gothenburg, May-Britt walked up to the front desk and asked in her broadest Småland's dialect if they had a room available. We were given a room on a lower level. As we got on

Visiting with my maternal Grandfather.

the elevator one of the hotel employees got on with us. Noticing the travel tags on our bags, she told us that the room we had been given was for locals only, because it was cheaper, but since we had already registered we were allowed to stay there.

May-Britt's sister, Linnea, and her ten-year old son, Roger, came the next morning to pick us up. We drove up along the coast to Oslo, Norway. From there we drove up through the beautiful, rugged Norwegian countryside towards Värmland where their sister, Birgitta, and her husband, Erik, live. I had never met May-Britt's relatives and enjoyed getting to know them. After a couple of days we were on the road again towards Småland, where May-Britt grew up.

We arrived in the evening and met Linnea's husband, Helge. He would become one of my dearest friends. Although the Scandinavian languages are similar there is enough of a difference to make conversation difficult. During our first visits to Sweden I had a little trouble communicating with Helge, but we were always at ease in each other's company. Later, when I had become somewhat proficient in Swedish, we could converse easier but I still made some rather humorous mistakes that Helge was quick to pounce on and relate to others.

171

ACCORDING TO ME

I enjoyed getting reacquainted with my father-in-law, Gunnar Samuelsson, who lived nearby. He had visited us in California for six months in 1966-67. I used to take him with me out on my painting jobs and put him to work. He didn't really like some of the things I had him do, like scraping paint off the windows, but it was better than sitting around at home. We had fun together, although communication wasn't what it could have been. He had a hearing problem and I didn't speak Swedish well at all. More than forty years later there is one episode that we all still chuckle over. I asked him about the time. He looked at his watch and said, "She is 10:30." I thought that was funny and asked him if he always called the watch a "She?" I repeated the question three times, but he didn't understand me. Finally, after the third try, he responded, "Ya, so!" Which is the Swedish equivalent to "Uh, huh," and the way he responded to any question or comment that he didn't understand.

I truly enjoyed myself in Sweden. May-Britt has a large family, all of them pleasant. Ywonn, her youngest sister, had come to California in 1963 and worked as an au pair for a couple of years. She returned again to California with her father in 1966. In '67 Ywonn was back in Sweden planning her wedding to Bengt. We were, of course, invited to the wedding, a lovely church ceremony followed by a scrumptious dinner. Afterwards we all drove out to the old farm where they were holding an old fashioned barn dance to celebrate the newlyweds. The hay barn had been dressed with birch branches creating a large dance floor. Bales of hay were piled up near the wall for the musicians to sit on. The musicians were to be paid in Vodka, but Gunnar, my father-in-

law, blundered by paying them ahead of time. By the time the guests showed up for the dance, the minstrels were dead drunk and couldn't perform. Linnea and a couple of other people were pressed in to service as second stringers. I must say that they did a remarkable job and everyone had a magnificent time.

But what really made a lasting impression on me was something that happened later in the evening. The barn dance was an open invitation affair and people from all over the community showed up. Some of the young men, friends, and possibly former suitors of the bride, arrived in rather high spirits, powered by several bottles of vodka, hollering for the bride and groom to come out. They even detonated four sticks of dynamite right outside the old barn. Every time a stick would go off, I thought that the barn would rise off its foundation. It was downright hazardous. The explosions were felt a kilometer away, even cracking a window in house across the yard, a fair distance from the barn. All the same I had a fantastic time and the knot that Bengt and Ywonn tied that day is still holding, more than forty years later.

Our fourth and final week we decided to take a camping trip, driving through Denmark, Germany, Austria and Switzerland. We took Helge and Linnea's car, with them and their daughter, Els-Marie, accompanying us. Our plans were far too ambitious for one week and we spent more time just getting from place to place than actually sightseeing. It was exasperating to reach our destination at a campground after dark, pitch the tent and eat by the headlights, getting up early the next morning to continue on our way. One evening after getting settled at a campground in southern Germany, we decided to have a wiener roast. It had been raining and the trees were dripping wet, but I found some dry dead sticks and made a little fire. As we were roasting our wieners, the manager came over, raving in German about the fire danger we were causing. When he was through, I told him that I didn't understand him. With that he became completely irate, stamped his foot in the middle of the fire and told me to get some water quick. Then he stomped off. That was probably the funniest thing that happened on that trip. We did make it over the Austrian border but, to Els-Marie's great disappointment, never made it to Switzerland.

Our trip had come to an end and we were soon winging our way back to California to our two wonderful kids. We hoped that they had not forgotten us.

LONDON

Traveling was now in our blood and we decided in June 1969 to return once again to Scandinavia, this time traveling via London. On the recommendation of a friend we stayed at the Home of Rest, a large house that catered to missionaries, charging a nominal fee of five dollars a day for a room, breakfast and dinner. When we checked out, the lady asked if we had taken any baths. We told her that we took baths every day. That would be five cents extra per person, per day.

London is so interesting with all its old historical locations. We learned to use the subway system and the busses, taking them everywhere we wanted to go. We visited Piccadilly Circus, where we, very possibly, just avoided being robbed. Crowds of people were sitting on the steps lining the fountain in the middle of the square. A man came up asked me to exchange some money for him. I almost took out my wallet but, thinking better of it, told him I didn't have any to give him and that he should go to the carnival area to get change. I had the feeling that he was just waiting to rip my wallet out of my hand and run away with all our money. You can't be too careful while traveling in big cities.

Around the World in *Almost* 80 Years

We fed the pigeons on Trafalgar Square, saw the changing of the guard at Buckingham Palace, toured Westminster Abbey and the London Tower. One day we took an all day excursion to the Windsor Castle, returning to London by boat on the River Thames. Renting a car we drove down to see Stonehenge, which was fascinating. Driving the car, though, was frustrating. Everything is backwards. The steering wheel is on the right side of the car, with the gearshift on the driver's left and the turn signal on the right. It wasn't too difficult out in the countryside, but once we got back in to the city it became downright nerve-wracking. It was dark and, since they drive on the wrong side of the road, I had trouble positioning the car often coming too close to the curb. To make matters worse we managed to lose our map and the streets seemed to change names for no apparent reason; we didn't know where we were going and I don't know how we ever found our way back to the house. When we took the car back to the rental agency the next day, May-Britt insisted upon taking the wheel, she had enough of my driving.

After four days in London we flew to Sweden to be with May-Britt's family again. I had a lot of fun with Helge, accompanying him on hunting trails. Summertime is between hunting seasons, but hunters get together to practice and compete with their hunting skills. About a dozen stations are set up on a circuitous trail throughout the forest. At each station a wire is strung up between the trees. A metal target in the form of an animal, like a bird or a rabbit, slides across that wire at a realistic speed. In the target is a 2x2 inch hole where a piece of paper can be inserted. The shooter fires his shotgun at the moving target trying to fill the paper with holes. Ten holes is a full count, anything less and you get one point per hole.

We were going to one of these hunting contests in the forest and I asked Helge if he was ready to go out and shoot at paper targets in the forest. Laughing, Helge went into the kitchen to tell the women what I had said. Apparently I had mispronounced one word, which gave my question an entirely

175

different meaning. I had inadvertently asked, "Hey Helge, are you ready to go out and shit on a piece paper in the forest?"

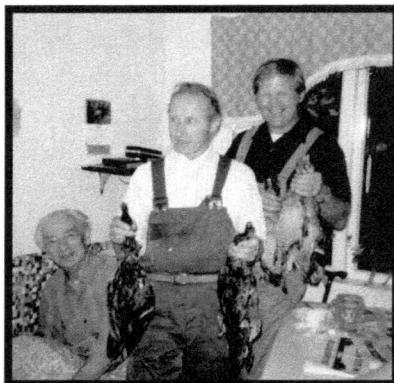

I was going to take the train to Denmark to spend a few days with family and May-Britt, Linnea and Helge were going to join me in a few days. We had a rather unpleasant incident on the way to the railroad station. I was driving Helge's car. Approaching a railroad crossing the bells started ringing, but I figured I could make it across before the booms came down and kept driving. May-Britt, always nervous when crossing a railroad, screamed out loud and I slammed on the brakes. The booms came down around us and we were stuck on the tracks with a train fast approaching. Luckily, there were several tracks and the train passed by, narrowly missing our car. May-Britt was so infuriated with me that she wouldn't talk to me and refused to kiss me goodbye. I really couldn't blame her. By the time she joined me in Denmark she had cooled off a bit and had bought me a present. A small sign for the car that read (translated from Swedish), "Who's driving, you or me?"

After being in Denmark a few days, we boarded a ship in Esbjerg and sailed back to England for our charter flight home again.

Swedish Christmas

Christmas 1971, we finally took the children with us to Scandinavia. We spent some time in Copenhagen before continuing on to Sweden by train. Walking around the city we happened to see Princess Margrete who was out shopping just like everyone else. Just a few weeks later her father, the King, died and she became Queen.

176

AROUND THE WORLD IN *Almost* 80 YEARS

We celebrated Christmas with May-Britt's family and the children had a great time. From then on they traveled with us to Scandinavia and other places. We visited Denmark together with my parents in 1973, continuing up to Sweden for a couple of weeks. After that we traveled to Sweden almost every other year. LaVonne married a young Swedish man, Stefan and moved to Sweden. Our visits became even more frequent when our first grandchild was born in 1989. LaVonne and Stefan live near Gothenburg with their five children. Bringing the entire crew, they have visited us in California, Colorado and now Missouri. When they don't come to us, we come to them.

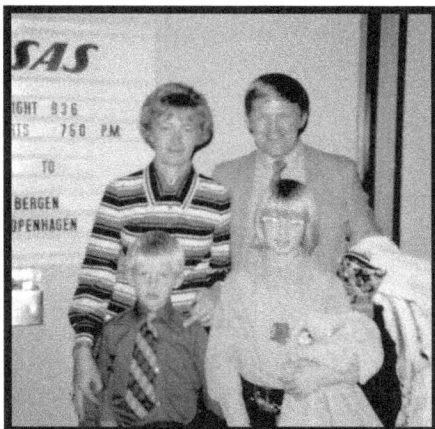

YUGOSLAVIA

In 1993, while visiting in Sweden, we decided to take a side trip and visit our friends, Hans and Vivian Sandstrom, who spent their summers in southern Austria. In their large, four-story home, located in a beautiful valley by a lake, they ministered to youth groups, pastors and pastor's families coming from behind the Iron Curtain. There they were allowed to rest and fellowship, returning home after one or two weeks refreshed body, soul and spirit. Primarily from former Yugoslavia and Romania, many had suffered through war and persecution. Feelings were sometimes sore and emotions ran high. Hans told me that it was exciting to bring people together who, upon arrival, were antagonistic towards each other and, after a week, see them kneeling together in prayer.

According To Me

War had been raging in the former Yugoslavia for several years with terrible devastation and loss of life. As usual the civilian population suffered the most, leaving many widows and orphans with no place to live. Hans and Vivian had acquired a beach resort hotel in Crikvencia, Croatia, a city on the Adriatic coast. Before the war it had been a very popular destination for western Europeans who came to enjoy the beaches and restaurants. At the hotel they were able to house up to 100 people, primarily widows and children. At the time of our visit the surrounding area was in ruins and refugees wandered about not knowing where their next meal would be coming from. Less than 100 miles away the fighting continued. Armed soldiers wandered the streets and there was a lot of hatred and resentment among the populace.

One evening, while we were there, a young man from the hotel had gone to a little shop to buy a coke or something. He met some soldiers there and said something that infuriated them. Finding out where he lived they threatened to blow up the hotel and everyone in it. Stevo, the manager, spent hours talking to the soldiers and managed to defuse the situation. We didn't find out about any of this until the danger had passed.

All in all it had been an exciting week. We enjoyed connecting with our friends and seeing their ministry. Driving back to Munich to catch the plane, we arrived sooner than planned. (I tend to have a lead foot.) Since we had so much time before our flight, we decided to go to Dachau and see the concentration camp that is now a museum. We had been to Dachau before and have also been to the holocaust museums in Jerusalem and Washington, D.C. I always come away with an indescribable feeling of sadness, realizing that this unspeakable evil occurred in my lifetime, not by savages, but by a civilized nation. By people who look just like me.

Between trips to Scandinavia I have had the opportunity to travel to many other countries, often without May-Britt. I am thankful to her for letting me go, she has never tried to hold me back.

THE GREEK ISLE CRUISE

My first solo trip, without May-Britt, I took in 1973 together with my brother-in-law, Leroy. We booked passage on a Greek Isle cruise together with a group of Russian-Americans from the Los Angeles area. We began our trip flying on a 747 airplane to Chicago. In those days the flights weren't full. At the back of the plane there was a large open area with a piano and a small dance floor. Since one of our ladies could play, we had a dancing party. It was rather fascinating to perform a waltz at 37,000 feet. We had a six-hour layover in Chicago, which we spent in the beautiful elite Olympic lounge. Onassis owned Olympic Airlines and his wife, Jackie, the former US First Lady, had reportedly decorated the lounge. The airline, however, left a lot to be desired. It wasn't really dirty, but it wasn't clean either. The 11-hour flight became very uncomfortable and we were all super tired because we just couldn't sleep in the seats.

We finally arrived in Athens, that ancient city with so much history, both pagan and Christian. After getting a good night's rest, we went on a city tour and saw the 2,500-year-old Acropolis with the Parthenon and several other temples in the area. We ate baklavas on the street and at night we went to a fine restaurant from where we could view the Parthenon all lit up.

After spending a day and a half in the city, we were taken by bus to Piraeus, where our ship was docked. It was an old cruise liner, recently remodeled, but it seemed that they had not quite finished the job. One of the toilet seats wasn't attached and one of the men in our group found himself sliding off and sitting on the floor. He was not a happy customer!

179

According To Me

Although the ship left something to be desired, the food was fine and the entertainment superb. I learned to enjoy Greek music and we danced every night. Of all the cruises I have taken, this was probably the most interesting.

We left Piraeus in the evening and sailed into Irakleon, Crete, arriving just as the sun was coming up. After a hardy breakfast, we piled on busses and rode to the ancient Minoan palace-temple at Knossos, the cradle of civilization. According to legend the Minotaur, half man and half bull, roamed the labyrinth that had been created to hold him. The walls were decorated with frescoes depicting young people jumping over bulls. After spending several hours with a knowledgeable guide, we went back to the ship.

Our next stop was Santorini, a volcanic island once part of the Minoan empire. About 1,460 BC the volcano either blew up or imploded, precipitating a tsunami that destroyed Knossos on the island of Crete and, it is speculated, aided the Children of Israel in crossing the Red Sea as Moses was leading them out of Egypt. Because of the steep slopes a serpentine stairway with 600 steps leads up to the settlement and the shops. From there one has a breathtaking view over the Aegean Sea and all the many islands scattered around.

In the evening we weighed anchor and sailed for the island of Rhodes, arriving the following morning. The island is a favorite vacation spot for Scandinavians. I was surprised when I walked into a shop and found that the shopkeeper could speak Swedish. We spent most of the day taking a bus tour to see some ancient Roman ruins.

Our next stop on our adventure was Kusadasi on the Turkish mainland. We took a bus to Ephesus where we had an outstanding guide who made the place come alive with his descriptions. We were told that Ephesus was a very modern city when St. Paul visited here, with streets paved with marble. We could still see the ruts worn into the stone by the chariot wheels. We visited the amphitheater where Paul preached about

AROUND THE WORLD IN *Almost* 80 YEARS

Jesus Christ and His saving grace, angering the idol mongers in the city who started a riot.

Sailing into Istanbul we were stopped and forced to wait in the Bosphorus Bay for four hours before they would allow us to enter the harbor. I have no proof, but I have always suspected that the animosity between the Turks and the Greeks could have been the reason for the delay.

When we had disembarked, Leroy and I joined a couple and went to the Istanbul Hilton hotel for dinner. The restaurant was on top of the very tall building with a fabulous view over the city and the large inlet called The Golden Horn. A beautiful young Turkish lady, dressed in what looked to me like a national dress, was our waitress. Our friend wanted a picture of her, so I told him that I would take one of him and his wife with her. There were some plants on the far wall that I thought would make a better background. Taking the girl by the arm, he escorted her across the room. Suddenly a young man burst out of the kitchen and told him in no uncertain words to get his hands off her. She was his fiancée and no man was supposed to touch her. He did allow us to take a picture, but only if he could be in it too. That was my first experience in a Muslim country.

After dinner we joined up with our group, about 300 people, for a scheduled visit to a Turkish nightclub. When we arrived there, we were escorted down a very long and narrow staircase that ended in a large gathering place with the stage off to the side. The walls were covered with drapery and I thought that if this place caught fire, we would have no chance to get out. We would all be cremated right there. I told Leroy and a couple of the others that I didn't like the place and was getting out of there. Apparently I was not the only apprehensive one in the group because a general exodus followed. Some of the people were angry at the ship's tour guide for arranging such an outing and really gave him a piece of their minds. He apologized profusely and promised to make it up to them.

According To Me

The next day, after touring the sites in Istanbul, the tour guide announce that he had hired a troupe of musicians and a belly dancer to come on board and entertain us. This was much better and everyone was pacified. I was sitting on the floor because there weren't any seats left. As the belly dancer was doing her routine she stopped and asked if any of the men would come and dance with her. When nobody accommodated her, she grabbed my arm and dragged me out on the floor with her. She rolled up my pant legs and pulled up my shirt so my belly was exposed, it wasn't as big then as it is now, and I was supposed to go through the gyrations with her. I'm sure I wasn't very good, but everyone had a good laugh.

From Istanbul we sailed back to mainland Greece, stopping off at the Cyclades and Mykonos Island. It had been an incredibly out of the ordinary adventure. I had seen a lot of things that I had only read about in books. Anything less than 2,000 years old now seemed almost modern. It is a trip I would love to take again.

MIDDLE EAST

ISRAEL

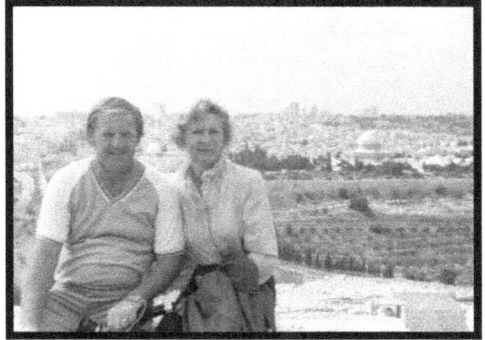

If I would rate any of my trips a "Ten," it would have to be my first trip to Israel. For years May-Britt and I had dreamt about going there, but we really didn't know whom to go with and we didn't want to go there on our own. There were so many organizations offering tours to the Holy Land, but we wanted to go with someone who could really make it meaningful.

I had a men's Bible study group, which met weekly in my office. One of the men in the group highly recommended a pastor named, Dr. Roy Blizzard. A Texan who spoke with a real Texas drawl, Dr. Blizzard held a Ph.D. in Middle Eastern Study with an emphasis on Israel and could even speak Hebrew. My impression of him was that he was a man with a colossal ego who thought that he knew more than anybody else about the subject of the Holy Land. Nevertheless, we decided to join one of his groups and go with him to Israel.

We were a group of 35 pilgrims making the journey that, for most of us, was our first visit to this historical and holy country of which Isaiah had once prophesied:

Though you were ruined and made desolate and your land laid waste, you will now be too small for your people, and those who devoured you will be far away. The children born during your bereavement will yet say in your hearing, "This place is too small for us; give us more space to live in." Isaiah 49:19-20

ACCORDING TO ME

When Israel was finally destroyed in 70 A.D. and the Jews dispersed all over the world, the country was ruined and made desolate. But, just as Isaiah had prophesied, God had restored the land and today seven million people make their home in Israel.

We were riding on the bus to Tel Aviv after having gone through entry procedures at the airport. Dr. Blizzard was standing up in front telling us about what we were to experience for the next two weeks. He explained that it is illegal in Israel to proselytize Jews to Christianity and that if any of us had any tracts for evangelizing, to throw them in to the trashcan located at the front of the bus.

We stayed a few days at the beautiful Tel Aviv Hilton Hotel, located right by the Mediterranean Sea. May-Britt and I went swimming one afternoon when we were free from sightseeing. The first night at the hotel we were served roast beef with potatoes and vegetables, and wonderful bread rolls, but no butter. I realized then, that in Israel everything is kosher and you don't mix meat with dairy products. For breakfast, though, there was plenty of bread and butter, many kinds of cheeses, all sorts of fish and a whole array of other foods. I like the Israeli breakfasts. The following evening we were served margarine instead of butter, which was fine with us.

Dr. Blizzard was a great tour guide. After having taken several subsequent trips to the Holy Land, I would say that he was one of the best guides I've ever had. Touring the country in the bus, he would stand in front with a map hanging from the ceiling and lecture about the areas we were passing. He really made the Bible come alive for me in a way it had not done before. One area he pointed out was where Samson was going down to Gaza to court Delilah. We came to a place with two hills with a dry creek bed in between where David slew Goliath. We all got out of the bus and looked around trying to picture the event. Some of the people picked up rocks to take home as souvenirs. Dr. Blizzard told us that most of the bus tours stopped there and

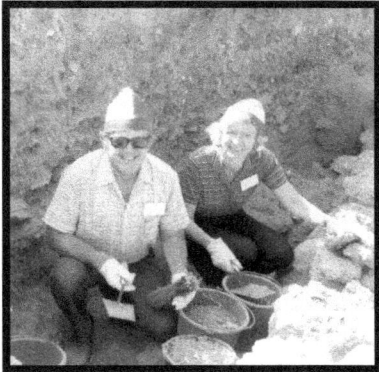

people would take rocks with them. Once in a while some creative Arab would bring a load of rocks and leave them for the tourists.

We spent the first three days working at an archeological dig just north of Tel Aviv at a place called Tel Qasile. May-Britt and I were assigned a small area, which looked like the remnants of a foundation barely visible on the ground. We dug with a small shovel and carried the soil away in a bucket. At day's end we had only come down about four feet and were getting bored with the project. The next day we asked to work someplace else and another couple was put to work in our place. At the end of the day they got to the bottom and found a clay jar, which had been there since the Roman era. May-Britt and I were a little envious of our friend's good fortune, but we'd had our chance and walked away from it. There are pottery chards all over Israel at different strata and you can tell the age of the civilization by their location.

From Tel Aviv we traveled to Tiberius on the Sea of Galilee. Staying at a hotel near the lake, we made day trips to places in northern Israel. Caesarea Philippi, at the foot of Mount Hermon, was particularly intriguing, I thought. There is a large cave going in to the mountain, called the Gate of Hell. Ancient Greeks and Romans carved niches into the rock where they placed their idols. It was here that Jesus asked his disciple who they thought He really was. Simon Peter answered, "You are the Son of God."

"Blessed are you, Simon son of Jonah, for this was not revealed to you by man, but by my Father in Heaven. And I tell you that you are Peter, and on this rock I will build my church and the gates of Hell shall not prevail against it."
Matt.16: 15-18.

185

According To Me

We crossed the border into Lebanon through a gate in what was called the Good Fence. The Maronite Christians living in Southern Lebanon were friendly with the Israelis. They were allowed to cross the border into Israel to find work and to take advantage of the free health care.

Nimrod's Fortress, located on top of a mountain ridge in northern Golan Heights, was built by the Arabs in the early thirteenth century to ward off the coming Sixth Crusade. An enormous structure stretching over a large part of the peak, it is now a ruin, but with some imagination one can picture the impregnable stronghold it once was.

We took a boat across the Sea of Galilee from Tiberius to a kibbutz on the eastern side of the lake where we were served St. Peter's fish for lunch. This fish species has been in the lake since biblical times. Jesus, having been told he should pay taxes, asked Peter to go and catch a fish. Doing so, he returned with a fish that had a coin in its mouth with which Jesus could pay His taxes. Amazingly, when my fish was brought to the table it also had a coin in its mouth, but since I didn't have to pay any tax I just put it in my pocket.

Finally, we came to Jerusalem where we stayed for several days making excursions from there. One can easily spend a month in Jerusalem looking at the innumerable sights, but we had only a few days so we hit just the highlights.

It is a fascinating place with thousands of years of history. Originally built on top of a mountain called Mt Moria, it is the site where God told Abraham to sacrifice his son, Isaac, reneging on that request at the last minute and providing a ram for the sacrifice instead. Solomon later built a temple where the Jews, for several centuries, worshiped Jehovah. It was destroyed and rebuilt several times until its final destruction in 70 A.D. The most important remains of the temple is the western wall where Jews gather to pray for its restoration.

Walking up the steps to the temple mount, I was in awe, thinking that Jesus had once walked where I was walking. It was on those very steps that Peter and John met a man who had been lame for 38 years. Not having silver or gold to give the beggar, Peter healed him and told him to get up and walk, which he did.

We went to Masada where Herod had built his fortress palace complete with steam baths and a swimming pool. During the final destruction of Israel 900 zealots took refuge on Masada, holding out against the Roman siege for three years. Finally gaining access to the mountaintop, the Romans entered only to find that everyone inside had committed suicide.

Twelve hundred feet above the desert floor, the only access to the top was a narrow winding path called the Snake Trail. May-Britt and I hiked up that long trail, getting very thirsty in the hot sun. We had one can of coke between us and by the time we reached the top we were completely parched. Luckily we found a Good Samaritan who offered us water. Tired after our long trek, we decided to take the cable car back down the hill.

From Masada we drove down to the Dead Sea, the lowest point on earth. Swimming in the Dead Sea is a bizarre experience. The high mineral content makes it impossible to sink and you just float on the surface. It doesn't taste good, though and if you get a drop in your eye it is very painful. After our dip in the Dead Sea we drove to En Gedi and hiked about a mile up in the hills to a refreshing waterfall, where we could wash the salts from our skin.

Driving back to Jerusalem, we stopped off at Qumran where the Dead Sea Scrolls were found. At the time of the destruction of Israel the Essenes living in this area sealed their holy scrolls in clay pots and hid them in the many caves at Qumran. Centuries later, in the 1940's, a young shepherd boy, throwing rocks at the caves to pass time, heard a crashing sound and went up to investigate. He found several clay pots that held ancient scrolls. Since then, over 900 scrolls have been found containing invaluable historic and religious texts, including the oldest known surviving copies of Isaiah the Old Testament of the Bible.

According To Me

Isreal and Jordan 2001

In February 2001, my friend, Jim Davis, called and offered me an incredible deal. His daughter worked for a travel agency that organized tours to the Holy Land. They had a last minute cancelation on a two-week tour and were now offering the spot at half price. But we only had an hour to make a decision and the tour was leaving the following week. I didn't need an hour; I was ready to go!

Traveling with Jim is always adventurous and this trip was up to par. After spending the night in Los Angeles, having dinner with Jim's daughter and son, and going to church on Sunday morning, we boarded a plane to London. Landing in London, we found a hotel and went to a quaint old pub for dinner. It was located in a building built in the sixteenth century. People must have been a lot shorter in those days, because we had to stand with our heads in between the beams and Jim, who is quite tall, still couldn't stand straight. The next morning, after a wonderful English breakfast, we rode the shuttle bus back to the terminal. I thought we would never get there on time, Heathrow is so big and spread out, but we made our flight and arrived in Israel about three o'clock in the afternoon, well rested. It was the easiest long distance flight I have ever experienced.

Joining the group we met the pastor and his wife, Jack and Lisa Hibbs, who were the spiritual leaders on the tour. Our Israeli guide, Avi, was former military and an excellent guide. He took us to most of the locations that May-Britt and I had been before, but also showed us some old military encampments on the Golan Heights.

After touring Northern Israel, we crossed over to the Kingdom of Jordan, where we changed busses and guides. An armed policeman also rode along with us, for what reason I don't know, but he was a very pleasant fellow and was willing to talk with us.

Our destination was Petra, a rock city in Jordan, south of the Dead Sea. Our hotel was located a short distance from the opening of the Siq, a mile long deep chasm split in the sandstone leading to the ancient fabled city. It was a palatial hotel with fascinating Arabic décor and the food was also wonderful and different from the Israeli fare we had been eating.

Petra is considered one of the Seven Wonders of the ancient world. The Naboteans arrived there in the seventh century B.C., finding a secure valley where they could raise their sheep and goats in peace. It must have taken centuries to carve the enormous facades that have been found all over the hundred square miles. Less than 20% has been excavated and there is no telling what archaeologists will find at later dates.

Leaving Petra we drove down to Eilat, the most southerly Israeli city on the Red Sea. We spent all day on a tour boat, swimming in that wonderful water. I even went parasailing for an hour or so. Later, Jim and I rented some snorkel gear and swam around looking at the fish.

The next day we drove to Jerusalem. Passing through the Negev desert we stopped to see the ancient Children of Israel Tabernacle, an exact replica of the one in the Bible, set up in a little valley between some low mountains. We saw the desert bloom, passing orchards with every kind of fruit. We also passed several Bedouin settlements, people, whose lives seem unchanged by the passage of time, living like Abraham in big black tents and moving from place to place.

In Jerusalem we toured the sights, including Yad Vashem, the Holocaust museum. After viewing most of what there was to see in that enormous building, I wandered outside to look around. I came out onto the Avenue of the Righteous among nations, a walkway lined with trees planted in honor of all the Non-Jewish people from many nations who risked their lives saving Jews from Hitler's gas chambers. Walking around the building I saw a rowboat on a stand against the wall. I was curious as to what that represented, and coming closer, I saw a sign above the boat.

According To Me

The inscription said that in October 1943, Denmark saved 7,200 Jews by transporting them over to Sweden. Denmark was the only country in Europe that was able to save most of its Jews from the Nazis. The Germans incarcerated about 500 Jews and took them to Theresienstadt, Czechoslovakia. Somehow the Danish Red Cross was able to prevail upon them not to send them on to death camps. After the war, all but 50 of the Danish Jews returned to Denmark. Arriving at their homes they found that their neighbors had taken care of their properties in their absence, so they could just move right back in.

I have been to Israel a total of five times. Although the tours follow basically the same route, the experiences are unique. It is always wonderful to return to the Holy Land. In 2008 May-Britt and I were booked on a trip with our church in Branson, Missouri. In the last minute May-Britt had to back out because of medical issues, but we were able to transfer her booking to our son, Orla Jens, who jumped at the chance to accompany me. We had a memorable time experiencing the places where our Lord once walked. Mostly it was fun to be able to spend time with my son.

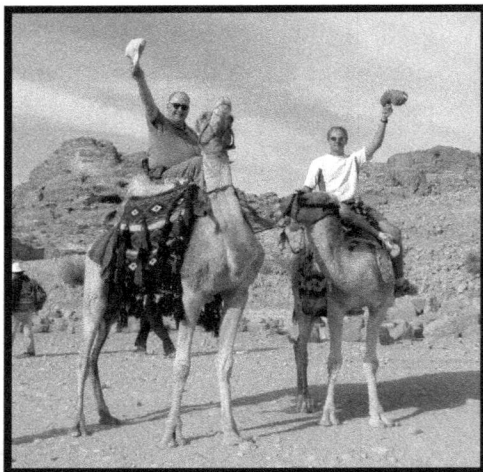

May-Britt had been longing to return to the Holy Land ever since our first visit in 1983. Disappointed over having to cancel in 2008, she booked another trip in 2009 and this time she was able to go. If she had her way we would move to Jerusalem and live out our last days in the Holy City. I don't think that will happen but you never know what the Lord has in store. Some day we will live in the "New Jerusalem" and that will be more than wonderful.

ASIA

MY FIRST TRIP TO SRI LANKA

In April 1983 our new son-in-law, Stefan, invited me to join him while he was working in Sri Lanka. Stefan is a documentary and natural history filmmaker and has worked all over the world. While in Sri Lanka he was also trying to establish a leather bag factory for export to Europe and the United States. As it was my first time to travel to the Far East, I was really excited to experience something really different.

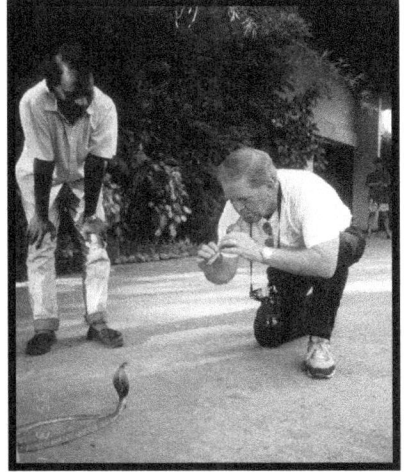

Flying to Japan, I lost an entire day. I left Los Angeles on Monday afternoon, crossed the dateline and arrived in Japan on Wednesday. Tuesday never existed. From Japan I flew on to Singapore where I had decided to layover two nights. I'm glad I did. Singapore is such a beautiful place. Super clean, it's illegal to chew gum there for fear that people will drop it on the tile-covered sidewalks. Graffiti is punishable by caning. I wish they would do that here.

In Singapore I attended a Rotary meeting, held in my hotel. I have always liked to go to Rotary meetings wherever I have traveled and I have many souvenir banners from all over the world. As I was coming out of the hotel after the meeting, I saw a city tour bus getting ready to leave. I asked the guide if I could come along. She said sure and sold me a ticket. It was a great tour. We saw a lot of the city and went to a two-acre aviary totally covered with netting. There were thousands of birds of all kinds and beautiful flowers and trees. Later on

191

we went over to Malaysia across the strait. It was like crossing the border to Mexico from San Diego, a much less developed country.

I left Singapore in the evening, landing around midnight in Sri Lanka where Stefan and his friend, Yaya, picked me up in Yaya's old broken down car. And the adventure began.

The automobile, if you could call it that, was an Australian Holden and should have been scrapped years earlier. Driving along the pot-holed road towards the town of Panadura, where Yaya lived with his widowed mother and three brothers, the car was hopping and skipping because the shock absorbers were worn out and also had a broken rear spring. With every bounce the floor of the car would hit the drive shaft and reverberate through the entire car. My feet prickled like they were full of pins and needles from the vibration. The drive shaft had worn a hole in the floor allowing plumes of dust to engulf me in the backseat. Suddenly, smoke billowed out around the hood. Yaya pulled over to the side of the road, got out and opened the hood. A three-foot wire was shorting out and was aglow with fire. Some people, asleep on the sidewalk, woke up from the commotion and came over to see what was happening. Someone brought a jar of water and dowsed the fire. Yaya grabbed the wire and yanked it out of there. I figured that the car was now beyond hope and resigned myself to spending the night on the street. But Yaya was able to start it up and we were going again. I have no idea what kind of wire it was; it may have been for the horn. The lights worked intermittently but

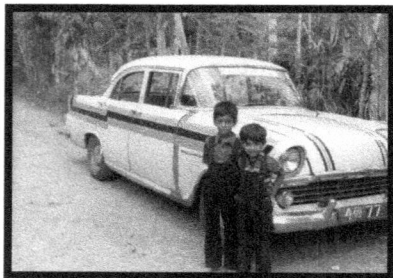

we were moving along at moderate speed. I realized later that the car didn't have any brakes either. Coming to a 90-degree turn, Yaya bounced off a block wall before going up the hill to the house where he lived. He was going a little too fast to turn into the drive way and rolled down to the bottom of the other side of the hill where he turned around and then drove slowly up to the house and parked. This was my introduction to Sri Lanka, my home for the next three weeks.

It was a fairly nice house by local standards. Built with cement blocks, it had concrete floors, eight foot interior walls with exposed rafters holding the roof. Sometimes we could see a rat crawling around up there. There was no glass in the windows, but there were bars to keep out intruders. Stefan and I shared a bedroom. It was so hot that all we had on the bed was a sheet; there was no need for a blanket.

There was no bathroom, but there was a toilet, a 3 by 3 foot room with a hole in the middle of the floor with a foot imprint on each side of it to facilitate aim. We took a bucket of water with us in there to flush with and rinse the floor off in case we missed a little. In the morning we'd go outside to the back of the house where there was a well. Filling a bucket with water, we would shave and then pour the rest over our heads; that was our shower. There were a couple of fish in the well which, I suppose, were to keep the mosquitoes under control. It is also possible that some kid threw them in there.

Amma, Yaya's mother, was very nice, although we couldn't communicate with her. Her four sons, however, all spoke fairly good English. Not wanting to be a burden, Stefan and I bought tea and bread rolls for breakfast and took our other meals in the city.

Every morning we walked a quarter mile to catch the bus to downtown Panadura. We were the only white people around and the neighbors came out of their houses to stare at us. We were an anomaly in this part of the world. We'd say hello and smile, and they would smile back. I think we were well accepted.

According To Me

In Panadura we jumped on the slow train to Colombo, where Stefan had to visit many different government offices to get a license for his leather business. It was too hot to sit inside, so we would sit outside on the steps and watch the countryside roll by. I was amazed at the lack of protection around the tracks. In the villages kids of all sizes played right next to the tracks. I would later see many people who had been maimed for life, with limbs cut off by the wheels of the train.

Sri Lanka is a beautiful, lush tropical country with lots of flowers and fruit, and several animals that I hadn't seen before. In the city park in Colombo there are two big trees where Flying Foxes or Fruit Bats hang out. They have a wingspan up to about six feet and have a face like a little fox. They are as cute as anything. Observing them, it occurred to me that everything in this world fights with his neighbor. I thought bats slept during the day. Not these, they were screaming at each other all day long. After a while when one had had enough of the insults, he flew to another part of the tree, where the squabble continued.

It was interesting to see the old colonial buildings, built mostly by the English. Even the office furnishings are remnants from colonial days. We stayed in several old hotels where one could imagine the English Gentry and their ladies enjoying the good life.

After following Stefan around for a couple of weeks, dealing with government bureaucrats, we decided to have some fun. We took a bus down the coast to Hikkaduwa where there was a Swedish diving club. Stefan wanted to do some underwater filming. When we arrived there, the place was closed. We went down to the beach where we met a couple of boys who had a boat. For a few rupees they would take us out in the ocean a little distance from shore where we could snorkel and view coral formations. The area was called Coral Gardens. It was a sight to see. The coral was formed in a long reef and looked a lot like asparagus spears. The sea was moving up and down about 3 – 4 feet and we found ourselves drifting with the current over the coral. I think I panicked, because I thought that there was a very good chance that I would be eviscerated on the sharp spines that were coming very close to my body as I moved down with the wave action. Kicking to get away from the dangerous situation, I kicked the coral a couple of times cutting my legs and feet badly. I found out that those kinds of cuts don't heal very fast. Something in the coral, they tell me. My doctor had prescribed some medicine for traveling, which I took every day. He told me later that it helped prevent infections in those sores.

I don't remember if we did any diving, but we had a real nice time lounging around the hotel for a couple of days. Funny thing happened while we were there. We had been out swimming in the magnificent Indian Ocean, where the water is always the right temperature. Stefan had his bathing suit on, but I had taken a shower and was lying on my bed in my birthday suit. All of a sudden the door opened and a woman walked in. She took one glance at me and said something in a language that I didn't understand and left in a hurry. She had obviously made a mistake and walked into the wrong room.

People are very friendly and helpful in Sri Lanka. We rented a motorcycle in Hikkaduwa and, after a couple of miles, ran out of gas. A boy ran over to us and asked us what the problem was. He said that his father had some gas in the shed behind his house that we could have. It got us to the nearest gas station and we were off and riding.

We decided to visit Yala National Park, a couple of hundred miles away. Yaya picked us up in his old bucket of bolts. By now the starter had also died and we had to push it to get it started. Once we pushed the car down a hill to get it started and then had to run to catch up with it, jumping in as it gathered speed. The brakes worked when there was enough brake fluid, but it leaked out in a short while and then we could only hope to be going up a hill to stop. We were driving at night when we suddenly discovered a herd of buffalo. With no horn and no brakes, and lights that functioned occasionally, all we could do was close our eyes and pray. Miraculously, we sailed unscathed through the herd coming out on the other side. We did make it to Yala National Park safely.

Stefan and I were walking around a lake near the hotel where we were staying. All of a sudden a crocodile ran out from under a bush and crashed into the water. That actually happened four times. Stefan decided that he wanted to film the crocs and we went back to the hotel to get his equipment.

As he was setting up his camera Yaya and I wandered off into the bush. Suddenly Yaya said that he saw a big elephant up ahead. I looked in the direction he was pointing and saw the biggest bull elephant I had ever seen, standing by a bush. I called to Stefan to forget about the crocs and focus on the huge behemoth. The elephant was coming toward us. Stefan was filming. I was snapping pictures like mad, hiding behind a bush, as if that would save me. And Yaya was gone like the wild goose in winter. The elephant, obviously aware of our presence, continued on his path towards us but then veered off, staying about a hundred yards away, crossed the lake and disappeared into the woods. It could have been very dangerous, but as I always tell people, "I didn't have to outrun the giant; I only had to outrun Stefan."

After a few days viewing wildlife in Yala, we started back in the old rattletrap. It was late and we made it as far as Hikkaduwa where we decided to spend the night. There was no one in the hotel reception, so what do three adventurers do in a situation like that? We found an empty room, recently vacated, and crawled into bed. There were a few extraneous hairs on the sheets, but that didn't bother us. Yaya slept on the floor, he was used to doing that, and we had a good night's sleep.

Three adventurous weeks had passed and it was time for me to say goodbye to my newfound friends in Sri Lanka. After spending the last night in Hotel Taprobane in Colombo, I said farewell to Stefan and boarded the magnificent Singapore Airline, which was going to carry me home to California. The service on board was wonderful; the stewardesses were gorgeous and accommodating.

Staying overnight in Singapore was a bit of a culture shock. I had gotten used to sleeping on an old bed with only a sheet for cover, no glass on the windows and bugs that ate me alive before morning, and showering, shaving and brushing my teeth in a bucket. But when I saw the bed with clean white sheets and took a shower in that beautiful bathroom, I kind of had to pinch myself to realize that I wasn't dreaming.

I left Singapore at nine o'clock Sunday morning, flew to Japan where I had a couple of hours layover, and continued on through the night, arriving in Los Angeles at ten thirty, and it was Sunday morning! Again I had crossed the Dateline, arriving almost before I had left!

THE INDIA ADVENTURE

We met Sam and Adela Kamaleson in a real estate office when they were in the process of buying a home in Arcadia. He was Vice-President at Large for World Vision, a large international humanitarian organization, headquartered in Arcadia, California. Both born in Madras, India, they had three children, Mark, Ruth and Paul. Our daughters were the same age and LaVonne and Ruth became great friends. Ruth would come over to our house and the girls would lie by the pool. LaVonne in the sun, trying to get tan (a lost cause since she has inherited my Danish complexion,) and Ruth in the shade, avoiding getting darker. I called them "Salt" and "Pepper."

197

ACCORDING TO ME

When Sam and Adela found out that I was in construction they hired me to remodel their bathroom. Working late, I was sometimes there for dinner and they would invite me to sit down with them and partake in Adela's wonderful, but very spicy Indian cooking. Indians don't use utensils when they eat, they use their fingers. Sam showed me how they only use three fingers, but I noticed that his whole hand got a bit messy. They offered me a fork, but I didn't use it. I told them that, when in India, I do as the Indians do.

In January 1984 we had the incredible opportunity to accompany Sam and Adela to India. The four of us left LAX, flying business class to New Delhi. On such a long trip it was nice to be in business class. After going through immigration formalities, we went to the Ashoka Hotel, where we spent five nights. Sam and Adela were very great tour guides. They took us to places normal tourists never see. Introducing us to their friends, we were invited into homes and got to see how people live.

One evening they took us to the old Red Fort a few miles away for a Light and Sound show. Arriving at the Fort, the cab driver told us that he would wait for us and take us back to the hotel after the show. I thought that was a little odd, but then they do things differently in India. The show, which was fantastic, told about the history of India. Sure enough, when we came out the cab driver was waiting for us. We got in his car and left. After a couple of miles he ran out of gas right in the worst slums in India. Grabbing a big bottle from under his seat, the driver took off, running up the road towards another taxi, where he siphoned out some gas and came running back. Lifting the hood of the car, he somehow attached the bottle to the carburetor and we were off again. We soon came to a gas station but it was closed. No problem, there was another standing taxi there. Getting out his trusty bottle our driver siphoned some more gas and we were on our way. Both times he had permission from the other drivers. Apparently people in

India help each other however they can; either that or it was the code of the taxi drivers. We were within eyesight of our hotel when he ran out of gas again. Paying him off, we walked the rest of the way.

Sam and Adela really didn't want us to roam around in the city by ourselves. But one day, while they were resting, we decided to go sightseeing in the old town of Delhi. Our hotel was in New Delhi, a modern city with wide boulevards and parks, not too crowded. But Old Delhi would be swarming with people. Hailing a taxi, we told the driver where we wanted to go. Even he objected, claiming it was unsafe for us to go there, but we insisted he take us. He let us off a little short of where we wanted to go. I'm not sure why, maybe he was afraid to go there. Undaunted, we took a rickshaw, a tricycle with a seat for two mounted behind the driver who, in this case, was a fast pedaling teenager.

Delhi must be one of the most remarkable cities in the world. We found ourselves on a broad road, devoid of cars, but crawling with humanity, not dissimilar to an anthill. In the middle of the crowd a herd of about six white cows moved amiably down the street. No one was driving them on or trying to shoo them away; cows have the right-of-way in Hindu India. Nobody bothered us. We did a little window-shopping along the street and returned, unmolested, to our hotel.

We took a side trip, flying from New Delhi to Agra to see the Taj Mahal, a marble mausoleum built in the 17th century by the Mughal Emperor Shah Jahan, in memory of his favorite wife, Mumtaz Mahal. It is considered to be one of the Seven Wonders of the World.

We went shopping, looking for something to take home with us as a memory from Agra. We found two gorgeous tapestries with peacocks embroidered on them in bright, beautiful colors. We really liked them but they cost $650.00 and we weren't sure that we wanted to spend that much on a souvenir. Walking around town we ran into the storeowner. We explained that we couldn't make up our minds and said that we would probably have to flip a coin. Obligingly, he said he had a two-headed coin in his pocket! We laughed, went back to his store and bought the peacocks. They are now hanging in our dining room.

From New Delhi we traveled south stopping for a couple of days at an orphanage that Sam had founded with some associates about 20 years previously. It was an absolutely stunning place. I don't remember how many kids lived there, but outside the classroom there were oodles of shoes. On our last evening Sam spoke at a youth conference with about 1,000 attendees. Sam, a great orator, spoke of the 800 million people in India who need Christ. When he finished the young people in the auditorium were ready and eager to go out and conquer India for Jesus.

The next day Adela, May-Britt and I took the train to Madras. Sam, who was staying behind for a while, would come later. In Madras we stayed at a nice hotel near a golf course. Now in their hometown, the Kamalesons wouldn't let us spend any money. They sent a car for us every morning and took us sightseeing, bringing us home to their relatives for dinner, which was very enjoyable.

The day after we arrived in Madras we were invited to a wedding. Sam was supposed to officiate but his flight was delayed and he came too late for the ceremony. He had been a great influence in the bride's life when she was a young child and the family was very disappointed. When he finally arrived in time for the dinner the whole family seemed to be quite upset with him and the mother of the bride served him a piece of her mind! The dinner was held outside at a country club and we were served chicken with mashed potatoes and gravy. There were no utensils, being India, so we used our fingers.

In church the next day Sam preached and we all laughed when he sang, "No one loves me like Jesus." He was still not in good graces with the bridal party, having missed the wedding.

It seemed that every time we took out our camera in Madras, we almost caused an international incident. Driving through the countryside, we noticed some long gourds hanging from overhead trellises. Stopping the car we walked out into the field to take a picture. All of a sudden half a dozen men appeared out of the bushes and told us to get away from there. They believed that taking photographs would bring a curse on the crops.

Another time, I saw a couple of small, black, potbellied pigs lying next to a man who was lying on the beach. When I took a picture of the pigs, he jumped up and both he and the pigs began chasing me. I can't remember if I gave him money, but nothing happened.

One evening, as May-Britt and I were walking around downtown Madras, we saw big flat wagon loaded with kids, drawn by a team of highly decorated oxen. May-Britt took out her camera and snapped a picture. As soon as she did that, all the kids jumped off the wagon and chased after us, screaming and hollering. They wanted money for the candid photo. We kept on walking, hoping that things would calm down. After a while a storeowner came out and hollered at them to leave us alone. Surprisingly, they calmed down and turned to enter a Hindu temple. They even invited us to come along. We were tempted, but we didn't want to leave our shoes outside among a thousand others. We were afraid we wouldn't find them again.

Probably the funniest, and perhaps scariest, incident on our adventure was the elephant escapade. Our trusty driver had brought us to an orphanage for girls, run by a friend of ours, Prema, whom we had met in Arcadia while she was visiting the Kamalesons. As we were waiting for the gate to open, we saw a young man riding on an elephant. The animal was all painted and decorated like it was going to be in some kind of parade. May-Britt jumped out of the car and took a picture. The next thing we knew the man, still sitting on the elephant, was standing by our car demanding to be paid. I was still sitting in the car with the window open and the elephant was standing next to me rubbing it's trunk back and forth on the roof and slobbering all over the windshield. I thought it might reach in through the window and drag me out of the car. The gate opened but our driver was busy wiping off the windshield, all the while the guy on the elephant was yelling at us. The driver eventually got in the car and drove in through the gate and up to the house with the elephant and its rider following after. Prema came out on the front porch and told him to get off the private property, but he kept insisting to be paid. May-Britt told me to give him something just to get rid of him. I took out a 5-rupee bill and gave it to the elephant just to see what it would do with it. To my amazement, it took it very gently with its trunk and held the money up to the man sitting on its back. They then turned around and lumbered off.

Before going home we decided to take the short hop down to Colombo, Sri Lanka. I wanted to show May-Britt where Stefan and I lived the year before. I had made arrangements with Yaya to meet us at the airport. This time he had a better car. The old Holden was probably resting alongside a road somewhere. It was a lot of fun to go back to my old stomping grounds again. We went to Yaya's house and I think the same rat was still crawling around in the rafters. We saw a lot in the day and a half we were there, a couple of factories where young children painting woodcarvings, a little woodshop where a man was reproducing the Swedish Dala horses (probably illegally,) and another factory where young girls were sewing shirts, maybe the one that I am now wearing.

Yaya had a little eight-year-old niece, Nangi, who we fell in love with. We even discussed bringing her with us home to America, but that never worked out. We did take her with us to spend the night in the old colonial Mount Lavinia Hotel. She had never been to a fine restaurant but she acted like a fine little lady.

We flew back to Madras and stayed for a couple of nights until it was time to get on that long weary flight back to California. It had been a wonderful trip, traveling with the Kamalesons, who know the culture so well and were so willing to share it with us.

SNAKE CHARMING IN SRI LANKA.

April 1995 found me winging my way back to Sri Lanka for the third time, this time to spend 10 days with my adventurous son-in-law. He and his friend from Sweden, Nisse, picked me up at Negombo airport. This time he had a much better car and a driver called Siri, with whom I became the best of friends. We spent the first night at Mount Lavinia hotel. I've stayed there a couple of times, but it seemed to have lost some of its shine since my last visit 11 years before.

The next day we went to the see the Secretary of Interior to obtain a commercial filming license for Stefan. The Secretary, however, proved to be a very stern official who was not about to issue a permit. Stefan walked away empty-handed, but he wasn't without resources. He had connections with the Sri Lanka Tourist Board and they were able to secure a permit for him. We had lunch at the Casicade restaurant, on top of a building in downtown Colombo with a view over the entire city. The food was good, but it was a challenge to eat because of the very hot spices. After lunch we went to a 30-story building still under construction. Getting permission, we boarded a wiggly construction elevator and rode it to the top. Stefan wanted to do some filming of the surrounding area. Seen from that height Colombo is a beautiful capital, with the ocean, the harbor and parks scattered around the vicinity.

According To Me

In the afternoon we drove south along the coast through familiar areas to Panadura, where we turned inland toward the mountains. The highest point in Sri Lanka is 8,200 feet. We were going to a town named Nuwara Eilya, located at about 6,000 feet and much cooler than the coast. The roads were terrible with large potholes everywhere and, although the distance isn't great, it took many hours before we arrived at our destination, an old colonial hotel. It had been a wonderful hotel with perfect climate overlooking the lush valleys with all kinds of fruits and vegetation. You could still feel the presence of old British aristocracy and their ladies enjoying life and partaking of high tea. There was a lot of deferred maintenance, but it was still quite comfortable and the food was fine.

After breakfast the next day, we drove north to Anuradhapura, where we spent a week in a very nice hotel by a lake. Again this hotel was built in the colonial times and had a large covered veranda with comfortable seats, where we relaxed in the evening and enjoyed a cold beer.

This is where the real adventure began. I found myself involved in something I had never imagined I would experience. Stefan's plans were to revisit a small Gypsy village called Kudagama. In 1982 Stefan had produced a film about two snake-charming gypsy boys. They are the Ahukuntakayo, "the snake people." Their primary occupation is to clear the rice fields of snakes so that the harvesters can wade out into the paddies. The snakes are necessary to control the rodents that would otherwise destroy the crops, so the Ahukuntakayo do not destroy them after they've been collected. Most of the snakes are simply caught and released a short distance away. Some are kept for a month or two and used by the Ahukuntakayo in their secondary occupation, snake charming for the tourists.

Kudagama was a collection of small mud huts scattered in the jungle. A canvas sheet, stretched over poles in front of the hut, provided shade and some protection from the elements. This, I learned, was where the family slept. The huts were only for storage and shelter in case of inclement weather. It was like going back in time thousands of years. People lived off the land using only primitive tools. Nobody had cars and there were only a few bicycles. Wherever they went, they walked. If they were going to the city, they took the bus. They are, however, not really welcome on buses or in hotels. It seems that gypsies are discriminated against all over the World.

Stefan located the chief of the village and we were invited into his hut. It was a little fancier than the rest of the huts because it had a door. We sat on a clay ledge against the wall and beside me was a stack of wicker baskets. I had seen these baskets before and knew that they all contained Cobras. Suddenly the chief reached over and removed the lid of the top basket. A Cobra rose up, standing within a couple of feet of my face. Although I'm not really afraid of snakes, it did kind of give me the willies.

It didn't take long to familiarize myself in the village. The people were all excited to have visitors, especially white men, who they seldom saw. They also enjoyed being actors in a movie. Stefan spent several hours every day filming their way of life, from catching cobras to rocking their babies to sleep.

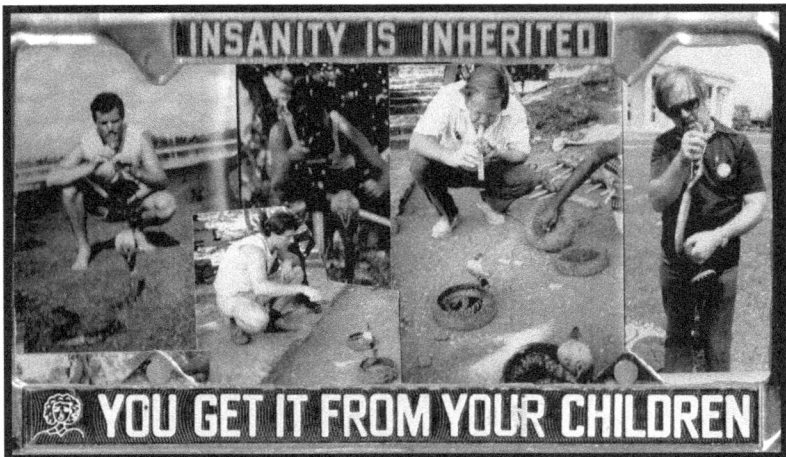

205

ACCORDING TO ME

Every day we would go down to the lake to go swimming. With nearly the entire village accompanying us, we waded into the shallow water, hollering and splashing at each other. They brought soap, washing their bodies along with their clothes, combining pleasure with purpose. The women even did their laundry; they were the workers. The men didn't do much, but I saw the women bringing water from the lake in big containers on their heads. They were also the ones to sweep up the leaves falling on the ground around the family hut.

I learned that when they get married, the bride is expected to bring a dowry: a monkey, a snake, a dog and a gourd flute. They marry young, fourteen or fifteen years old. I didn't see anybody having marital problems and I never heard any fighting between anybody. They seemed to live like a big happy family.

The men did work with their snakes. I saw them feeding a Cobra, which was very interesting. One man held the mouth of the snake open while another laid a strip of meat across and shoved it down with a stick. It reminded me of stuffing a sausage. Another time I observed a snake eating a chicken egg. The snake curled itself around the egg to hold it still, while it opened its mouth over it and slid it in without breaking the shell. Once the egg moved past the head you could see the bulge moving through the body. By this time I had become quite comfortable with the Cobras and was going to pick it up before it squirmed away, but was told to be careful with it because if the egg broke inside snake, the crushed shell would cut the inside of the stomach before it could be dissolved. Apparently the stomach juices in a snake are so strong that it can dissolve almost anything.

Not only do they keep snakes, they also have small trained Macaque monkeys. Traveling from city to city, they settled near a hotel and performed with their animals for the tourists. The money they were given for their act was thrown into the snake basket, as good a safe as any with the snake as a watch guard.

One evening they organized a party for the whole village. There was singing and dancing. One man beat on a drum and another played on his gourd flute. He kept playing the same melody over and over; I guess he only knew the one he played for his snake. Stefan showed the film he had made 12 years before and everyone, seeing themselves and others on screen, laughed so hard I thought they would pass out! Instead of going back to the hotel we spent the night in the village, pitching a tent and borrowing some mats to lie on. It wasn't very comfortable and the night seemed very long.

Stefan told me that during his first visit to Kudagama in 1980, there was a lot of drunkenness and it was really kind of dangerous to be there. In fact the village chief had told him that if he was going to film, he should come early in the morning and leave by ten o'clock. He could only promise that they would remain sober until then and one never knew what a drunken snake charmer might do. He might put a Cobra around your neck just for fun. Something like that could ruin the rest of the day.

But in 1995 the situation had changed dramatically. Living conditions were better, the children were clean and well cared for, and the drinking had ceased almost completely. On Sunday the entire village went to church, walking a couple hours to get there unless they could catch a bus.

According To Me

What had caused this great conversion?

During the 1980's Sri Lanka was infested with a sinister and unusually brutal Marxist-Leninist terrorist group. As a young man, Nimal had become a member of the group and had tortured and killed many people, burning homes and buildings, especially churches. One day Nimal was in a store buying supplies. He struck up a conversation with another man who told him that he was the pastor of a small church in the area. When Nimal showed interest, the pastor invited him to come to the next meeting that, because the church had been burnt down, was being held under a tree. Nimal, thinking this would be a good way to infiltrate the group, agreed to come.

On Sunday Nimal found himself sitting among the parishioners listening to the pastor's sermon, which seemed to be directed towards him. After the service some of the people talked with Nimal and told him that they knew that he was the one who had burned their church building. Fearful that he had wandered into a trap, he tried to deny it, but they insisted that he was the one. Then, to his great surprise, they told him that they forgave him and that he was welcome to come back. Not quite sure what to make of such treatment, he decided to go back the next Sunday. The people were friendly to him and invited him to eat with them. When he asked why they forgave him and accepted him into their church, they answered that they were followers of Jesus, who taught that you are to love your enemies. Nimal kept coming back to the little congregation under the tree, listening to the pastor telling about a better life for those who accepted Jesus into their hearts. One Sunday Nimal told the pastor that he had accepted Christ and wanted to be baptized. I can only imagine the delight in that church that day. One of their archenemies had become one of their own.

Nimal, now in trouble with his former gang members,

had to go into hiding or he might be killed. He was also in trouble with the government, which had just launched a massive offensive against the terrorist group. The pastor found him a safe location at a seminary somewhere on the island where Nimal began studying the Bible in earnest and felt the call to the ministry. After a couple of years of study he was ordained and began searching for a place where he could begin his ministry. Coming to Kudagama, he witnessed the squalor and depravity brought on by generations of alcoholism and felt called to minister to the Ahukutakayo people.

He made friends with the children, inviting them to come and hear stories under the tree. He arranged for a mobile medical clinic to come to the village and offered the villagers treatment and food in exchange for their liquor. Eventually the village chief became a Christian and the rest of the village followed. They dried out and began sending their children to school. Nimal held his services in the village under a tree until someone offered him a church building. It was a long ways away, but he decided to take it and the Ahukutakayo walked there on Sundays to hear him.

We visited one Sunday and the little place was packed out. Today the church has grown and expanded to include a seminary with housing for students.

It was a wonderful experience to meet and play with the snake people, who seem to be as happy as anybody on the planet, even though they have so little of the world's commodities.

But all good things must come to an end and Stefan brought me back to the airport. I said goodbye to him and to that wonderful island, which I will probably never see again. I flew straight home without a layover in Singapore. It was a rough trip. I don't sleep well on airplanes. I don't know why because I sleep great in cars and anywhere else, but that's how it is.

ACCORDING TO ME

THE TOUR DOWNUNDER

NEW ZEALAND

May-Britt and I took a 17-day first class tour to New Zealand and Australia in 1997. That part of the World is beyond a doubt unlike anywhere else one might wander on the Earth. The flora is different, there are animals that cannot be found anywhere else, and the landscape is dramatic and desolate. New Zealand is a variation of lush agriculture, thermal eruption, high snow covered mountains and deep fjords. Australia is mostly desert with beautiful verdant areas along the coast.

Arriving in Auckland, we were taken to a very pleasant hotel where we met the rest of our group. All were Americans except for an elderly Jewish couple from Montreal. We had a lovely dinner that night and went to bed early to catch up on our sleep and combat our jetlag.

The next day we boarded a beautiful new tour bus. The driver/tour guide kept up a running commentary about the sights we were passing. He told us that the bus was his own, recently acquired property. It was a big investment for him, but he and his wife had discussed it and decided that it would be a good thing to do. He liked being his own boss and he was quite knowledgeable about the north island.

There are more sheep in New Zealand than people and the first place we visited was a sheep show. It was in a large building filled with hundreds of people, primarily sheep farmers, who had come to see the show and bid at the auction. I didn't know that there were so many kinds of sheep. There was also a demonstration on how dogs worked with sheep. We watched, amazed, as the dogs drove the sheep from one end of the building to another without barking. They just ran around and stared down the sheep and the sheep obeyed without a bleat.

Back on the bus the driver took us up in the hills around Auckland where we had a great view of the city and the ocean. We have, of course, similar views in California but we still never tire of looking a beautiful landscapes and seascapes.

We drove south to the city of Rotorua. Located in the midst of a geothermal area it is surrounded by geysers and bubbling mud pots. Walking through the area we were careful to stay on the walkway, one misstep would cause severe burns if not instant death. We live in a dangerous world.

That evening we went to a Maori show. The Maoris, Polynesians native to New Zealand, told stories of their ancestors who traveled miles in flimsy outriggers across the Pacific, navigating by the stars.

We flew to the south island and were picked up by another driver/guide in a luxurious bus. The snow-covered mountaintops reminded me of Norway's rugged landscape. December is summertime in the southern hemisphere and the temperature was moderate, similar to a Scandinavian summers.

We had an unforgettable boat ride on the Shotover River. (Interesting names they have for lakes and rivers.) Piling 10 people into a jet boat they zoom down the river at breakneck speed, coming very close to the rocky sides, and then, spinning around, continue backwards at almost the same speed. It was an exhilarating adventure.

Having survived the Shotover River we continued our tour of the South Island. Driving past the 200' bridge,

211

where bungee jumping first became popular, we decided not to press our luck and stayed on the bus. We took a more peaceful boat ride through the deep chasms of Milford Sound, one of the many fjords on the South Island.

AUSTRALIA

After ten days in New Zealand, we flew to Sydney, Australia, where we stayed in the magnificent Ritz Carlton Hotel. After settling in we boarded a ship for a lunch cruise in the beautiful Sydney Harbor. The sun glittered on the water as we sailed under the old Sydney Bridge and past the Sydney Opera House, designed by a Danish architect. Later, we were given a tour of Sydney. Built on several hills it reminded me of San Francisco.

Our last evening in Sydney we attended the New Years Eve Concert at the Sydney Opera house. The first part of the performance was classical music. At midnight we went outside to witness the most fantastic fireworks display that I have ever seen. It was like a war, first with the fireworks on one side then it came from the other side. I thought they were going to blow up the old Sydney Bridge. But the bridge, decorated with a smiley face, remained standing with no harm done to it. We returned to the Opera House and listened to the final part of the performance. The musicians were now playing modern and rock music. We had all received streamers, which we threw all over the auditorium. By the time the concert was over there was a terrible mess.

From Sydney we flew to Canberra, the capitol. We had a tour of the government buildings and saw and read a lot of Australia's history. Later we were taken by bus to a sheep farm, owned by two old brothers, who showed us how they sheared sheep and took us out to meet their kangaroos. We were given cups of tea to serve them and were told that they would only drink out of blue cups. I found that interesting, I thought that they were colorblind.

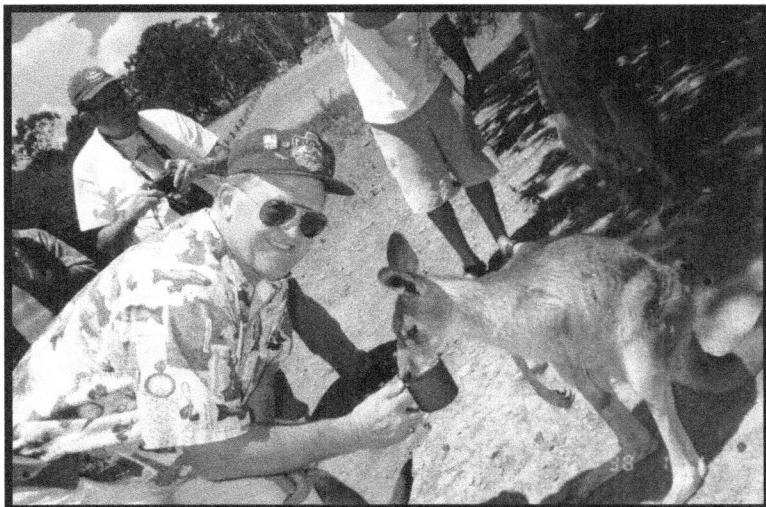

That evening we flew to Melbourne for the last couple of days of our tour. One day at sunset we went out to Philip Island where we saw the penguins return from the sea. Walking to the beach we noticed many holes in the ground and were told that the penguins dug them for their nests. We sat waiting for a long time for the birds that apparently don't operate on a schedule. Eventually they came, waddling across the beach on their short legs. Only the size of pigeons, I was impressed with the distance they covered from the ocean to their burrows, stopping every few feet to utter a quack or two to their neighbor, probably commenting on the crowds of people standing on the beach with nothing better to do than stare at them! Passing the burrows again on our way to the bus we could hear the murmuring of parents returning to their young with offerings of food.

The next day we were deposited at the airport for our flight back to New Zealand where we laid over a few hours before continuing the long journey across the Pacific, home to the "Good Old USA." It had been a memorable trip, but it is always good to be home again.

AFRICA

WEST AFRICA

I became acquainted with Dr. Ted Engstrom, president of World Vision International (WVI), through the Arcadia Rotary Club, where we were both members. In the eighties there were terrible famines in Ethiopia and World Vision was heavily involved in humanitarian efforts in that country. One day, when I was sitting next to Dr. Engstrom at lunch, I asked him if it would be possible to go with him on a journey to Ethiopia some time. He answered that it would be very possible. Sometime later I got a call from somebody in his office who asked me if I would be interested in going to West Africa on a presidential assessment expedition since the tour to Ethiopia hadn't materialized. We would be visiting World Vision projects in Senegal, Mauritania and Mali. I, of course, jumped at the chance. The man said that he would handle all the arrangements; all I had to do was come up with the money. He even ran a tab for my expenses while I was on the trip.

We were ten men who, in September 1985, flew from Los Angeles to Washington D.C., where we met up with Dr. Engstrom, who had been meeting with government officials. After dinner at Dulles airport we flew on to Dakar, Senegal. We had just arrived at the hotel when it was announced that we were going back to the airport for a flight to Nouakchott, the capitol of Mauritania. Located on the Atlantic coast at the edge the Sahara Desert, Nouakchott has to be one of the most horrible places in the world to live. Nearing our destination, I saw what I thought was smog rising up to about ten thousand feet. I realized that wasn't possible

214

since there are no industries or cars of any consequence in the city. It was actually a great dust plume rising up from the desert. In the early 60's Nouakchott had about 20,000 inhabitants but by the mid-80's the city's population had grown to half a million people. Once nomads, the people had lost most, if not all, of their animals due to a 20-year drought, and had moved into the city. The entire capital is a shantytown. There is no sanitation, no running water or electricity, and dust everywhere. Fine sand covered every surface in my hotel room. Disease was rampant. You could probably contract any number of illnesses just walking down the street.

John, who ran the WVI office, lived with his wife, Stephanie, and their small children in that grimy outpost of the world. Because Mauritania is a Muslim country John, a missionary, worked as a teacher and could only witness to people if they asked him about his faith. Had he tried to preach in open meetings, the religious police would have arrested him. John, who had a good command of the French language, translated for us during our stay.

We toured a medical clinic World Vision had established together with a Swiss organization, where one doctor was attempting to treat 3,000 people. Sick patients and mothers with babies sat in the dust, shaded by a big tarp, waiting to be treated.

John and I and a couple of the other guys were invited by Dr. Engstrom to join him in meeting with some government officials. First we met with the American Ambassador to Mauritania, a very nice gentleman. I wondered what infraction he had committed to be assigned to this grimy outpost on the planet. Next we met with the Secretary of Health for Mauritania, a very well fed man, who pretended he only understood Arabic. His aide, who spoke several languages very well, transcribed the entire meeting. As John translated for Dr. Engstrom, the aide wrote notes first in French, and then he wrote backwards in Arabic under the line he had just written. When he was finished with the page, every other line was French or Arabic.

215

According To Me

After lunch in John and Stephanie's home, we drove south across the desert in two Land Rovers. Other than a herd of wild camels, we saw nothing but sand in all directions. Every 20 miles or so, we had to stop at military checkpoints and explain what we were doing and where we were going. It got really interesting when we crossed the border to Senegal. Our visas, which were single entry visas, had already been utilized when we landed in Dakar. It took an hour or two to get new visas, this time with multiple entries since we were going to Mali and returning again to Senegal.

Overcoming that debacle, we continued on to St. Louis, a city on the coast, where we stayed overnight. The accommodations were better than they had been in Nouakchott the night before and there was a decent restaurant in the hotel. Some people ordered frog legs, a French delicacy. I've had frog legs in the past and I didn't care for them so, luckily, I didn't order them. The frog eaters suffered from food poisoning all night, but recuperated the next day.

Our next stop was a village further south where WVI was teaching the people to grow vegetables. It was amazing to see. There were several acres with beautiful cabbages, beans, carrots, etc., growing right out of the sand. It was the best vegetable garden that I have seen in Africa. The people were diligent in keeping the weeds out and made sure that every plant was fed and watered. It was truly a community project where everybody gave a helping hand to make it a successful project.

Returning to Dakar in the evening we attended a party with dignitaries, from several West Africa countries, who were there to meet with Dr. Engstrom. It was a real pleasure to partake of the exotic foods and mingle with influential Africans who professed an interest in helping their fellow man.

The following day we took a ferry to Goree Island, just off the coast from Dakar, where thousands of slaves once waited to be loaded on ships bound for America. Conditions on the island were crowded and primitive, but nothing compared to what awaited them aboard the ships. Animals were never treated so poorly. No wonder a lot of them died.

Our next destination was the country of Mali. We flew in to Bamako, the capitol and met and dined with the people from Mission Aviation Fellowship, who were going to provide our transportation in this landlocked, god forsaken desert nation with nothing but sand as far as the eye could see.

I had heard about Mission Aviation Fellowship (MAF), but knew little about them. Missionaries and pilots, they are sent to remote areas of the world where they fly planes transporting people and goods to hard to reach places. Facing a host of challenges like tropical diseases and dangerous flying weather, not to mention homesickness and separation from loved ones, they serve for four years before returning home to recharge mentally, physically and spiritually. During their year on furlough they travel around the country raising support for their stint in the mission field. One of the pilots told me that, having raised the required support and returning to the field, they might receive a questionnaire from one of the churches or service groups who had agreed to monthly support. If their answers weren't satisfactory their support could be cut off. Traveling around the country raising support must be grueling, but having desperately needed funds cut off in midstream would be devastating indeed.

MAF had two airplanes at our disposal, both single engine Cessnas. One was a six-seat 210 with retractable gear. The other was a much bigger plane called a Caravan that could carry a very large load. When they found out that I held a pilot's license I was allowed to take the controls on the 210 airplane.

The next morning we flew to Timbuktu, located on the southern part of the Sahara desert, about 8 miles from the Niger River. I had, of course, heard about Timbuktu, a place most people refer to as being so far away as to be almost unreachable and that few realize really exists. It does exist and is actually a good size town, considering where it is located. For centuries it had been an oasis that, growing into a city, reached its peak during the fourteenth century. Since then it has declined in importance.

We stayed at a hotel on the outskirts of town that was built in a large quadrangle with St. Augustine grass in the courtyard. That was the only green I saw in Mali. Looking out the front door, all I could see was sand. Camels were lying around, chewing their cud, and people wandered around dressed in long robes and enormous turbans. Most of them wore sunglasses so you couldn't see their eyes. Standing there, gazing at the mesmerizing landscape, a young man came over and offered to sell me the decorated spear he had in his hand. Claiming he had the best deal in the world, he told me the price was $ 130.00. I told him that he was out of his mind. I met him again the next morning when we were leaving to go to the airport and was able to barter him down a bit, but not enough. I knew that he would come down further.

In the evening, we hired a car to take us into town to meet a young missionary family. Arriving at a small mud hut with a sand floor, we were greeted by a man and his wife and their two small children. There were no chairs so we sat outside in the sand. His name was Nouh AF Infa Yatara. With one of the pilots translating, he told us his story.

Nouh was the son of a nomadic, Muslim man who had four wives. As a child he had been told that white people liked to catch little nomadic children and eat them. Mr. Marshall, a white missionary living in Timbuktu, had a garden with many kinds of vegetables. One day Nouh and a couple of his friends decided to go into the garden to steal some carrots. They had done it before and figured that they wouldn't get caught because they could run fast. But this time the missionary grabbed Nouh, who was scared stiff and thought he was going to be eaten. Instead, the missionary gave him the carrots and also some cards with Bible verses printed on them. He told Nouh that if he read and memorized the verses, he would give him a ballpoint pen. He learned the verses, became convinced that Jesus is real and accepted Him as his savior. The next time he saw the missionary he recited the verses he had memorized, and Mr. Marshall gave him the ballpoint pen.

Finding out that he had been to the missionary, Nouh's teacher and parents beat him severely, but he refused to deny his newfound faith.

His mother, desperate because her standing in the community was in jeopardy, decided to kill him. Lacing his food with poison, she gave it to him and he ate, but nothing happened. His brother, however, ate a few bites and became gravely ill and is still partially paralyzed. Seeing God's intervention, the family and the town's people were afraid to make further attempts on his life, but condemned him as an outcast. His father threw him out of the house.

Mr. Marshall, fearing that taking Nouh into his home would put his life in danger, gave him a Bible and a few books about people who had suffered for their faith and sent him to Dakar to study at a seminary. He studied diligently for a few years and decided to become a messenger of the Good News to his own people in the desert.

Dr. Engstrom asked if there was anything he needed. Nouh said that walking around out in the hot, burning sand was a little difficult. Dr. Engstrom asked if a bicycle would help, but Nouh said a donkey would be a lot better means of transportation. When he told us that he could buy one for about $40.00 we all dug in our pockets and collected the money. I imagine he is still riding his donkey.

The following day we flew east to Menaka, a city near the Niger border on the edge of the Sahara desert. People live in houses made of mud with sand floors. When the sand gets a little uneven, they use a little rake to level it again. When it rains, once in a blue moon, and the mud gets washed off the house, they just apply another layer. As you can imagine, it is a very hot and dusty place.

We were met by a WVI worker who led us to an aid station where they provided nourishment to starving people. These people were all destitute. Tears came to my eyes when we saw a small boy who was only skin and bones. They said he was 12 years old but he didn't look older than five. The lady said that when they found him they thought at first that he was dead but, noticing slight movement, they brought him to the aid station and nursed him back to life. But I fear that the damage he'd suffered affected his health for the rest of his life.

For lunch we were driven about an hour further east to a place where Touaregs, a nomadic tribal people, had laid a table for us in the desert. Under the shade of tarps we were served a whole roasted lamb that we tore apart with our fingers. They also served couscous out of a five-gallon bucket.

We returned to Menaka just in time to climb into the Cessnas for our flight back to Timbuktu. According to Mali flight rules we had to get off the ground in time to reach our destination before dark.

My friend with the spear was waiting for me when we got back to the hotel. I had to disappoint him again, telling him that his price was still way too high, but I told him I would see him in the morning.

As we were leaving for the airport, I gave him my final offer of $13.00 and told him to take or leave it. With the saddest expression you've ever seen he took my money and gave me the spear. I didn't feel too sorry for him, though. I didn't force him to sell it to me, and he has probably sold lots of those spears, at exorbitant prices, to sucker tourists. I walked away with a grand souvenir from that enchanted place.

Flying back to the States, we stopped over in Paris. Three of us took advantage of the time and toured the city for four hours. We visited the Notre Dame Cathedral and ran through the Louvre museum in twenty minutes, stopping briefly for a superficial glance of the Mona Lisa and the Venus de Milo. I can't understand how someone without any arms could be considered to be the goddess of love! We walked up the Champs Elysees to the Arch de Triumph and even had some refreshments at a sidewalk café. I've heard that the French can be unpleasant, especially to Americans, but I don't believe it. I found them all to be very nice.

SOUTH AFRICA

I met Neil Pagard in 1994 at a dinner party that I attended by myself because May-Britt was still in California. We were seated at tables for four. Introducing ourselves, Neil told me his name and I said that it sounded Danish. It was and, after comparing notes, I learned that I had gone to school in Denmark with some of his cousins. Small world!

His parents had come to America when they were young and Neil was born in Los Angeles. While he was still very young the family returned to Denmark but didn't stay very long. Neil's parents had become Christians in America and felt called to be missionaries. They were soon on their way to Swaziland in southern Africa. Neil grew up in Swaziland, attended boarding school in Durban, South Africa, and college at Fuller Seminary in Pasadena, California, before returning to South Africa as an adult where he was, among other things, a missionary/pastor. Now retired, Neil divides his time between his home in Colorado Springs and his home in Greytown, South Africa. Fifteen years prior to our meeting Neil and his wife were involved in a terrible auto accident and his wife suffered severe brain damage and was being cared for in a nursing home in Greytown. Although she seldom recognized him, Neil visited her daily when he was in South Africa. Their daughter, Colleen, lives there and Neil has a wonderful relationship with her. She, too, is a lay pastor in the Anglican Church in Greytown.

Neil and I became great friends and often got together for lunch or dinner. Both culinary adventurers, one of our favorite meals is sushi. He told me a lot about the beauty of South Africa. The greatest place to visit, he told me, is Kruger National Park where you drive around and observe all the wild animals in their natural habitat. The more he told me the more interested I became. Not that it takes much to spark my interest and desire to go to new places! Neil said he would be delighted if we came to visit. We made plans for a trip in March 2004 but, for reasons I no longer remember, May-Britt was detained and I made the trip on my own.

After a grueling trip with a twelve-hour layover in Frankfurt, followed by an interminably long flight to Johannesburg and a three-hour layover, I finally landed in Krueger where I was to meet Neil and his daughter, Colleen. Wanting to make a good impression I had bought a small bouquet of flowers in Johannesburg. By the time I could hand them over to Colleen they had, of course, wilted, but it's the thought that counts.

Driving about an hour from the airport we arrived at the park entrance and saw, waiting on the other side, a large herd of Impala and a group of Baboons. I was already excited. Entering the rest camp was like coming into a traditional African village with round, thatched huts arranged near a watering hole. Everything was modern, though, with each cabin outfitted with a private bathroom. We had a wonderful dinner and then I retired, completely exhausted, to my cabin. Five thirty the next morning Neil was banging on my door telling me to hurry up, "We don't want to miss the window!" The animals were most active before nine o'clock and he didn't want me to miss a thing. We had just driven through the camp gate when we encountered a large elephant meandering down the road. Cautiously Neil followed at a safe distance. He didn't want to antagonize the animal by trying to pass it. Elephants can be unpredictable and

have been known to attack cars. Eventually the elephant turned off into the bush and we continued on our way.

It had been raining for a few days and the animals were kind of docile. We didn't see lions for a couple of days. When the weather improved we saw more animals. One day we spotted a herd of Cape buffalo coming over a rise towards the road where we were parked. As we waited, the herd became larger and larger, moving down the hill and crossing the road right in front of us. There must have been about 400 animals. It was an extraordinary sight.

Every day followed the same pattern. Leaving early in the morning to "catch the window," we drove around the park looking for animals. Around nine o'clock we'd park near a lake filled with hippos or crocodiles and have coffee and rusk, a very dry crumpet that we dipped in the coffee. Half an hour later we would be on the road again. Around noon we'd stop at a picnic area and Colleen would rent a propane tank with a 2-foot pipe attached to the top of it. On the end of the pipe was a disk about 2 feet in diameter. This was the grill upon which she made fabulous lunches every day. I marveled at how she had planned everything food wise for the entire trip. One day she even prepared lamb chops for us. At every picnic area little, gray monkeys tried to steal our food, driving Neil wild. It all made for an amusing and enjoyable time.

Neil had impressed on me the dangers of being outside the car when we were in the park. We hardly dared to step outside to take a leak for fear of getting attacked by a lion or a leopard. One day after stopping at a rest camp to pick up supplies, we saw two guys on bicycles with rifles tied to the crossbar. I told Neil to stop; I wanted to talk with those brave individuals. Something didn't add up for me. Here we were among all these very dangerous animals, afraid to even get out of the car, and these guys were on bicycles. They told us that they were park rangers looking for poachers and illegal aliens coming over from Mozambique and that they had everything under control. Later,

on a night safari with a guide, I mentioned the rangers we had met. He told me that they call them "meals on wheels!"

After six amazing days we left Krueger and went to Neil and Colleen's home in Greytown. On the way we drove through Swaziland where Neil had grown up. A very poor country, Swaziland is run by a young dictator who calls himself a king. Every year he takes an additional wife from a different part of the country. At this writing he has about 15 wives. We spent the night in Mbabane, the country's capital, in a very nice bed and breakfast. The next day we went to the southern part of the country, to the mission station where Neil had spent so many years and where his mother is buried. Wanting to show us her grave we drove up to the graveyard that was totally overgrown with weeds. A little wary of snakes possibly lurking among the weeds we picked our way around the graveyard and eventually located Mrs. Pagaard's grave. After our visit, Neil hired some people to clean up the graveyard and cut the weeds.

Arriving at Neil's home, we spent one day just relaxing. But there wasn't time to just lounge around for long. Colleen and her husband, Wally Slatter, own a wonderful animal preserve, located on thousands of acres with a magnificent lodge and comfortable accommodations.   Neil and I spent a couple days in this blissful place. He took me around the preserve to view the many different animals, like wildebeests and other kinds of antelopes.

We spent my last week in South Africa in Durban, a beautiful city located on the Indian Ocean. Neil took me to a crocodile farm where they raise thousands of crocodiles for their hide. Crocodile leather is very beautiful and desirable for purses, shoes and coats. We had a delectable lunch in the restaurant there on the premises. Crocodile. Tastes like chicken!

Later we went to Shakaland Zulu Cultural Village where we learned some of the traditions of the Zulu and of their violent past.   Shaka, born in the late eighteenth century, ruled over 250,000 people. His ten-year reign has been noted for reform and innovation but condemned for brutality. With an army of over 50,000 soldiers he is said to have killed more than 2,000,000 people. At Shakaland we saw a reenactment of how they used to prepare for war. The old chief, Shaka, who looked to be at least 80 years old, walked back and forth in front of his warriors and encouraged them to go on the warpath and be brave. It was a great show with dances from both men and women, and afterwards we were invited to the restaurant for a very fine lunch, as good as I have had anywhere.

Three weeks flew by all too fast and it was time to leave my good friend and return home. We celebrated our last night together by going to a Japanese restaurant for a fine sushi dinner. We have gone for sushi many times but this was a little more than our usual fare. When May-Britt and I go out to eat we don't want to sit where we can see the kitchen. Here we were sitting in the kitchen, watching as the cook prepared the delicacies.

The next morning I began the long, grueling flight home with the dreadful 12-hour layover in Frankfurt again.

According To Me

Mercy Ships

The "Caribbean Mercy"

I met Larry Ott, a representative for Mercy Ships Ministry, shortly after coming to Colorado Springs. Started by Don and Deyon Stephens in 1977, Mercy Ships provides medical services in third world countries. When I met Larry the ministry had two ships. One was the Anastasis, serving West Africa, and the other was the Caribbean Mercy, serving Central America. Both hospital ships preformed thousands of free operations on patients who were too poor to pay. Larry showed me pictures of people in Africa grossly disfigured by enormous tumors that, without proper medical treatment, would eventually kill them. The Caribbean Mercy was primarily an eye clinic. The ships would come in to a port, tie up to the dock and stay there for five months and then move on to another location. Both ships set up dental clinics on land, where dentists and their assistants provided dental care for thousands of people.

Knowing that I enjoyed traveling, Larry asked if I would like to accompany him to Guatemala to visit the ship, which was docked at Puerto Barrios on the Caribbean Ocean. I decided that would be interesting so, in April 1997, Larry and I flew to Guatemala City. We stayed over night in a nice hotel and the following day took a bus to Puerto Barrios, a three-hour ride through the country.

The Caribbean Mercy was a relatively small ship with only one operating room for eye surgery and a few beds for patients needing to stay over night. I witnessed one eye operation. The surgeon had a microscope with three sets of lenses, so that people could observe the operation. Using very fine tools, and

226

with incredibly steady hands, the surgeon looked through the microscope and very skillfully cut open one side of the eyeball and removed the opaque cornea, which was causing the blindness. He then inserted a little plastic lens and the patient could see again. I was very impressed by what I saw. In America an operation like that would cost thousands of dollars, but on Caribbean Mercy it was performed free of charge to the patient. I heard a story about a grandmother who lived in the mountains and had been blind for years. Her family heard about this wonderful white ship with doctors who made blind people see again. Her 12-year old grandson, whom she had never seen, guided her for two days to the ship where the doctor replaced her corneas with a new lens and she saw her grandson's face for the first time.

We had breakfast, lunch and sometimes dinner on the ship. At every meal we were accompanied by different crewmembers that explained the diverse functions on the ship. On Thursday evening we gathered in the big lounge for church service. Speakers come from all over the world to encourage the crew and medical personnel in their work.

Although I found my visit on the Caribbean Mercy both interesting and worthwhile it was not as touching as the trip I would make a few years later on the Anastasis.

THE "ANASTASIS"

Nearly five years passed and I couldn't forget my experience with the Caribbean Mercy. I decided that I would like to return and help out for a couple of weeks. Larry suggested that I come to Africa and work on the Anastasis. I told him that I wasn't really that crazy about Africa; the trip with Dr. Engstrom had left me with an aversion to that continent. I had done a lot of work in Mexico and I liked the Hispanics and felt that I would rather go to Central America. But Larry persisted, arguing that he and his wife would also be on the ship, and I was persuaded.

The Anastasis was in The Gambia, a narrow, finger-like country that borders the Gambia River for a couple of hundred miles, splitting Senegal. I decided that I would be on the ship for ten days, a plan that at first seemed to meet the approval of Mercy Ships. I had acquired the visa, paid for the plane ticket and was ready to go, when I got a call from one of the officials at the head office in Lindale, Texas who explained that since I was only going to be on the ship for ten days, they couldn't use me, their minimum requirement was two weeks. I called Robyn Balcom, a lady on the ship that I had been in contact with by phone. I explained that I had all my travel papers in order but had just been told I couldn't come. "You just come on down," Robyn told me. Apparently she had the authority to make that decision, and I was grateful indeed.

On my layover in Denver, I called May-Britt to talk with her one last time before leaving the country. She informed me that Larry had just called her from Africa. He and a group of people from Jersey Island were remodeling a school and he wondered if I could buy six tool bags and bring them with me. I told May-Britt that since I had a couple of day's layover in England, I would go to London and try to find them there.

The morning after I arrived in England, I rode the train up to London to look for the requested tool bags. Getting off the train, I walked the streets for a while but found that I was in a residential area and decided to take one of those double-decker busses. Sitting on the upper level I had a great view as we drove along the streets of London. I changed busses several times, sometimes because the one I was on came to the end of its route and I had to get off and find another one. Eventually, after a couple of hours of my adventure, I spotted a hardware store. I jumped off the bus and ran across the street, only to find out they didn't have the bags, but they did direct me to another store a few blocks away and told me to try my luck there. The store turned out to be a miniature Home Depot. They had the bags and I was very happy that I could fulfill my responsibility to Mercy Ships.

The next day I boarded the plane to Banjul. Su Jin Lee, the Chief Operation Officer onboard the Anastasis, met me at the airport. Su Jin, a Chinese gentleman from Singapore, and I became good friends. He is now back in Singapore with his family and I wish that I could have an opportunity to go there and visit him.

I thought that, since I was going to be among Missionaries, I would be drinking lemonade and water. I was pleasantly surprised when, on the way to the ship, Su Jin told me that we were going to stop at a Chinese restaurant for dinner. There I met the Captain and his wife, the Chief engineer and a couple of other people and they were all enjoying a beer. I thought to myself that I was really going to like this place.

One of the first people I met when I came onboard was Dr. Gary Parker, Chief Medical Officer, whom I found awe-inspiring. Dr. Parker is a facial maxilla surgeon and has given his life to help the destitute of Africa. He had graduated from the University of Southern California, worked for seven years at a hospital in England and, hearing about the Anastasis, decided to donate some of his time. Seeing the misery the people in West Africa endured, he decided that his life's work was going to make their existence more tolerable. He met his wife, Susan, on the ship. She claims seniority, having been there two weeks longer than him. They have now served onboard for 22 years and have two children, who are going to school on the ship together with 25-30 other children who are kind of in the same boat as they are.

Since I wasn't to do any work during my ten-day stay, a detailed program had been planned for my benefit. The first morning I was told that I was to spend some time in the operating room with Dr. Gary. They asked me if I thought I could handle it. I said that I would try. If it got to be too much, I would just leave.

ACCORDING TO ME

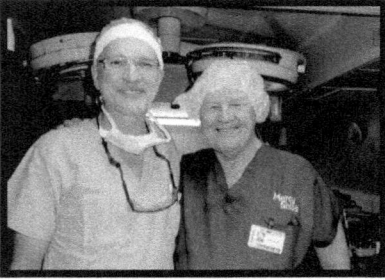

Dressed in sterile clothing from head to toe, I entered Dr. Gary's domain. He had 12-year-old boy on the operating table, out cold. The poor kid had been mauled by a hyena a couple of years earlier, and his right eye was missing. The right side of his face was caved in, the right ear was gone and he had a very large scar on top of his head. Dr. Gary was going to repair as much as he could of it.

He told the nurse and me that he would begin by harvesting a rib. He opened up the boy's ribcage and cut out one of the bones. As he showed me the rib, he told me that whenever I went to the Outback Restaurant, I would think of him. He has a great sense of humor. He told me that since he didn't completely sever the membrane around the bone, the rib would regenerate it self in six months. That, I thought, was really amazing. It explains why men are not missing a rib, even though God took one from Adam to make Eve. He then split the bone and put half of it above the eye and the other below to build up the child's facial structure. There was a box full of artificial brown eyes of different shades and he found one that matched the boy's good eye. Then he blew me away. He cut open the kid's scalp from front to back, loosening it from ear to ear. He installed two balloons and sewed the scalp together again. Dr. Parker told me that the balloons would be inflated a little at a time every few days and that in a month's time, the kid would be about four inches taller. Then he would remove the balloons and be able to use the excess skin to eliminate the scar tissue. A few days later I asked how the boy was doing. I was asked to take him up on deck and play with him, because he was running wild in the patient ward. I found a soccer ball and we kicked it around for a while. I got a little scared when he stumbled and fell once, but he was fine. It felt good to be able to help a little.

230

A couple of days later Su Jin told me that we were going on an all-day outing. After breakfast we climbed into a Zodiac speedboat and crossed to the other side of the inlet, a couple of miles away. Since there was no dock we had to wade to shore. There were some young men who offered to carry us to land. Su Jin accepted the offer and laughingly told me later that the guy carried him like a baby. There was no way that I was going to let anybody carry my 200+ pounds over the water. I was afraid he would drop me and ruin my camera.

After visiting briefly with some ladies and observing one of them teaching Bible to a bunch of small kids, we took a car to a village miles away in the bush. One of the men from Mercy Ships was holding a class for the men, teaching them about sanitation. Drawing on a white board, he showed them how to make a latrine for the village by digging a deep hole in the ground and building a hut over it. Apparently they used the bushes for their natural functions. The instructor told them that if the village grew to a thousand people, it would become a terrible health hazard.

At noon four ladies appeared, each carrying vats of food. We were five people from Mercy Ships and we got one of the vats. It was filled with some kind of rice or millet with peanut gravy on it. There were no utensils, so we dug into it with our fingers. It tasted fine but, as I always say when I tell this story, it was cooked in a village with no sanitation.

Ingvar Haraldsson was the leader of the advance team, which visited the country months before the ship would come in, making all the necessary arrangements. They secured a place for the ship to dock for five months, arranged for the necessary security and for supplies and water to be delivered to the ship. Ingvar is Swedish and we hit it off from the very beginning and went out to dinner together several times.

Su Jin asked me Saturday evening if I would go with him to church the next morning, to which I readily agreed. He warned me that the service was four hours long but, he promised, it never seemed that long. The church was a building that looked like it had been haphazardly enlarged several times, with tree trunks holding up the beams for the corrugated metal roof. There were probably 400 people in the congregation. A dozen ladies were up front singing praise songs accompanied by a keyboardist and a drummer. They sang in English since The Gambia is an old English colony and English is the official language. The music went on for over an hour with the drummer beating his heart out to the point that I figured that he was going to beat a hole in one of the drums. After a while he became tired and another guy took over.

A women's conference had been going on during the week and the keynote speaker stepped up to the podium. Originally from Philadelphia, she had served as a missionary in Dakar, Senegal. She spoke for almost an hour, concluding the conference. Included in her recommendations, she told the ladies not to be doormats for their husbands, but be assertive in their lives and strive for independence. Good advise, but I wondered how it would work in that society.

When the lady stepped down, the pastor came up and gave his sermon, followed by another preacher from Guinea, who only spoke French. The pastor decided that he would translate for him, but as the sermon went on, the pastor realized that he didn't know French well enough, and one of the congregants was pressed into service.

After three different speakers I thought the service was about to conclude. But oh, no! Every lady, who had anything to do with the women's conference was recognized and called up on the stage, complimented, and given hugs and kisses and bouquets of flowers. I must say that, though I really enjoyed the service, it did seem at least four hours long.

Several of us were invited on a boat ride on the Gambia River one day. We sailed for several hours upstream and came to the village where Alex Haley, who wrote the book "Roots," had many distant relatives. These people knew the story of Roots and reenacted some of it for us. For centuries people from this area had been captured and enslaved. On the way back down the river we stopped at an island, which had been a holding station for slaves waiting for the next slave ship to come for its wretched cargo.

One of the last nights on the ship I invited Robyn, Paula Kirby, a lady I had become good friends with, and Dominique, the director of the dental clinic for a nice dinner. Of course I didn't know where to go so, telling them that I wanted to take them to the best place in Banjul, I let them pick the place. And boy, did they! It was a fabulous place where they grew all the food they served. It was a French cuisine and we had a scrumptious meal. When I was presented with the bill, which was twice as much as I expected it to be, Robyn, that rascal, looked at me with a smirk on her face and said, "You don't have enough money to pay for this, do you?" She was right, of course. She knew how much money I had because she handled the currency exchanges. For some reason I could only exchange a few dollars at a time and I couldn't use a credit card in The Gambia. Thankfully, between the two of us, we had enough to cover the tab. I paid her back the next day.

Robyn told me that she and her husband, Perry, and their three kids would soon be moving back to the United States. I invited them to come to Colorado, if they had a chance. A few months later Robyn arrived at our house with her oldest son. We were all invited for the weekend to Don Stephens' home in Cimarron, Colorado, where we met Lord Ian and Lady Jean McColl from England. Lord McColl sits in the Upper House of Parliament in London and was Prime Minister John Major's personal doctor. Both McColls are surgeons and spend between 3 - 6 months every year on a Mercy ship.

Perry arrived a few days later with the rest of the family and they stayed our home for two weeks. In fact, we went to Sweden while they were still in our house. We just told them to lock the door when they left! They have become wonderful friends and have visited us several times since.

According To Me

The "Africa Mercy"

Shortly before the turn of the century a lady in Scotland donated six million dollars to Mercy Ships to buy one of the retired Danish ferries to be converted into a new hospital ship. The ferry was built in 1980 and was put into service to carry railroad cars between the islands in Denmark. It was 500 feet long with a displacement of 16,500 tons. After the purchase, it was sailed over to Newcastle, England, and put in dry dock, where it remained for eight years. Returning from The Gambia in 1988, Larry Ott took me to see it at the shipyard. They had only just begun to rip everything out before the remodeling could begin. Over the years I received progress reports, but there were times when I wondered if the project would ever see completion.

But in late 2005 I received a letter with an invitation to the commissioning of the new Mercy Ship, which was to be christened "Africa Mercy." I was so excited and honored that my presence was requested at that exceedingly auspicious occasion. The commissioning was to be in London in early April 2006. May-Britt and I decided to make our annual trip to Sweden early that year. We flew to London where May-Britt transferred to a plane to Gothenburg. I would join her later, after the ceremonies.

The ship was still in Newcastle undergoing the finishing details. There had been some discussions about sailing the ship to London for the commissioning, but it was determined that it would be too expensive. A better alternative was to transport everyone to Newcastle by train.

Early in the morning about 80 invitees arrived at the London railway station to board a First Class train, where we were treated to an English breakfast with all the trimmings.

234

Rolling through the English countryside I remembered that at one point in time this part of the country had belonged to Denmark. I don't remember how the Danes lost it, but they don't have it anymore. I spotted almost a dozen nuclear power plants, which I thought was interesting since there is such a strong opposition to them in America.

Arriving in Newcastle we boarded busses that drove us the short distance to the harbor. It had been four years since I had seen the ship that was now the Africa Mercy, a beautiful white hospital ship, ready to embark on her maiden voyage to the third world to perform wonderful healing to the poor and needy. Now serving West African countries, she is equipped with six state-of-the-art operating rooms and 100 hospital beds. A crew of 450 people, not including doctors and nurses, are required to keep everything running smoothly. Medical personnel, as well as crewmembers, are volunteers from over 40 countries who are required to provide their own support, paying $700 per month for room and board.

The ceremony and reception lasted several hours, with many speeches and recognition of people from diverse parts of the world. I saw a few of the friends I had met in The Gambia. Afterwards, we were taken back to the train where we were served a filet mignon dinner on our return trip to London.

The next day there was lunch at Kensington Palace and Lord McColl gave us a tour of the Houses of Parliament. In the evening we had a cocktail party and dinner in the spans of the London Tower Bridge. Again there were several speeches about the efforts of Mercy Ships and several people wrote out checks, one was for a million dollars.

Our last morning was spent cruising on the Thames to Greenwich Village. I spent the afternoon wandering around the city with a couple of friends and went back to the hotel and relaxed for the evening. The next morning I flew to Denmark to spend a week with my relatives, before continuing on to Sweden.

According To Me

There were very few people on the plane and I was assigned to a seat next to an older couple that weren't very friendly. I noticed that there was no one sitting in the emergency door row so, when they closed the door, I moved up and took one of those seats, not realizing that it was actually business class. There were three flight attendants, one man and two women. They were looking at me and conferring with each other. After a while the male attendant came and told me that, although I had not paid for that seat I would be allowed to stay there. I would, however, not be served any food. I thanked him and told him that I had eaten breakfast and wasn't hungry.

As the plane began to taxi, one of the young female attendants came and sat in the seat next to me. We began a to talk and she told me that she had been a psychology student, but was now taking a break. I told her a little about what I was doing and asked her about her life in general. She said she wasn't dating anyone, because in this kind of work there weren't many opportunities. "Well, what about all the guys working on the plane?" I asked her. "They are all gay and not interested," she informed me.

When we reached flying altitude she got up to resume her work. In a little while her colleague brought me a food tray. I told her that I wasn't supposed to have it, but she said to just go ahead and take it. After a while my little friend came by and asked how I was doing. I told her that I was as happy as a pig in mud. She said she wasn't allowed to offer me a drink, but if I asked her for one, she would give it to me. I gave her my biggest smile and asked for a beer, which she promptly provided.

As we were making our descent into Copenhagen, she came back to sit down next to me. I told her that she had observed a psychological lesson. "Which one?" she wondered. "It's easier to ask for forgiveness rather than permission!" I answered. She got a big laugh out of that.

For more information about Mercy Ships,
visit their website at www.mercyships.org

236

MISSION TRIPS

BRAZIL

Dan Williams, my son's father-in-law, invited me to go along to Brazil on a 10-day construction-missionary trip. I met Dan and the rest of the group, men and women of all ages, at the Atlanta airport. It was going to be a rough trip. The oldest in our group was a lady that was nearly 80 years old and she almost died before we got her home again.

Arriving in Natal, a coastal town in Northeastern Brazil, we were loaded into vans and driven to a missionary home, which also served as a school and church. The lower level of the building was a large room with several pew-like wooden benches. Several of the men, obviously more initiated than I, were quick to shove two of them together, forming a platform for their air mattresses. Not having so much forethought I had not packed an air mattress. Looking around I found some thin mats and, with no more pews available, laid them on the concrete floor. Upstairs there was an apartment with several bedrooms furnished with real beds but, chivalrous as we are, we let the women sleep there.

It was a miserable first night. My mats were not enough to protect me from the hard concrete floor and I hurt all over. Later I was able to find a few more mats that made my nights slightly more bearable. Not only was my bed excruciatingly hard, the noise level took some getting used to, with the snoring of a dozen men and the noise of the busy boulevard just outside. Early in the morning somebody would drive by making loud announcements over a loudspeaker.

237

ACCORDING TO ME

We weren't there to sleep and, thankfully, our days began early. We woke at 6am and showered. There was no hot water but the climate was so warm, the cold water was refreshing. Breakfast was served at 7am, so we could be ready to get into a couple of taxis at 7:30 and be on the job site at 8am, where we would toil till 5pm.

Our task was to begin construction on a 2-story school building behind a small church. We also removed the roofing tile from the church building in order to strengthen the rafters. The man in charge was a remodeling contractor from Indianapolis. He was a very committed Christian and had been to Brazil numerous times doing construction work. He was a very pleasant person, but as time went on, I became more and more disenchanted with his management of the project. It was a difficult job and he managed to make it even more complicated. I made a few suggestions but they did not fall on good ground, so I just went along with his program and kept my mouth shut. Rather than go into great detail, suffice it to say that I will never go on another missionary construction program again.

CUBA

Although my first missionary experience was a disappointment, to say the least, I longed for a travel experience where I could meet and interact with the people in the countries I visited. I've been all over the world but mostly as a tourist.

I first met John Maisel, and heard him speak, at a High Ground Ski Conference in Beaver Creek, Colorado in February of 2003. President of East-West Ministries, John is a spellbinding orator. Introducing myself after his talk, I asked if he ever came to Colorado Springs and, if he did, would he have dinner with my wife and me. He called me some time later saying that he would be in the Springs in a couple of days and we arranged to meet at an Outback Steakhouse for dinner.

We had a great time getting better acquainted with each other. John brought along a big folder with information about East-West ministries. They form short-term missionary teams to all the former Iron Curtain countries, including Cuba, telling people about Jesus Christ and His plan of salvation.

I had never been on that type of missionary trip, in fact I had never really witnessed to anybody, but doing a trip to Cuba fascinated me. Under sanctions from the U.S., Americans are not supposed to go there. I have to admit that the illicitness added to the attraction of the idea.

John sent me the application a few days later and I filled it out and sent it in along with a couple of passport pictures. On June 6, 2003 I boarded an airplane and flew to Cancun, Mexico, where I met up with the rest of the group of about 20 people. Although East-West has a letter of approval from the American government allowing them to go to Cuba as a humanitarian organization, it is still difficult to fly directly to Havanna. In Cancun, we purchased tickets to Havana and applied for visas to Cuba. Arriving in Cuba, the authorities stamped our visas but not our passports. When we left, they took our visas. So although I've now been to Castroland twice, I can't prove it.

One couple had trouble getting through customs in Havanna, having to explain why they had so much Christian literature and a whole suitcase of small gifts. When we finally got to the hotel, it was very late and we were all very tired. It felt good to go to bed. My roommate was quite unhappy. Whoever had unloaded the luggage had dropped his duffel bag in a puddle of water soaking most of its contents.

After breakfast the next morning we went back to the airport and boarded an old, Russian four-engine prop plane for Santiago at the east end of the island. It reminded me of the plane we flew to America on in 1951, however this plane had not aged well. It was truly a rattletrap, but it got us there safely.

According To Me

In Santiago we boarded a bus to Guantanamo City, near the American base. We had been admonished not to talk about politics or about the conditions in Cuba with our translators. We were also told not to mention that we were affiliated with East-West Ministries. John had once been caught preaching and handing out tracts on the streets of Havana. He was arrested, deported and told never to return, and East-West Ministries was blacklisted in Cuba.

We stayed in the Guantanamo City Hotel and took a bus every day to our host church in a village east of town. There we were paired up with a translator and a guide. Our translators were wonderful people. I was paired with a young man named Jose, who was studying to be a pastor. A young lady from the church was our guide in the village. I had never really witnessed to anybody before and was getting increasingly nervous. I had a little tract printed by East-West Ministries called, "May I ask you a question?" If I read through the tract I would pretty much cover all the points about the Plan of Salvation. We knocked on a door at the first house we came to and were greeted by a lady who invited us in. We exchanged pleasantries, I explained where I was from and that I had grown up in Denmark. I complimented her on her garden and said it reminded me of my mother's. Then I began reading from the tract and told her that we are all sinners that, were it not for our Lord Jesus Christ providing the supreme sacrifice, we would be bound for Hell. But now everyone who believes in Him can be saved. Jose was a very able translator for me and was a great help. Nearing the end of the tract, I asked the question, "Is there any reason that you cannot accept Christ as your Savior today?" To my great surprise and delight she said, "No." We told her that now that she had accepted the Lord, she was assured of her place in Heaven. Then I asked Jose to pray for her.

Crossing the street we came to a home where several people were gathered. After chatting for a little while, I went through the plan of salvation but they were not willing to give their lives to the Lord. I must have made a good impression on them though, because they filled my backpack with mangos and papayas when we were leaving. We stopped at a couple of other houses, but I don't remember that we had very much success. Coming back to the church I ate some of the wonderful fruit I had been given. They warned me to be careful with the mangoes, but I have always eaten a lot of fruit and I have a cast-iron stomach.

In the afternoon we went to a different location and I believe that a few more people accepted the Lord. Still, I felt very uncomfortable witnessing. Finished for the day we returned by bus to Guantanamo and to the Baptist church where we ate dinner every night. The pastor, a big and very black man named Marciano, was so friendly. Except for his color, he reminded me a lot of Earl Lee, our pastor in Pasadena. He used a lot of the same mannerism. One night there was a church service with close to 400 people attending. When the service was over, we all stood by the door and greeted the passing worshippers who bestowed God's blessings on us.

We were supposed to witness for four days, but on the forth morning, just as we were leaving, a government man showed up at the hotel, took our names and passport numbers and told us not to continue with our activities. We went to the church, where we learned that the pastor and our Cuban coordinator had been called to the government office.

We waited several hours for them to return and were wondering what was going to happen to us. Worst-case scenario would be a visit to the Cuban jail. We could also be deported, effective immediately. After a couple of hours Pastor Marciano and our coordinator returned and told us that we had to stop and that for the rest of our stay we would have to be regular tourists. After lunch we took the bus to a pavilion on top of a hill overlooking the American base at Guantanamo Bay. Looking through a telescope I tried to locate the area where the terrorist prisoners were held but it was difficult and I couldn't quite make it out.

The next morning, after a very severe scrutiny by security, we boarded the old, Russian plane bound for Havana. That evening at dinner we were discussing our experiences, but were reminded that we were still in Cuba and ought to be careful with our conversation. The next morning we flew back to Cancun and then home to the US. Reflecting on the journey, I was glad for the experience. I had stepped out of my comfort zone and witnessed about my faith. I didn't keep score of how many came to the Lord but He knows, and I pray that He will keep hold of them.

UGANDA

At the High Ground Ski Conference in February 2003, the same conference where I met John Maisell, I also met Bob Fischer from Rapid City, South Dakota. When the conference was over, Bob asked me if I could take him to Eagle airport. On the way he told me that he was going on a short-term missionary trip to Uganda. I, of course, found this tantalizing and told him that I would be very interested in coming along. He told me that he was traveling with a group from International Commission, located in Texas. (It seems that all the missionary organizations I am involved with are based in Texas.) Bob said that he would be glad to have me along and would send me an application. After filling it out and getting a recommendation from my pastor, I sent it in and was accepted for the trip.

I flew to Minneapolis on September 10, 2003, where I met Bob and a couple of other people. After a few hours' layover we boarded the flight to Amsterdam, where we met the rest of the group. We were now 35 people intent on going into the darkest part of Africa to save the lost.

Around the World in *Almost* 80 years

Arriving at Entebbe Airport gave me some feelings of foreboding thinking of the events of 1976 when brave Israeli commandos rescued over a hundred people taken hostage by Idi Amin, the brutal dictator of Uganda.

It should have taken us an hour to drive from Entebbe to Kampala, but the van ahead of us had a flat tire and we had to stop and help them. It was an ordeal, since they didn't have the equipment needed to change the tire. Tired after our long flight, we didn't appreciate the delay. We were hot and thirsty when we finally arrived at our hotel. It was not a bad hotel, but there were no elevators and Bob and I had to drag our luggage up four flights of stairs. That got the sweat rolling.

The next day, Saturday, we all went to the big Baptist Church in Kampala, which was full of people who had come to meet the foreigners whom they hoped would bring in new believers to their congregation. The service was nice, although long. We were paired off and assigned to our respective churches.

Bob and I were assigned to a church in a village called Kikandwa, about a one-hour drive northeast of Kampala. I was happy for that as it was much more pleasant than wandering around in the grimy city. On Sunday morning we piled on the busses that would take us to our respective locations. Driving through the city on the badly paved roads, dodging the many potholes, I was impressed by the scene I witnessed outside my window. There were people, cars and bicycles everywhere and I was worried that we would have an accident or run over somebody. It is amazing what they can pile on a bicycle. I saw one man riding along the road with a bedstead. Others lugged half a dozen 5-gallon cans full of water. There is no running water in the villages, so the people have to go to a well somewhere and fill their containers.

Bob and I arrived at the church an hour before the service was due to start. Precisely at ten o'clock, even though only a few people were present, a couple of guys began beating on bongo drums and a lady began to sing. Within fifteen minutes the church was full. The young pastor, Bruno Mkevezi, with his wife and two little boys, sat up front. One of the boys came over and crawled up in my lap. Delighted, I looked into his eyes that were gazing at my face, fascinated by my white skin.

Mrs. Mkevezi led the small choir in singing several songs. I recognized some of the melodies and it was interesting to hear them sung in the Ugandan language. Then Pastor Bruno stood and spoke for a little while. I heard him say my name and motion to me to come up on the platform. I had promised to give a sermon on our first Sunday and had spent quite some time preparing. I had five pages, which I decided that I would simply read, so as not to become totally discombobulated. The singer, Dorothy, joined me on the platform. She was going to be my translator. A schoolteacher, she spoke perfect English and together we muddled through my first experience of being an evangelist. At the end of my sermon, I gave an altar call and 13 people came forward to make their decisions for Christ. I had a Polaroid camera and took a picture of each one, giving it to them as a memento of the occasion.

After the service we went to a nearby house to have lunch that was prepared by three young ladies. Under a canopy of galvanized tin they built several small fires on the ground upon which they set their cooking pots. It was a very simple lunch, but certainly adequate. There were yams, fried bananas, mush made from millet and several other dishes. There was not much meat because the people are very poor and meat is too expensive. We ate lunch there every day and the girls always prepared many dishes.

After lunch it was time to go out to visit people. I was introduced to my translator for the week, a young lady by the name of Annit, who was a schoolteacher. One of the drummers, Peter, came with us. We visited 3-4 homes in the area, there wasn't time for more since my presentation and Annit writing down the names took close to an hour, but several people accepted the Lord.

Every day Annit and Peter led me around the countryside. There were no roads, only trails between the mud huts with roofs made of corrugated tin or palm fronds. Peter told me that he was a farmer, but the farming I saw was very primitive. Except for the highway that now crosses the country, little has changed in thousands of years. Still, I enjoyed being there, and felt very comfortable. I just loved the people.

Walking along the highway I noticed the tall termite stacks and commented on them. Peter told me that they eat termites. Being the culinary adventurer than I am I said that I wanted to try some. Peter collected a little package of leaves with termites and, when we got back for lunch, gave them to the girls who fried them in oil. When we all sat down at the table there was an extra dish, sautéed termite. Bob lost his appetite but I dug in to them and, together with my native friend, devoured the lot of them. They tasted sweet but I had to pick the legs out of my teeth afterwards.

When Sunday rolled around again we met at the Baptist Church to report on the results of the crusade. As Bob and I sat waiting for the service to begin, Pastor Bruce came over to us and asked us to go with him to visit his sick father. We felt that we should stay for the service, but he said that visiting his father was more important. One of his church members drove us to the house where his father and stepmother lived. Both were very pleasant people. As we were witnessing, some younger members of the family came in and we witnessed to them also. Both the father and the young people prayed to receive Christ. The stepmother, however, couldn't make up her mind. When she saw that her entire family had accepted Christ and she was the only one left, she also accepted Him as her savior. Feeling jubilant we left the house with an ecstatic and thankful Pastor Bruce.

245

ACCORDING TO ME

On the way to the airport the next day, we stopped at a flea market to buy some souvenirs and then relaxed at a park in Entebbe before heading to the airport for our evening flight. We had a long trip ahead of us but were thrilled and grateful for the experiences we'd had in what Churchill had referred to as the "Pearl of Africa."

SECOND MISSION TO CUBA

A couple of years later I went back to Cuba with East-West Ministries. This time we were on the west end of the island, in Pinar Del Rio, about a two and a half hour drive west of Havana. The hotel was a little better than in Guantanamo and the staff was friendlier, too, and gave us good service. Every morning after breakfast we met in a little church downtown, run by a young minister, Juan Carlos, with whom I became good friends. Juan Carlos had a heart for church planting and we drove out into the countryside where he had established small house churches with lay pastors.

As usual we were teams of two assigned to a house church and one of the parishioners would lead us to an area of town where they wanted us to witness to people. We had again been told not to discuss politics with our translators but two of them, disillusioned with the Cuban government, complained so loudly about the conditions in Cuba, that I was afraid we would all go to jail. One had been a government lawyer in an office with big windows overlooking the capitol square. He was fired when he became a Christian, I don't know what he does now.

Another had a soft drink business in Havana. He admitted that he watered down Coca Cola and added some sugar. As long it was cold, nobody complained. Somewhat overweight, he was

246

already under suspicion since it was assumed that anyone who could afford to eat that much, must have been doing something illegal.

He was the only one I met in Cuba who owned a car, all be it a '49 Plymouth. He had modified it by adding propane power, which was illegal. Propane is much cheaper than gasoline. He had the filler tube hidden in the trunk under the spare tire and some other junk. Inside he had a control lever so, if he saw the police as he was driving around town, he could quickly switch to gasoline. That way they couldn't smell the propane. He told us that in the cities every neighborhood has a commissar who keeps track of the comings and goings, and sends regular reports the secret police. What a country!

I was appalled by the abject poverty on the island. The people have next to nothing in the way of worldly goods. Typical of communist countries, everything is poor and run down. The buildings have not been maintained in 50 years. Every hurricane seems to hit the area twice. Passing over once, they bounce off the coast of Mexico and return again, destroying what they missed the first time. I remember one lady, who was living in a house destroyed by hurricanes. Her husband had run off leaving her and their three children destitute. She broke down in tears telling us about her situation.

After five days it was time to go back to Havana for a little sightseeing. Bob West, our leader, told us to be sure that we had all our papers in order for departure the next day. That's when I discovered that I was in big trouble. On my arrival to in Havana I had torn the tags off my suitcase and gotten rid of all the junk in my travel folder including, I now realized, my return ticket. Bob tried to get a copy of my ticket but was unsuccessful. Somewhat apprehensive, I arrived at the airport the next morning and had to pay $200 for another ticket to Cancun. I figure I got off easy; I would have paid a thousand for it! It is one of those experiences that you look back on and laugh at, but that certainly was no laughing matter at the time.

ACCORDING TO ME

SIERRA LEONE

In the spring of 2007 I was invited to return to Africa on a missionary trip to Sierra Leone with International Commission. We were a group of 22 individuals including my friend Bob Fischer from Rapid City, South Dakota. International Commission president, Rodney Cavett, and his wonderful wife, Debra, were also along. We all met at the Dallas airport and had an uneventful flight to London and continuing on to Freetown, Sierra Leone. The airport is located on an island a short ferry ride from the mainland. It was here the journey became eventful. The ferry was a real rust bucket and they piled on as many cars and people as they possibly could, and then some! Wary of pickpockets, I moved my wallet, passport and other valuables to my front pockets but I forgot about the small digital camera that I had on my belt. Disembarking among the throng of people, I was aware of someone rubbing against my arm a couple of times, but didn't pay any attention to it. All of a sudden a young kid ripped my camera off my belt and ran away. I took off after him screaming, "THIEF!" The Sierra Leonians reacted by hollering, too. A policeman actually caught the culprit who, of course, no longer had my camera. He probably passed it on to an accomplice in the crowd. It was a terrible thing to have happen right at the beginning of this great adventure, but fortunately Rodney had an extra camera that I could use for the duration of the trip. As it was, when Rodney sent out reports later the pictures he used were all mine since he downloaded them onto his computer and let me have the memory stick to take with me home for my own usage.

We stayed in a run down hotel the first night in downtown Freetown. Getting up early the next morning, we were served a simple breakfast while the hotel personnel loaded our luggage on

the roof of the bus that was going to take us across the country to an area called the Kono District. We boarded the bus, sitting as cozy as sardines in a can, and began to drive away only to discover that the luggage had been piled too high to clear the archway of the hotel portico. We all got off the bus and waited while the personnel removed the luggage from the roof, drove the bus outside the portico, and then reloaded the luggage. It was a long delay but finally we were on our way.

It took eight hours to make the 200-mile trip because the road was poor with crumbling asphalt and potholes. We were grateful when we finally arrived at our destination and drove into the gated courtyard of the hotel where we were going to stay for the next eight days. It was not a bad hotel, but there were not enough rooms to accommodate all of us the first night and extra beds had to be added to the already small rooms.

Dinner was served when we arrived and we were told to eat quickly because people were waiting for us outside. Stepping out into the street after our meal we were met by about 200 people holding large signs welcoming us and proclaiming the great International Commission Conference. When we had greeted as many as we could, we began marching down the street toward the church a mile away, singing and dancing to the beat of drums. I joined in with my usual enthusiasm. Although I couldn't join them in song, I could dance with the best of them, raising lots of dust as we proceeded up the dirt road.

By the time we arrived, the church was packed and we were asked to sit up front around the platform. I was sitting on a bench by the platform, together with some other people in our group, listening to the preacher when a little girl, about two and a half years old, stepped out of a door, walked right up to me and crawled up in my lap where she stayed for the duration of the service. There must be something about me that appeals to

African children, because I never saw any of them crawl up in anyone else's lap. At the end of the service we were called forward, one at a time, to meet people from the church we were assigned to for the week. When my name was called I took the little girl with me in my arms to meet my hosts, to the great delight of the congregation. After a while I set her down and she scurried off. I never found out whom she belonged to and I still wonder why, out of all the people in the congregation, she chose me to be her friend during that church service. I felt greatly honored.

Sunday morning, after breakfast, we were transported to our respective churches. I was teamed up with Julius Raines, an evangelist from the state of Georgia, who would become a dear friend of mine. The regular pastor, Teh, wasn't there, but a young pastor, John Kargbo from the central part of the country, performed the service. I was to deliver the sermon that morning and John was my translator. My sermon went ok. After several mission trips I'd become, if not proficient, at least more comfortable in the pulpit. Afterwards John asked me if I was a Baptist. I answered, "No, I am a Christian." John laughed! He thought that was the funniest thing he had heard in a long time. Baptists are, of course, also Christians, and I was traveling with a Baptist organization but I, myself, am nondenominational.

I was invited to lunch there at the church after the service. A terrible civil war, lasting 14 years, had finally ended just a couple years prior to our trip, leaving the people of Sierra Leone in extreme poverty. Lunch was a thin black soup enriched with only a little rice and fish, not very appetizing but I ate a small portion, not wanting to offend my hosts.

In the afternoon John and a couple of the church members took Julius and me to some homes to witness about the Lord and we had good results. Everybody we met made decisions for Christ.

We were supposed to be picked up by a van at five o'clock in the afternoon, but it never showed up. After waiting for an hour Julius and I decided to find our own way back. It was about five miles to the hotel so we began walking, accompanied by John, my translator, and several other people from the village. After a while one of the men, Isaac, took off running towards the main road, he had spotted some taxis. The first one already had two passengers so we climbed into the second taxi, but John and the taxi driver almost got into fisticuffs over the fee he wanted to charge. Third times the charm, we caught the next taxi, agreed with the driver on a fair price, and Julius, John, Isaac and I were delivered to the hotel in no time. John insisted on paying for the taxi, which took them back to the village.

We met at the church every morning at about eight o'clock. Pastor Teh, a small man, about 5'3" tall, had returned from wherever he had been on Monday morning. He was very excited about what we were doing and really wanted his church to grow. He was also quite proficient at English and was a good translator. Some of the homes we came to had 20 people waiting to listen to us. After witnessing to them, they would all accept Christ as their savior.

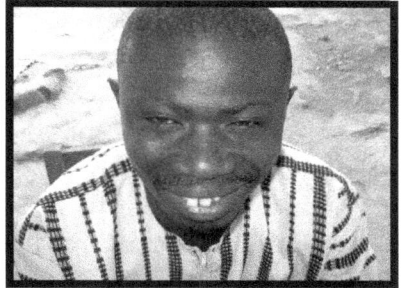

One morning Pastor Teh asked me if I would be able take a long walk. Confident that it would not be a problem, I answered, "Sure!" I think we walked about six miles, arriving at another village where a couple of hundred people were waiting outside of a medical clinic. John and I witnessed to a group in front of the clinic and Julius and Teh went behind the building where there were even larger groups. Everyone we spoke to made decisions for Christ. When we compared notes Julius had reached 200 and I had reached 90. We were excited about that harvest. Many of the people waiting outside that clinic bore witness of the atrocities committed during the war. I saw two men whose fingers had all been chopped off, and a woman who had lost both of her hands, not for anything they had done, only because they were in the wrong place at the wrong time.

We were finished around noon and began walking back to our village. The sun was now high in the sky and it was getting excruciatingly hot. By the time we were back at the church I was totally exhausted and looking for a place to rest. I pulled out one of the church benches to the shade and laid down on it. After a while Pastor Teh came with an old chaise lounge, which was much more comfortable, and I was out of commission for the rest of the afternoon. I'm not as young as I used to be.

During the week we spoke to a lot of people in many places. We met a couple of village chiefs, spoke to several hundred kids in a school, and even talked to a group of policemen. Many Muslims made decisions for Christ. The harvest was astonishing. At the end of the week 9,300 people had asked Christ to come onto their hearts and 500 asked to be baptized. Julius baptized forty people in a pond created by an abandoned diamond mine, while I stood on the shore taking pictures with my Polaroid camera, handing a picture to each believer as they came out of the water.

Sunday arrived again, all too soon, and we gathered at the main church for the Victory service. Once again, the place was packed and everyone was singing and dancing. Pastor Teh came over and dragged me into the crowd and we jumped around, too, for a while. There were several ladies that Julius and I had become acquainted with, who had laughed and joked and shared their food with us during the week. Now it was impossible to get a smile from them, they were so sad to see us leave, they were almost in tears. I must say, I left a small piece of my heart there too. It was good to come home again, but the memory of my experience in Sierra Leone and meeting so many wonderful people there will be with me for the rest of my life.

Around the World in Almost 80 Years

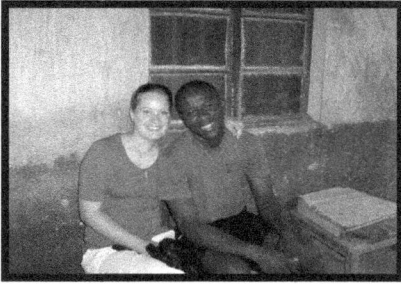

I have kept in contact with Pastor John Kargbo over the years. Some time after I came home, John met a young lady, Lindsey, from Washington State, who was in Sierra Leone on a short-term missionary trip. They fell in love, got married and are now living in the Seattle area. John recently spent three months in Sierra Leone helping with projects that he and Lindsey became involved with prior to their marriage and move to the USA.

THAILAND

Bob Fischer talked me into going on another missionary tour in April 2008. This time we were going to Northern Thailand, to an area called "The Golden Triangle," near the border to Burma and Laos. We would be witnessing to the Lahu tribal people. Suffering discrimination in China these people had fled to Burma only to find that they had gone from the frying pan into the fire. Eventually they were able to leave Burma and flee to Thailand where they have found peace.

Since we were at our home in Branson, Missouri, I was scheduled to fly from Springfield to Minneapolis and meet up with Bob. But when I arrived at the airport I was told that the flight to Minneapolis had been cancelled. This was a fine kettle of fish; what was I going to do now? Airline personnel offered to rebook my entire itinerary sending me to Bangkok via Chicago and Tokyo. I would in fact arrive in Bangkok a couple hours earlier than Bob, which was fine I thought, I could get a few extra hours sleep before we had to get up to catch the early flight to Chiang Mai in Northern Thailand.

After a very short layover in Chicago, I was on my way to Japan. Landing in Tokyo I located the gate for my flight to Bangkok only to find that my name was not on the computer passenger lists and the flight personnel would not let me board. I explained the entire situation of how I was originally booked on Northwest but had been rebooked because of a cancellation. Finally, after several hours, a kind and helpful representative from Northwest Airlines showed up. There were no direct flights to Bangkok that evening but she offered me two alternatives. I could fly to Singapore and then onto Bangkok or she could put me up in a hotel for the night and I could fly to Bangkok the next evening. A bed and a shower sounded good by that time so I opted for the hotel. As compensation for my troubles, she told me, she would bump me up to Business Class and arrange for someone to meet me at the airport in Bangkok who would put me up in a hotel. All of this, free of charge. After retrieving my luggage and clearing Japanese immigration and customs, she took me out to the street and placed me on the bus that took me to my hotel. She was so gracious, a true ambassador for the airline and for her country. I wish I'd had time to see Tokyo, but the airport is located far outside the city and there wasn't time. Some day I would like to return to Japan for a real visit.

I flew to Bangkok the next day and, as promised, was met at the airport by an airline representative who took me to a hotel. I was 24 hours late but had been able to email several people in the group so they knew what had happened and that I was on my way. I slept fitfully, waking often to check my brand new alarm clock, not sure if it was trustworthy. Finally, at 4 a.m., I decided to get up and take shower. My flight to Chiang Mai wasn't until 8:30 a.m., but I wanted to be sure to have enough time to find the terminal and get through check-in procedures.

Around the World in <u>Almost</u> 80 Years

I'm glad I went early. The airport in Bangkok is huge and I walked for what seemed like miles before I realized I was going the wrong direction and had to walk all the way back. When I finally arrived at the check-in counter there was a long line. I checked in, got my boarding pass, cleared security and located the gate where I had to wait for a bus to take me out on the tarmac to a big 747 plane. I was surprised that so many people were flying to Chiang Mai. On this relatively short flight, only about 400 miles, they even served a meal.

Phil Crust, our fearless leader, met me at the airport in Chang Mai. I had missed the orientation session but, since I was a "veteran" having been on several similar missionary trips, I was able to go right to the field. We met up with the rest of the group at a gas station, where I finally caught up with Bob. We only talked for a few minutes though, before we separated, each to our own assignment. I wouldn't see him again for five days when the group reunited in Chiang Mai.

I was assigned to a taciturn man, Li Po. It was the first time that he had been a translator for American missionaries and he didn't quite know what was expected of him. The Lahu village was in the mountains, about two hours from Chiang Mai. Terraces were carved out of the mountainsides where the people grew crops, primarily tea. I watched them drying the leaves on large canvasses laid out on a level area.

There were no paved roads and the people lived in split bamboo huts built up on stilts. There were no windows in the huts, because there was plenty of light coming through the cracks in the walls. They even used bamboo on the floors and I was more than a little worried that they wouldn't hold me. I am, after all, slightly larger than the Lahu people. I learned that bamboo is very strong, even when it is cut in narrow strips.

The "kitchen" was usually located in a smaller hut with a dirt floor. A pot hung over the open fire, bubbling with whatever was on the menu for the day.

Since there were no hotels in the area, we were to live with the people in whatever facilities were available. I was taken to a big empty building with a concrete floor. Used as a dorm to house young people, it was currently vacant and I didn't see a bed anywhere. I asked Li Po where I was going to sleep and he pointed to a place over by the wall. "I'm going to be dead in the morning." I thought to myself.

My fears were relieved when the housemother entered, carrying a couple of thick pads that she folded double and covered with blankets and pillows. Hanging a mosquito netting over the makeshift bed she created a cozy little nest for me. I was quite comfortable. Crawling into bed around 8 p.m. and reading by the light of my head lamp, I usually dozed off within 15 minutes, sleeping soundly until six o'clock the next morning.

The "facilities" were located at the back of the building. To call them "bathrooms" would be an overstatement, but there were four of them, two with toilets. The other two just had holes in the floor with a bucket of water for flushing. The shower was a simple hose. There was no mirror for shaving but I know my face fairly well and I shaved quite adequately without it.

Most of my meals were taken at the pastor's house. Breakfast was rice, sticky like glue, with some vegetables, fruit and tea. Dinner was more sticky rice with spicy vegetables, like cabbage, and very little meat.

I'm not sure the pastor understood that our mission was primarily outreach and that we were there to witness to non-Christians. For four days he took me around to the homes of

256

church members to listen to their joys and sorrows and I was asked to speak at three church meetings. While I enjoyed meeting the people in their homes, everyone I met was already saved and a member of the church and I never got to witness to non-Christians. I had been told that the Lahus generally frowned upon physical contact. They don't shake hands and would not welcome a brotherly hug as is customary in other countries. I broke that rule a couple of times when I was praying for the sick, laying my hands on their heads or shoulders and anointing them with oil, but there were no complaints.

When my tour was over, I met up with the group and we went back to Chiang Mai, where Bob and I roomed together in a fairly nice hotel. From our room we had a great view over the city.

We visited the Elephant Park one day and were all enthralled at the amazing things the elephants had been trained to do. They played soccer, kicking equally well with both front and back legs. While they performed many fascinating tricks, the most astounding was when they painted pictures. Gently taking the paintbrush offered up by the handler in its trunk, the elephant began spreading paint on a large piece of paper mounted on an easel. Within minutes it had painted a picture of a tree with red flowers! Walking around the park, Bob and I came upon an elephant kneeling. We both took the chance to sit on the elephant's knee while it wrapped its trunk around us in a loving gesture.

ACCORDING TO ME

Several of us caught an early flight back to Bangkok where we stayed overnight in a five star hotel. Heading back to our rooms after a lovely dinner, I observed several middle age men with young ladies on their arms. I wondered how those rather mediocre looking men had managed to attract such young beauties. It soon dawned on me, however, that I was naïve. Thailand is notorious for its sex trade and those "young ladies" were most probably prostitutes.

We got up at four o'clock the next morning to catch our flights home. Bob and I were on the same flight to Japan where we separated. I arrived back in Branson without incident.

THE PHILIPPINES

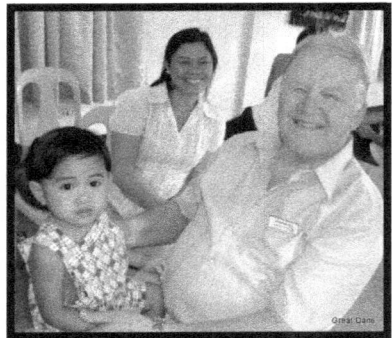

Of all my missionary trips the most pleasurable and memorable was my trip to the Philippines in April 2009 with International Commission. The people were so wonderful and hospitable, accepting me into their midst as if I was one of them, even though I was several generations older then the majority of the members.

Don Seltzer, my former pastor and dear friend, accompanied me on this trip. He had often mentioned that he was half Filipino, his mother having come from the island of Luzon outside of Manila. Don had been going through a rough time in his life and I wanted to do something for him to get his mind off his troubles for a while. He was reluctant at first and even his mother discouraged him from going, but in the end he came along and had a wonderful time. His relationship with his mother, strained prior to his trip, improved when they had some common ground and could talk about the country she came from. All in all it was money well spent.

AROUND THE WORLD IN *Almost* 80 YEARS

After clearing customs in Manila, we boarded a southbound bus and arrived after a couple of hours at our hotel located in a beautiful part of the island near a collapsed volcano. The old crater was now water filled, a lake encompassed by a multitude of flowers. A smaller volcano had emerged in the middle of the lake and apparently it, too, had a lake in its crater.

Rooming with someone, you get to know him quite well. I have never seen anybody go to sleep as fast as Don. He no more than laid his head on the pillow and he was asleep! Rising at three or four in the morning, he diligently made his bed, leaving it looking as though it had not been slept in, and retired to the bathroom to read. I told him he really shouldn't do that, housekeeping was likely to think we were sleeping together in the same bed! But he continued with his routine for the duration of our stay.

The following day, Saturday, we gathered in a church and were introduced to our hosts for the week. Box lunches were provided and devoured outside on a patio. Then we retired inside for a short devotional and to get acquainted with our respective hosts. I was assigned to Louie Echate, pastor of The Lamb's Baptist Church, and Bobby Grajales. Thinking about my experience in Thailand the previous year, I told them that I didn't want to preach to the choir but wanted to go out and win souls for Christ, to which they whole-heartedly agreed.

During my short stay I became very close to Pastor Louie and his wife, Nanette, and Bobby and Grace Grajales, and they have remained my dear friends. The church's rather large group of young people took me in as though I were one of them even though I was old enough to be their grandfather. Over a year later I still get messages from them on Facebook. There were at least 20 young people in the group. Breaking up into teams of five, they went out canvassing the area, getting hundreds of decisions for Christ.

I was suppose to deliver the sermon our first Sunday and was seated in the front row next to Pastor Louie and his wife. The sanctuary was as hot as a sauna and I, who can develop a sweat just combing my hair, was perspiring so profusely a puddle formed at my feet. Feeling sorry for me, Bobby Grajales brought me a fan, which helped a little. I managed to get through the service without too much embarrassment and, afterwards, was invited to lunch at the pastor's apartment. In the afternoon he and I went out and canvassed the area for a few hours, gaining some converts.

The next day, and for the rest of the week, I was picked up by one of the men from the church driving a small motorcycle with a very small sidecar. I could barely wedge into it but it was a blast to ride in that thing.

When we weren't out witnessing, I spent most of my time with the young people at the church, eating lunch or having refreshments in the afternoon when it was raining. Someone would pick up an instrument and we would sing praise songs, some that were familiar and a few new ones I had to learn. One afternoon they even tried to teach me a song in Tagalog, a very difficult language, at least for me. We really had an awful lot of fun together. One evening, meeting the rest of the group at the hotel for dinner, I told them that I was just having too much fun. Unimpressed, one of the ladies remarked snidely, "We're not here to have fun; we're here to witness."

Our last day was Victory Sunday. Once again I was supposed to deliver the sermon, but what a difference a week makes! I was no longer a stranger in their midst but had made a lot of friends and felt comfortable among them. One of the girls had told me that I spoke too fast, so I asked her to signal me to slow down if I started babbling while delivering the sermon, which she did several times.

Although I was only there for ten days I came away having gained many new and wonderful friends. I mention none of the fantastic young people that befriended me by name but remember each one dearly. With youth like them, the future looks bright for the Philippines.

Unto the Ends of the Earth

When I was a young boy I read about the Golden Hordes galloping from the East, taking over most of the known world in the thirteenth century. Ever since then I've been fascinated by Genghis Kahn and Mongolia and longed for the adventure of visiting this far-away country. I finally got my chance.

While I was in Thailand I mentioned to Jeff and Jody Chetwood, the Asian coordinators for International Commission, that I had a real hankering to go to Mongolia if ever an opportunity opened up. As luck would have it, they organized a project in late September 2009. This time it was me who called Bob Fischer and urged him to come along. He had, after all, pushed me in to several trips; not against my will, mind you, I love these adventures.

Stopover in China

Since we had to lay over in Beijing, China, we decided to leave a couple of days early, extending the layover for some sightseeing. Bob had made contact with a woman named Lynn Xu, who would show us around.

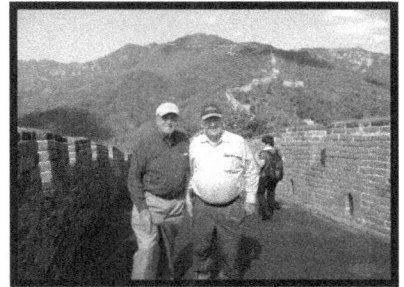

This time there were no flight problems for me. I arrived in Beijing ahead of Bob. Lynn and her driver, Bochang, met me as I was exiting the terminal taking me to a wonderful Konlun hotel, where we had reserved a room.

After my long flight I was glad to go up to my room and settle down. I had flown from Springfield, Missouri to Chicago that

261

morning and then nonstop to Beijing. The route we took was rather intriguing. A few hundred miles from the North Pole, we veered south and flew down over Siberia and Mongolia and on into China. As soon as I was somewhat settled, I crawled into bed and fell fast asleep. About 11 p.m. Bob entered the room and went to bed.

We were meeting Lynn and her driver at ten o'clock the next morning, which was no problem. Jetlagged, we both woke up early and went down and had a superb Chinese breakfast buffet. As usual, I ate too much. When we met Lynn, she told us that we couldn't go downtown. It was the 60th anniversary of the Communist takeover of China and security was especially tight. Later, we saw some of it on television. It was very impressive with parades that went on for hours and a speech by the president, which we, of course, couldn't understand.

Lynn suggested that we go and see The Great Wall. I was so excited! As a child I had read about the Great Wall of China and had seen pictures of it meandering over the mountains and valleys. Stretching over 4,000 miles, it is one of the wonders of the world, taking centuries to build and costing thousands, if not millions, of lives. The section near Beijing has been refurbished for the benefit of tourism.

The next day Lynn took us to the Olympic village. Beijing had hosted the Olympic games in 2008, spending billions to beautify the city. Now they are trying to keep it that way with people out sweeping the streets with brooms. The village was very impressive with great buildings everywhere. There was the enormous stadium, called "The Bird's Nest" because that is what it looks like from the outside. I took pictures of everything. I even asked Lynn if she could ask a policeman if I could take a picture of him. She told me not to bother asking, just take a picture of him. I liked Lynn.

When we had seen everything at the Olympic area, we drove over to the famous Tieneman Square ripe with history and national pride but also tragedy and resentment. A sea of humanity, it was difficult to move around in the crowd. This area was restricted the previous day because of the celebrations and now there were several floats left behind and decorative poles representing all the districts in China.

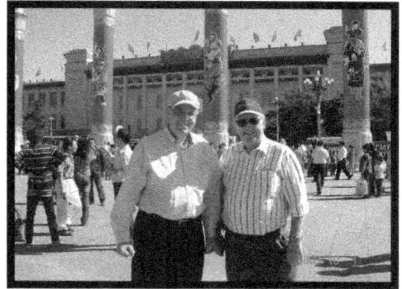

Across the great boulevard that runs past Tieneman Square is the entrance to the Forbidden City, an enormous locale that was home to the emperors for over 500 years. Constructed in the fifteenth century, it has 980 buildings with nearly 9,000 rooms of various sizes. It was fascinating to walk around looking at the ornately decorated edifices. We only had a couple of hours but I could have spent a week there getting oodles of pictures.

In the afternoon Lynn took us to a duck restaurant. What a delicious experience! After several kinds of appetizers, the chef brought out an entire roasted duck, which he carved by our table. First he sliced off some skin, laid it on a plate and shook a little sugar over it before handing it to us. Then he carved up the whole bird. We topped off that delectable meal with ice cream.

Bob wanted buy pearls for all of the girls in his family. Lynn had a friend in the business and took us to her shop, which was in a big two-story building filled with pearl shops. I have never seen so many pearls in one place. Sunshine, Lynn's friend and the proprietor of the store, was a very nice young lady. My experience with Chinese people is that they really know how to bargain, but they don't hold a candle to Bob's expertise in the art. Watching him in action was an education in itself. He negotiated with Sunshine for two hours, never coming to an agreement. Finally he told her that we would be returning in a week and they could pick up their negotiations. We then went back to the hotel and said goodbye to Lynn since she was leaving the city. Bochang would meet us early in the morning and take us to the airport.

According To Me

Mongolia

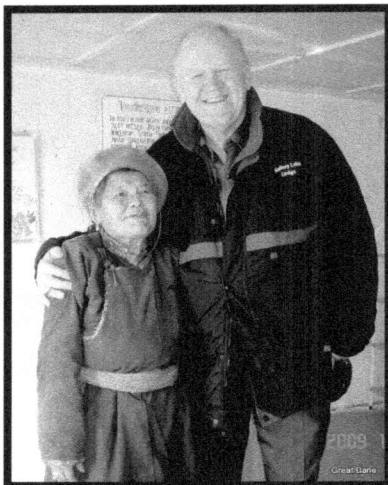

We arrived in Ulan Bator around ten o'clock the following morning, a Saturday. Odgar, a pleasant middle-aged man, met us and took us to the Genghis Khan Hotel. After checking in, we were taken to a museum where we met the rest of the group of about twenty people. After walking through the museum, we went to a restaurant for lunch. In the afternoon we did a little sightseeing by foot, went shopping and exchanged some money into the Mongolian currency.

On Sunday we attended a church service lasting two hours. Everything was in Mongolian, of course, a language that is different from anything I've ever heard, but was translated into English by an American lady, Penny, who had been in Mongolia for seven years. After the church service we were introduced to our translator, Gantuya, Gany for short. Since there were two of us, Bob and I really felt that we needed two translators with us. We prayed about it and told Gany of our concern. Later, Tom, a friend of Gany, showed up as a second translator and we were in great shape.

In the evening around nine o'clock, the four of us went to the train station and boarded a train bound for the little town of Selenge near the Siberian border. From there we would have to get a taxi to an even smaller town located directly on the border. I was praising the Lord. This was the kind of adventure I had dreamt about and I was so grateful. The journey to Selenge would take nine hours. We were assigned a sleeper car lined with bunk beds, fifty beds to a compartment. I thought it was fun and not uncomfortable. Everyone was friendly; with such close quarters it was a necessity. The conductor locked the toilet whenever we approached a station and I understood that the toilet emptied right out onto the tracks when the train was in motion, just like the trains did in Denmark when I was growing up.

We arrived in Selenge at 6 am, hailing a taxi as we stepped off the train. Billye, the driver, would become our driver and friend during our entire stay in northern Mongolia. From the station we drove ten miles to the little border town of Altan Bulag, population about 4,000. On arrival we found that there were no hotels available and had to return to Selenge where we found a simple hotel with one three-bed room for Bob, Tom and me. Gany had her own room across the hall. There was no housekeeping service, so we made up our own beds but we do that at home. Breakfast was included, but always the same, two fried eggs, a slice of toast and tea or coffee. Sometimes there was no hot water for showers. With Mongolia's cool climate we usually opted to wait until hot water became available.

Mongolia is now an independent country with freedom of religion, so we were not harassed for witnessing the way we were in Cuba. A part of the Soviet Union until 1989, Mongolia was pretty much left to their own devices when the reign of communism disintegrated. A developing country, only 20% of the population has indoor plumbing. Of the three million Mongolian inhabitants, one third live in cities, the rest are nomads and living in "Gers," a round tent-like structure that is easily moved. I got the impression, though, that a lot of the nomads are wealthy, owning many kinds of animals. Mongolia is a large country, about half the size of the U.S.A., with very sparse population and we drove for miles seeing only a couple of Gers here and there.

ACCORDING TO ME

Eventually we located the pastor of the Baptist church in Altan Bulag, a very pleasant lady in her early forties named Towshin; I never learned her last name. During our four-day stay she took us around to people she thought would be receptive to hearing about and possibly accepting the Lord. I found that the people were wonderful. They don't have much in the way of worldly goods but what they had, they wanted to share with us. Most of the homes we entered offered us food, which we accepted although we had never seen anything like it before and sanitation wasn't up to the standards we are used to, but I would never dream of offending them by refusing their hospitality.

One morning Pastor Towshin asked us to come to her house and witness to her husband who was not a Christian. We met him as we entered the home, which, compared to the general standards of the area, was a well-built house. I had the honor of presenting the gospel to him. As I was talking to him I noticed Towshin sitting in the other room with her eyes closed, praying. I asked him about what kind of work he did and he told me that he was in construction, building houses wherever he could find work on either side of the border. Since I had been in the same business we found that we had something in common and hit it off fairly well. After a while I worked into the "Plan of Salvation" and he listened politely. I kept talking with him for almost a half hour with Tom and Gany taking turns translating. When I was finished, I asked him if there was any reason why he could not accept Jesus Christ as his Savior. He said, "No."

I have a little tract with the sinner's prayer on the back. I gave it to Gany who translated the prayer with him repeating the words. We left the home with Towshin praising the Lord for saving her family. They have four children, two teenage boys and two younger girls.

For four days we went from house to house, going where Pastor Towshin led us. One day we entered a house where the people were especially glad to see us. They joked and laughed for quite awhile before finally asking why we had come. I began my presentation and, when I was finished, they all accepted the Lord. It may sound like I did all the talking, but in reality Bob and I took turns and he had the same success as I did. We didn't get a 100%, but close to it. There weren't a great number of decisions because we couldn't reach very many people. Often it was one on one and it takes the same amount of time, whether you are presenting the Gospel to one person or to twenty.

After four days we had pretty much exhausted all the places Towshin had in mind for us and we decided to go back to Ulan

Bator. Bob refused to go back on the train, so we hired Billye to drive us back, which was much more pleasant. Leaving Selenge around 10 a.m., we drove through the Mongolian countryside enjoying the view we had missed from our night train. I spotted a nomad with a big heard of Bactrian camels, the ones with two humps that are only found in Mongolia and Northern China. I screamed for Billye to stop, because here was a real photo-op and I wasn't going to miss it. The owner of the camels looked like someone you might meet in the city slums, but he had a horse and hundreds of sheep and goats, in addition to the camels.

Driving was considerably faster than taking the train and we arrived in Ulan Bator around four in the afternoon, meeting up with the rest of the group for dinner. The next day, while sightseeing in the country, we came upon the biggest statue in the world, an image of Genghis Kahn on top of a two-story building. We stopped the bus when we saw a man with an eagle and two huge camels by the side of the road. I paid for a short camel ride and the opportunity to hold the eagle.

267

ACCORDING TO ME

It had been a cold day in Mongolia and I got really chilled. By the time we came back to the hotel I had developed a fever. That was disconcerting since we were soon returning to Beijing. I knew that they would monitor my temperature when we arrived. As you disembark the plane you have to walk past heat sensors that register your temperature. If you had a fever you would be quarantined until you were well again. I stayed in bed all day Sunday, missing the Victory Service at church. I really would have liked to have been there since we had given our train tickets to Pastor Towshin and I would have liked to see her again and to say goodbye to our translators.

THE PEARL MERCHANT

On Monday I felt a lot better and was fever free. After many hours delay, we finally arrived in Beijing and, passing successfully through the sensors, was finally able to relax. Unfortunately our luggage wasn't as lucky. After waiting in vain for our bags to appear we put a search on them, informing the personnel of our hotel. We didn't know if we would ever see it again, but we prayed fervently that it would arrive before we had to leave Beijing.

The steadfast Bochang was waiting for us when we came out and took us to the hotel. While we were eating dinner Bob contacted Sunshine and told her that he was ready to do business. Sunshine showed up shortly, accompanied by four ladies carrying a big sack of pearls. In the room, Sunshine laid all the pearls out on the bed and the bargaining continued from where it had left off a week ago. It blew my mind how long it took. At one time Sunshine told Bob that he was killing her. A couple of hours later Sunshine finally bit the dust and told her girls to start making up the strands of pearls. It was fascinating to watch as they skillfully knotted each pearl and attached a clasp to each strand.

At eleven o'clock at night, after Sunshine and her girls had left, our luggage finally arrived at the hotel, and we felt very relieved.

Bob's flight left first the next day and, since Sunshine didn't have all the pearls he wanted, we made arrangements for her to deliver the rest to me in the morning. She came as promised and I, too, flew home without incident, totally satisfied after a most adventurous trip.

CAMBODIA

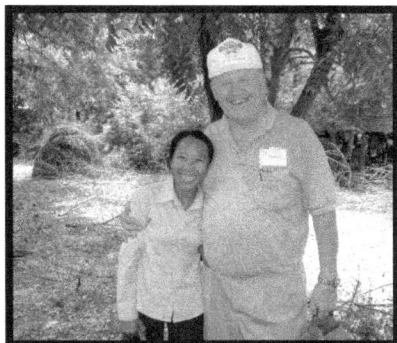

In October 2010 thirty-two Americans flew to Cambodia to preach the gospel. We were split into seven groups and driven out into the countryside to witness to the people. I'm not sure how far out the other groups were taken but we were always the last group to return to the hotel at the end of the day. We drove for an hour and forty-five minutes to get there on roads full of potholes and we usually couldn't drive faster than 5 or 10 miles an hour. It was extremely tedious and got old very quickly.

This trip was similar to the other missionary trips I've taken except that they warned us about eating food prepared by the people we visited, something about bacteria in the water. Culinary adventurer that I am, this really put a damper on

the experience. I usually eat anything people place in front of me, as long as it's cooked. I also didn't want to offend our wonderful hosts, but I thought it was wise to follow instructions, however I may not do that in the future.

269

According To Me

There were four Americans, plus our translators, in my group, trying to reap a great harvest for the Lord but the response we received upon presenting the Plan of Salvation was a bit disappointing. All of the people we met were Buddhists who had never heard about Jesus before and were both skeptical and disinclined towards conversion. Our leader consoled us, telling us that we had been given the most difficult area. We did, however, get a few decisions for Christ. The project as a whole, however, was a great success, yielding over 5,300 conversions. At the end of the week 1,100 people showed up at a muddy lake to be baptized.

The baptismal service was an experience in itself as all of those people arrive on pick-up trucks and other forms of transportation. I never thought that you could load 40 people into a pick-up truck but they can do it in Cambodia! Five or six people were crammed into the cab. There was a large raised rack covering the bed of the truck on which about a dozen people sat, with 12 -15 more people sitting below them in the bed. Then there were 3-4 people atop the cab and a half dozen hanging off the tailgate. It was an incredible sight to behold!

There were seven pastors baptizing people and they were quite efficient. As soon as one person came up out of the water, another person stepped forward to take their place and the whole thing was accomplished amazingly quickly. We were back in our four-star hotel in Phnom Pehn by afternoon and were able to relax after a rather strenuous week.

From our hotel room we had a pretty good view over the city and could observe the traffic, which consisted primarily of motorcycles that seemed to be driven so haphazardly it was a wonder no one was killed. Thankfully we never saw any accidents.

Sightseeing was on the agenda for Saturday and we were taken out to see the "Killing Fields." Between 1975 and 1979 the Khmer Rouge had control of the country creating a "hell on earth" for many of the citizens. In those five years over two million people were tortured and killed for no other reason than the desire of the diabolical rulers to rid the country of the educated and the rich. Anyone wearing glasses or who had smooth hands was at risk. One of the high schools in Phnom Penh was converted into torture chambers where victims were tormented prior to being taken out into the field where they were forced to dig their own mass graves. Adults were then clubbed to death while small children were slammed against a tree and thrown into the grave. Many victims were buried alive.

Today the area is a memorial over the victims with a 20 x 20 foot, four-story tower filled with skulls that have been exhumed from the field. Bones are still visible in the soil for people strolling the grounds. This was not the only killing field in the country, there are many more as such atrocities were committed everywhere. Finally Vietnam intervened and drove out the Khmer Rouge. Pol Pot, the vicious leader, escaped into exile and was never brought to trial.

It had been a rough trip, with the daily travel out to the village. By the end of the week I was ready to go home. As always, it was good to get back to May-Britt.

LAST WORDS

Well, I have had an unbelievable run of it. If someone could have told me when I was a kid that all this was going to take place in my life, I would never have believed it. As I was writing about how I met, fell in love with and eventually married May-Britt, I was just shaking my head. It was obviously meant to be. We have had 52 wonderful years together, and I certainly hope for many more with this wonderful lady.

We celebrated our Golden Anniversary early, in August 2008, because Stefan and LaVonne and their five children were visiting from Sweden. Together with them, Orla Jens and Darla, their two little girls, and about 60 friends and relatives we had a wonderful party in our home. There were speeches, music and singing by our kids and grandkids. Our friends took over 100 pictures for us to treasure.

Looking back over the last 76 years, I've lived a very busy life, yet it seems like fleeting moments in time.

It has been a life filled with excitement and a lot of hard work.

I have had two careers, one as a painter and the other as a building contractor. I have built homes and developed neighborhoods. I was a volunteer Deputy Sheriff, and have been involved in Rotary and the Chamber of Commerce and spent years working to improve the lives of orphans in Mexico. I have pursued and enjoyed many hobbies, flying, diving, sailing and, above all, traveling. It has been a privilege to travel around the world; something I'd always dreamt of doing, but never really had the time while I was working. Since retiring I've been blessed with, not only the opportunity to travel, but also to share the gospel with people who had never heard it before.

Of all these accomplishments, the crowning glory is my family. Although I take very little credit, (May-Britt deserves most of that,) our children have grown into wonderful, well-adjusted adults of whom I am very proud.

According To Me

LaVonne, our daughter is a gifted young lady. (Well, maybe not young anymore, she is nearly 50!). She is a writer and a graphic designer and the mother of five children. She and her husband, Stefan, have done a good job raising their children who are growing into delightful adults, all musically talented. They bring much joy and laughter to my life. And she loves the Lord. What more can I wish?

Our son, Orla Jens, is a successful developer and builder. His family is a priority for him. Although he is busy with work he always thinks of things to do with the family, for example hiking the Colorado Trail. Taking it in sections, 3-4 days at the time, it will take about six years to complete. But most of all he and Darla teach their kids to love and obey the Lord.

It's true that when you look back on a life lived you don't wish you had spent more time working, instead you regret not spending more time with family and loved ones. I wish I could multiply the time I spent with them, but time slips through your fingers like grains of sand. Before you know it you are 76 years old, the proud owner of a Smart Car, and writing your memoirs!

274

www.ingramcontent.com/pod-product-compliance
Lightning Source LLC
Chambersburg PA
CBHW031242090426
42742CB00007B/284